THE UNLIKELY
DISRUPTOR

SOUTH CAROLINA'S FIRST
BLACK WOMAN TO RUN FOR GOVERNOR

MIA S. MCLEOD, J.D.

The Unlikely Disruptor: South Carolina's First Black Woman to Run for Governor

Book Cover Design | Kelli Simone Rembert
Book Interior Design | Petya Tsankova
Cover Photograph | Ashley Martin Photography
Editor | Amy Tyler
Publishing Management | TSPA The Self Publishing Agency, Inc.

WHAT GOD MEANS TO ME

My faith in God is the light that guides, the love that restores, the courage that strengthens, the energy that fuels, the forgiveness that frees, the hope that heals and the boldness that beckons me to keep moving forward … no matter what.

I've struggled over the years to truly see myself the way God sees me. But when I think about all of the seemingly insurmountable challenges God has allowed me to overcome and all of the ways He has entrusted me to lead, I know beyond a shadow of a doubt that His plan for my life is so much bigger, bolder, and better than anything I could imagine.

Because I believe that my "steps are ordered by the Lord …" I also believe that my path to purpose is aligned with His Word, His will and His timing. Learning more about the true nature of God teaches me everything I need to know about my own.

As I reflect on the wisdom I've gained and the progress I'm making, "I am confident … that He who began a good work in me will see it through to completion…"

To my babies, BJ and Cam,

You are brilliant, beautiful young men. If I didn't know how much God loves me, the fact that He chose me to birth two of His most amazing creations would be all the proof I'd need.

TABLE OF CONTENTS

THE PILLARS OF MY JOURNEY

"Daddy, am I gonna die?"

"Yes, baby … all of us are at some point."

Without flinching, Daddy rubbed my left hand and wouldn't look at me. A tear rolled down his cheek. I could hear my heart beating faster and louder. "But remember this: Those who are afraid to die are also afraid to live," he said, almost as if he was reassuring himself and me at the same time. In that moment, I felt like I could kick death's butt just by not being afraid of it. Truth is, I was just a second grader and had already been hospitalized for a month. At the time, my doctors had diagnosed me with pneumonia but weren't sure why my body wasn't responding to the medications they prescribed to treat it.

As a young girl who was sick a lot, I often felt I was missing out on some of the fun stuff my friends did, like swimming in Lake Paul Wallace, cheerleading, or playing middle- and high- school sports. Each time I tried, I ended up in the hospital. Neither the doctors nor my parents knew what was making me so sick or why the excruciating pain seemed to randomly attack different limbs. Yet, there I was with oxygen tubes in my nose, IV lines in my arms, and pains so sharp in my legs, I could barely speak, eat, sleep, drink, or think—despite scheduled infusions of super-strong opioids to help manage the pain.

Doctors were baffled. I could tell my parents were scared. So when Daddy was the only one in my room and had promised to sleep in the recliner beside my hospital bed, I asked the question nobody wanted to verbalize. His wisdom and honesty in that moment would prepare me to confront that battle and each one that followed.

Born and raised in South Carolina, I grew up in rural Marlboro County, the second of four children in the heart of what America has come to know as the "Corridor of Shame." It's an area along Interstate 95 that is known for struggling schools, workforces, and communities, as well as significant health and socioeconomic disparities, and other systemic inequities, thanks to the government's failure to support the needs of the people in these counties and invest in critical infrastructure.

Yet, my parents never let us focus on what we didn't have. They taught us to be grateful for everything we *did* have ... a loving God, unconditional love for each other, life, health, strength, a supportive village, a roof over our heads, food on our table, and clothes on our backs.

I prefer to think of my hometown area as the "Corridor of Hope." Many amazing people who have contributed much to improve lives across our state and nation were born and raised there. If you ever wanted to get on Daddy's bad side, just look down on or speak negatively about Marlboro County, Bennettsville, South Carolina, or the good people who live there.

The entire county and folks all over the Pee Dee, a region named after the Pee Dee Native American tribe and the Great Pee Dee River that runs through it, knew Daddy as "Jimmy." He was an undeniably handsome, smart, outspoken, and gregarious mortician, funeral director, and small business owner, whose childhood memories of the deeply segregated South were always with him.

Daddy wouldn't let us shop at certain business establishments in our city or county that he believed mistreated Black community members during the Civil Rights Movement. Yet, in spite of his childhood experiences, he always found a reason to smile or a way to make us laugh. Daddy's voice was deep, as some might think an embalmer's or funeral director's would be. Yet, his demeanor was anything but dark or morbid. He enjoyed sharing nuggets of wisdom, often when we least expected it. I remember a friend coming over to play and casually saying she wished she had good hair like mine. Daddy didn't hesitate to jump into the conversation with his usual quick wit, big voice, and warm smile and say, "Any hair that covers your head is good hair!"

Back then, I had no idea what I wanted to be ... let alone who. I hated math, was fascinated with science, and loved to read and write. Mama, a public school teacher and librarian, kept our home filled with books and insisted that we read and take extra good care of them. Although she wasn't a native South Carolinian, I've heard many stories about how intrigued people were when Daddy first brought this brilliant, beautiful, soft-spoken, petite powerhouse to Bennettsville!

Originally from Alamance County, North Carolina, she had a compassionate heart for people and community—and a graceful elegance and eloquence that were all her own. Everyone who met and got to know her, loved her, including her students at Bennettsville Primary School.

One of my most memorable childhood moments was when my elementary school class went to the library where Mama was the librarian. She always read us a book with such expressiveness and enthusiasm and then let us go to the shelves and select one to check out. On one particular day, a classmate, who happened to be a white male, heard me refer to her as "Mama," and decided to correct me, since it was obvious to him that she was white like him, *not* Black like me.

Of course, I debated with him for a moment and then decided to take him over to her so that she could confirm that she was, in fact, my mom. She told him she was, and the sheer devastation and disappointment on his face were palpable. He even asked details like whether she was really Black like me or white like him. When she gently explained that she was a Black woman and that Black people come in a myriad of beautiful shades, he looked defeated, almost as if he had been betrayed.

Mama and I talked about it briefly when we got home. She hugged me, knelt to my eye level, and with both palms embracing my cheeks, said calmly and candidly in her soft, sweet voice, "If your classmate doesn't like the color of our skin, the issue is his, not mine, and certainly not yours."

Years later, I was preparing for my high school graduation. My inquisitive classmate had long since left the Marlboro County public school system and was likely preparing to graduate from his private high school. For a moment, I wondered whether race was still a big deal to him. Would it influence his decision to consider certain colleges? Had that encounter so many years ago influenced mine?

When it was time to consider colleges, none of my family members or friends were surprised that I wanted to go out of state. I visited Hampton Institute, now Hampton University, in Hampton, Virginia, where Uncle Gary went and Grandma Leah and Granddaddy Jim lived. I was equally enamored with North Carolina Agricultural and Technical State University (NC A&T) in Greensboro, North Carolina. Aunt Terry and my sister-cousin, Susan, were proud NC A&T Aggies. Both universities were near family.

After Mama and Daddy let me visit both Historically Black Colleges and Universities (HCBUs), Daddy abruptly announced, "I'm glad you really like those schools, baby, but your tuition is going to the University of South Carolina."

My parents weren't into explaining their decisions, so I might as well get over it because pouting and complaining would get me nowhere. They weren't gonna change their minds. It was a done deal. And I was devastated.

***

When I arrived on USC's campus in the fall of 1986, I felt like a small-town country girl in a big city. Before long, I was learning my way around and meeting other students who were from small towns too. About a month or two into school, I started feeling a dull ache that would soon turn into excruciating pain.

I thought, *Oh no! Not here. Not now!* My roommate, Natalie, suggested that I go to the health center on campus and told me how to get there. I remember being scared that I would probably have to go home and be admitted to Marlboro Park Hospital ... again.

It was during that visit to the health center that I was diagnosed with Sickle Cell Anemia, a genetic blood disorder where red blood cells become abnormally sickle-shaped, blocking blood vessels and causing pain, organ damage and other life-threatening complications. I knew very little about the disease and neither did my parents, although both of them had the Sickle Cell Trait. (Testing wasn't routine back then.)

During my junior and senior years at USC, a few near-death experiences sent me back to the hospital for lengthy stays. In 1989, a severe Sickle Cell crisis led to a life-threatening bout of double pneumonia. With tubes in my nose and IV lines in my arms, hands, and then hips, the doctors and nurses seemed to be running out of places to put them. I remember thinking there was no way I was gonna survive it. Everything I consumed came through an IV. By the time I was released—more than 40 pounds lighter—I barely resembled the vivacious person I was before.

In spite of the diagnosis, I was determined to live a normal life and not limit myself or allow others to limit me. During those early years, I wish I could say it didn't bother me to see my friends do things with ease that I wasn't able to do without facing swift and severe consequences.

Back then, other people's opinions impacted me too. I remember how hurtful it was to hear that one of my high school classmates started a rumor that I must have AIDS because I was so thin and frail after my release. After recuperating at home for several weeks, I finally had the strength to return to USC. At the time, I didn't realize that I had already begun to see myself differently and overcompensate for those areas where I felt most weak and vulnerable. Although I thought I was managing those feelings and that pain pretty well, the truth is ... I was starting to shrink and settle in ways that would later leave me full of fear and regret.

By the early '90s, I had learned how to manage the physical aspects of the diagnosis by eating healthier, staying hydrated, getting enough sleep, and not overexerting myself. Before I had my babies, doctors warned that the older I got, the more likely I was to experience serious and frequent Sickle Cell complications, especially during pregnancy. While I wasn't exactly sure what that meant or looked like, it didn't take me long to find out.

Brian and I dated in college and got married while I was in law school and he was in graduate school. I soon became pregnant with our first son, Brian James, or BJ, named after his dad and mine. I remember being sick with the flu at eight months pregnant. By the grace of God, I recovered and it wasn't until I went into labor about a month later that those labor pains were accompanied by an excruciating Sickle Cell crisis that lasted for well over a week after giving birth.

BJ's first two years flew by. In October of 1995, Daddy had a routine colonoscopy in Bennettsville that perforated his colon and led to peritonitis—an inflamed, infectious, and often fatal condition caused by a hole or leakage in the intestines. Our hometown hospital was not equipped to meet his medical needs. At the time, Richard Gergel, now a federal judge, was one of the founding partners at the law firm where I clerked during my last semester of law school. He made a few calls and had a medivac helicopter airlift Daddy to Richland Memorial Hospital in Columbia, where he had emergency surgery and stayed in the Intensive Care Unit until January 1996.

According to doctors, Daddy's prognosis was pretty bleak. At one point, the lead surgeon, Dr. Davis, looked me in the eye and said, "We're giving your dad the strongest antibiotic made. If it doesn't work, there's nothing else we can do other than pray." Dr. Davis probably didn't know that for us, antibiotics were the last resort. Prayer was the first.

When Daddy was released from the hospital in February 1996, Brian and I moved him into our two-bedroom townhouse. We brought BJ's crib into our second bedroom and gave Daddy ours to make room for his hospital bed, IV unit, and all of the medical supplies needed for his around-the-clock care.

By Easter, Daddy was strong enough to go home. And although he still had a lot more healing to do, the most challenging part of his recovery process was behind him. Our entire family was overjoyed about his miraculous recovery. His surgeons agreed and said they had never seen anything like it!

* * *

After graduating law school, Republican Attorney General Charlie Condon hired me at a time when our state was number one in the nation for women murdered by men as a result of domestic violence. My team and I wrote the protocols and curricula for law enforcement, solicitors, judges, and victim advocates to use when investigating, prosecuting, and adjudicating these violent crimes. This ultimately laid the foundation for every domestic violence policy South Carolina has enacted since.

In spite of all our family had been through, it seemed as though we couldn't catch a break. In 1997, Mama was diagnosed with Stage II ovarian cancer and Tracey with Stage IV breast cancer. Brian and I weren't exactly in a good place by then either, which only compounded the anxiety and emotional pain I was feeling. When our second son, Cameron, was born in 1998, Mama was living with us while taking chemo treatments in Columbia. I'm so grateful for the time we were able to spend with her.

Although my second pregnancy was easier in some ways than my first, Cameron weighed 10 pounds, 12 ounces. The physical impact of giving birth to such a big baby had its own unique complications and challenges that were exacerbated by Sickle Cell. Like his big brother, Cam was beautiful and healthy. The knocks on my hospital room door from members of the hospital's cafeteria and custodial team still make me smile today.

"Is you the one had the 11-pound baby?" the staff asked with delightful Southern drawls.

I chuckled and told them I was.

"Can we see him?" they asked with excitement and anticipation.

"Of course you can," I said.

By then, Mama's ovarian and Tracey's breast cancer diagnoses, coupled with the obvious stress of a marriage on life support, only fueled more anxiety and uncertainty about the future.

Mama died in 1999, just 15 months after Cam was born. In many ways, I felt the stinging juxtaposition of being a mom and motherless at the same time. On the day Mama passed, all of her children and siblings were there with her. I asked her if she could hear us, since her eyes were closed and she wasn't talking. She let me know she could by squeezing my hand. I told her I loved her and she whispered, "I love you too." We never got to hear her voice or see her sweet smile again. I held Mama's right hand when she took her last breath one day after her 61st birthday. She has held mine every day since.

As devastated as I was to lose Mama when I needed her most, the only thing that kept me from wallowing in that low place was my big sister Tracey and her battle with Stage IV breast cancer. We couldn't lose her too, so I was determined to be upbeat and encouraging as our entire family rallied around Tracey and quietly pleaded with God to not take her from us.

Thankfully, He heard our prayers.

* * *

When Democrat Jim Hodges was elected governor in 1998, he appointed me to direct the State Office of Victim Assistance (SOVA) and administer South Carolina's multimillion-dollar Crime Victim Compensation Fund. Coming from a rural area like Marlboro County, the first thing I did was open and staff satellite offices in underserved parts of the state, starting with my hometown of Bennettsville. When I traveled there with the governor to announce the opening of our first satellite office, Daddy and Tracey were there to welcome us!

After calling for the Crime Victim Compensation Fund's first actuarial study, restructuring the organization to ensure alignment, increasing professional development opportunities for SOVA's frontline employees, and expanding access to SOVA's services, South Carolina's Crime Victim Compensation Fund received national accolades for the very first time. Its services and sustainability efforts were showcased nationally as a model for other states.

I had just walked into my office at SOVA when the first plane crashed into the World Trade Center on September 11, 2001. It was SOVA's federal counterpart that assisted victims, survivors, and families impacted by the 9/11 terrorist attack and reimbursed them for medical expenses, mental health counseling, lost wages, and funeral and burial expenses, like our team did at the state level.

***

By 2002, my marriage was over. I was unprepared for the grief. The loss of our marriage and hopes for our future together as a family felt like a death.

Although our divorce wasn't exactly amicable at first, I prayed that God would continue to cover us and make sure our babies had everything they needed. It took a few months before we were finally able to talk without blaming each other. Thankfully, Brian and I found a way to put our differences aside and work hard to be the best versions of ourselves for our boys.

Raising our children separately together wasn't what either of us had envisioned, but with God's grace and guidance, we made it work. It's beyond beautiful to see the two exceptionally kind, brilliant, mega-talented, funny, strong, caring, and compassionate young men BJ and Cam are today.

***

With Governor Hodges' blessing, the South Carolina Department of Probation, Parole & Pardon Services (SCDPPPS) hired me in 2002 to direct the cabinet agency's governmental affairs division and secure bipartisan support for passage of the agency's landmark Interstate Compact legislation. It was a big deal for our state, and the governor held a press conference to highlight the bill's significance and impact.

When I left state government in 2003 to start my public affairs firm, my goal was to help clients navigate the political arena, build relationships with legislative and executive officials, and provide advocacy and strategic communication services. I really enjoyed my newfound freedom and flexibility as an independent lobbyist, in spite of losing my anchor contract with the SCDPPPS.

I'm so grateful that I stayed the course because when Republican Mark Sanford beat Democrat Jim Hodges in the South Carolina governor's race, Governor-elect Sanford cut my lobbying contract and offered me my old job back as SCDPPPS' director of governmental affairs. I trusted God and respectfully declined the governor-elect's offer. It wasn't an easy decision. I was newly divorced and BJ and Cam were just 10 and five years old.

Because of the Sickle Cell diagnosis, I needed health insurance coverage. After vacating my state government position, I enrolled in COBRA coverage and discovered that because of my pre-existing condition, I had a $1,300-plus monthly premium that practically equaled my mortgage. As a newly divorced mother of two with a mortgage, car, and student loan payments, some months I went without health insurance, praying I wouldn't have a Sickle Cell crisis that required an extensive hospital stay or any other costly medical emergency.

Not long after taking that leap of faith, God blessed me with an opportunity to represent all of South Carolina's private HBCUs, to help them navigate and engage within the political arena and ultimately gain access to funding generated by the new South Carolina Education Lottery. It was the contract that helped transform my business.

Word about the important work my firm was doing spread quickly, and, before long, I had more clients than I could handle as a solo practitioner. Fortunately, I was able to convince my bestie, Millie, to leave her position at a local law firm and join me.

When I decided to run for office in 2010, I consulted the State Ethics Commission to find out how my business and clients would be impacted if I were elected to the South Carolina House of Representatives. The Commission advised that I couldn't lobby, which I already knew, but I could continue to service our public relations and communications clients. My business partner was allowed to lobby as long as she registered with the State Ethics Commission and the changes were clearly communicated to our clients.

Just after winning the election, I promptly de-registered as a lobbyist and notified the firm's governmental relations and lobbying clients that my business partner would represent them as the firm's only registered lobbyist. I would handle the firm's public relations and strategic communications clients so that the lines were clearly drawn and the transition, seamless.

Not long after I was sworn in as a member of the South Carolina House, everything changed. The State Ethics Commission abruptly informed me that I would have to sever all business ties with Millie and my firm if she continued to register as a lobbyist. In addition, no lobbying activities could be performed under my company's name, although I had already de-registered and advised our clients of our separate roles and responsibilities based on the guidance the State Ethics Commission initially gave us.

Severing all business ties with Millie was senseless, especially since she had given up her job at the law firm to come work with me. And I was going through all of this because of a $10,400/year legislative job that the Republican majority designated as part-time, knowing it was anything but. For those who are retired and independently wealthy, like some of my Republican colleagues, part-time and full-time designations don't really matter. The best way to keep everyday working people like me out of the legislature is to keep the pay really low and the actual hours spent working, really high.

Another registered lobbyist, Todd Atwater, was also elected to the South Carolina House in 2010. The State Ethics Commission assured me that the same rules would apply to him. Unlike me, Representative Atwater was a Republican male who served as CEO of the South Carolina Medical Association, an organization that lobbied the South Carolina General Assembly. At the time, he reportedly earned a six-figure salary. My Republican colleague continued to serve as a state representative while maintaining his other job. As far as I could tell, he did so with no ethics violations, inquiries, or investigations, and kept his position and salary, seemingly without any consequences. Meanwhile, I struggled financially for years, living off my savings while serving in the House.

To be fair and provide some semblance of balance, all working professionals who serve in the South Carolina General Assembly should be required to adhere to the same legal and ethical codes of conduct.

I'm one of a handful of legislators who lobbied *before* I was elected to serve in the S.C. House or Senate. Because effective lobbyists advocate for their clients by engaging and influencing government officials on both sides of the political aisle, it is common for former legislators to become lobbyists *after* they have served, developed an understanding of the process, and forged relationships with other legislators who represent both political parties. I lobbied for eight years before serving a day in the House or Senate. This is a rare and much more challenging route, especially for a Black woman in South Carolina.

My previous work in the executive branch on both sides of the aisle gave me a very unique vantage point, allowing me to forge relationships and alliances with Republicans and Democrats, years before I was elected to the state legislature.

What I learned during those eight years as an outsider prepared me to better advocate, navigate, and infiltrate in some of the most challenging legislative environments imaginable during the 14 years that I served. And as much as it pains me to admit it, I had just as much political influence as an independent lobbyist, as I did while serving in the House and Senate. Probably more.

* * *

My interest in government began in the late '80s as an undergraduate when I was a page in the S.C. House. At that time, public servants were held in high esteem and "your word was your bond."

After State Representative Anton Gunn accepted a key role in the Obama administration in 2010, he asked me if I was interested in running for office. I quickly assured him that I wasn't. (Anyone who knows me would likely agree that I'm the last person they would expect to run for office.) I loved my work as a lobbyist and my public affairs firm was doing really well. Plus, I was making good money and had the freedom and flexibility to be actively involved in all of BJ and Cam's academic and athletic activities.

After trying unsuccessfully to help Anton find a successor, I ended up running for a position I never wanted because it was important to me that BJ and Cam continued to have a state representative who would be a fierce advocate for everyone, especially those whose voices were in jeopardy of being silenced. So, I prayed and talked about it with my family and decided to throw my name in the hat.

It was BJ and Cam who convinced me. They said, "Mom, you always tell us we can't sit on the sidelines. We have to get in the game and do what we can to make a difference." As difficult as it was to hear my own words coming back at me, the fact that my babies were listening, watching, and waiting to see how I would move in that moment was what ultimately compelled me to push past my fear and file. As a first-time candidate with no name recognition or elected experience, I was terrified.

House District 79 was a swing district at the time. The Special Primary was only a few weeks away and included some of Richland County, where I live, as well as a significant portion of neighboring Kershaw County, which is rural and Republican. With no political campaign or fundraising experience, I was grateful that Anton's campaign team agreed to work with me. Their guidance was invaluable. If I won the Primary, I would face a general opponent from neighboring Kershaw County who did have name recognition there.

I was excited that my campaign manager was a woman with experience and wins on both sides of the aisle. There was a lot to learn and a very small window of time to learn it. Right out of the gate, my campaign manager met with me and told me the three things I would have to do to win the House seat: park my BMW in my garage and drive a less expensive car in the rural part of the district; campaign at coffee shops and restaurants in rural, Republican Kershaw County from 7 a.m. to 7 p.m. daily; don't tell any of my prospective constituents that I was a registered lobbyist. When I told her I couldn't do any of these things, honestly ... I was scared to death. What if she was right?

Going against the advice and guidance of a seasoned campaign manager didn't seem like the smartest move, and I knew it. Yet, there I was, a first-time candidate with no clue about what it takes to run a winning campaign in one of South Carolina's fastest-growing swing districts, telling an experienced campaign manager that I wouldn't be able to do the three things she was advising.

"Why not?" she asked, astonished.

To start, I explained that as a single, working mom, I hadn't even considered the cost of a long-term car rental just to drive to the rural part of the district. That would be super expensive, impractical, and extremely inconvenient. I'm from a rural community too and have always known people who drove BMWs, so

I wondered why mine would be an issue for voters in that part of the district.

Next, BJ and Cam weren't running for office. I was. At 7 a.m. I would be helping them get ready for school. By 7 p.m., we would be finishing dinner and preparing for the next school day. Of course I was willing to campaign in Kershaw County, but spending 12 hours there daily wasn't realistic.

Finally, I was awfully proud of the work I was doing as a registered lobbyist. If Kershaw County voters had preconceived notions about lobbyists, I was ready to show them who I was and why I was running. I had to believe they would at least give me that chance.

"Sooo, you're saying you can't do any of the things I'm telling you it'll take to win this seat?" my campaign manager said.

I took a deep breath and tried to figure out a way to at least look like I was confident about the words that were coming outta my mouth.

"Ummm, yeah, that's what I'm saying."

She smirked and said, "Well, if you refuse to follow my advice, you won't win."

Not sure where the wisdom or words came from, but I politely and firmly replied, "Well then, I'll lose, but on my own terms." As we parted ways, I'd be lying if I said I wasn't absolutely mortified. Thinking back to that conversation, this I now know for sure—only God could've given me the courage to be authentic and resolute in that moment.

One day while campaigning in Kershaw County, I knocked on a door and an older white lady answered. I told her who I was, what I did for a living, how and where I grew up, and why I was running for the House seat. She asked questions. I answered the ones I could and promised to get back to her about the ones I couldn't. She told me about some of the issues impacting Kershaw

County residents and why she was concerned about them. I listened intently. We had a great conversation. As I prepared to leave her home, she mentioned that her homeowner's association was very active and engaged and asked if I would commit to attend their meetings. I smiled, looked her in the eye, and told her the truth: "I won't be able to commit to attend every meeting because I have two sons in school and they are my priority."

I assured her that I would attend some events in her neighborhood and around the county, but when my sons had school or athletic events, that's where I would be.

She hugged me and told me how much she appreciated my honesty. Then, she added that she had two grandkids and that she and her husband would be at whatever academic or extracurricular activities they had too. She said she understood and commended me for having my priorities straight.

Being honest with her allowed us to have a genuine conversation and connection. Before I left, she said, "I know everybody in this neighborhood. We're a close-knit community. Leave your cards with me and I'm gonna hand-carry them to all my neighbors and tell 'em to vote for you."

That encounter told me everything I needed to know about campaigning. Before I ever won a race or served a day, it was the courage to be honest and authentic that defined and ultimately distinguished my 14 years of public service.

The night we won the general election against a well-known Tea Party candidate from Kershaw County, I called Daddy to let him know. He was so proud of me. Yet, I could hear the concern in his voice. He knew firsthand how vicious politics can be. I'm convinced that having the courage to be authentic in my interactions with voters is what distinguished me from my opponent and offered the people of Richland and Kershaw counties a real choice.

By the time I won the House District 79 seat, another battle was ensuing. Daddy was in the fight of his life. Cancer had struck again. This time it was lung cancer.

Because he looked and sounded strong, I wasn't overly concerned. Daddy was a fighter and had beaten every medical battle he faced. He would beat this too. Still, my siblings and I are convinced that he never shared his prognosis with us because he didn't want us to worry.

When Daddy died the following year, I didn't really know how to navigate the storms of life without him. He was such a dominant force in my life. I tried to help Tracey as much as I could with our family's funeral business. Daddy had always been the face of it. And because it was family-owned and operated, we didn't have the time or space to grieve our own loss. And it was tremendous. Yet, somehow, we found the strength to pick ourselves up and continue moving forward.

Although his physical presence had left us, Daddy's words of wisdom never left me. What I missed most about him when I ran for the Senate and later, for governor, were his hugs, his laughter, his wisdom, his protection—and his deep bass voice that, like his cologne, warmly filled every room he entered and lingered for days.

Navigating life's challenges without Mama and Daddy, compounded by the stress of public service, caused serious health complications that soon had me fighting for my life again.

* * *

The morning of October 2, 2015, was beautiful, so I decided to walk. I had already gotten Cam off to school and was headed toward the back door to let our dog, Raider, out. Named after BJ and Cam's favorite NFL team, Raider was the cutest Black Lab and Border Collie puppy when we brought him home from the shelter.

By 2015, Raid was getting older and didn't always enjoy long walks, so I decided to go solo that morning to clear my head. It was the weekend of South Carolina's historic flood, and I had no idea what new challenges awaited my district and constituents.

As I approached the back door, my left leg felt like it was going to give. I thought, *Wow, why is my leg feeling funny?* I didn't remember hurting it the day before, so I went to my bedroom, and sat on my bed. My cell phone was on the nightstand to my left and Joyce Meyer, a Christian author who also leads a global ministry, was on television. I leaned back to catch the rest of Joyce and elevate my leg for a few minutes. While I was enjoying a moment of relaxation and a word from Joyce, my cell phone rang.

I leaned forward, picked it up off the nightstand with my left hand, and dropped it before I could bring it to my ear. I saw that the call was from my baby sister Erica. My bed is a little high, so I got down, picked the phone up off the floor to put it back on the nightstand, and planned to call Erica back during my walk. A few minutes later, I was still glued to Joyce's message and my phone rang again.

Thinking it was Erica, I picked the phone up with my left hand. Again, it fell from my grasp, this time landing on my bed instead of the floor. As I finally put the phone to my ear, I could hear my bestie, Millie, say, "Good mornin' dahling. What you doin'?"

I sighed. "Nothin' much. Just being clumsy. My phone just rang twice and I dropped it both times. How's that for a good Friday morning start?" We laughed and talked for a few minutes before I mentioned that I was about to go for my walk once my left leg felt a little stronger.

"What's going on with your leg," Millie asked. "Do you think you need to go to the doctor?"

"No, I feel fine," I assured her. "Besides, I don't have time to go to the doctor today, but I will call."

When I did, the nurse asked which hand I had used to pick up the phone. I told her I used my left hand, both times. I'm left-handed, so I didn't think it was a big deal. She did though and advised me to go to the ER. I insisted that I was fine and pleaded with her to let me come by the office so they could examine me and rule out anything serious. As I was preparing to leave the house, I could tell my balance was off and my leg seemed to be getting weaker instead of stronger. Yet, I was determined to make the 20- to 25-minute drive.

Could it be the stress of losing Granddaddy Jim on June 7 and 10 days later, my colleague and friend, Senator Clementa Pinckney, along with eight of his parishioners at Mother Emanuel Church? Were the sleepless nights and stressful days finally catching up with me?

I had just wrapped up my first series of town hall meetings on race relations in my district when I saw Clem on that fateful Wednesday afternoon in the State House parking garage. "Hey there, Senator!" I said with excitement as we approached each other. He gave me a big smile like he always did and said, "Well, hello there, Representative!" in his great big voice that I miss so much. I joked with him that he was going the wrong way as I headed toward the State House and he walked briskly in the opposite direction toward his car. We always hugged when we saw each other, but I could tell he was rushing that day, so we didn't.

I regret that.

Clem told me he had a big meeting at his church that evening. I told him to be careful on the road. Who could've imagined that several hours later, he and eight members of his Mother Emanuel Church family would be gunned down while they studied God's Word?

Early the next morning, after not sleeping at all the night before, I rode to Charleston for the prayer vigil with a few colleagues. Nothing unusual. We ride together all the time. But *that* day, the shock, horror, and sadness of the tragic night before was still so raw as reports began to come in about the shooter and his capture. This time, I was acutely aware that I happened to be the only Black person in the SUV and noticed how different our reactions and worldviews were. That day and in the days that followed, my thoughts were all over the place.

These guys will never know what it's like to be hated simply because of the color of their skin, I thought. They'll never truly understand the pain, anguish or fear of being hunted, stalked or profiled right here in our home state by people who refuse to see them as human beings—let alone equals. They'll never face a chief magistrate like Judge Gosnell, who, despite being publicly reprimanded by the South Carolina Supreme Court in 2005 for using the N-word in court, was still on the bench to look past the pain of survivors and grieving families, and advise them that the murderer's family members were "victims" too.

As my colleagues moved past the horrific events of the night before and started casually sharing their plans for the upcoming weekend and talking about where we should eat lunch after the prayer vigil, I stared out of the window, empty, without the words, desire, or the capacity to speak.

Everything in my world had changed.

During the prayer vigil, I sat behind Governor Nikki Haley, numb, while she and other speakers pandered and pontificated. Each time I closed my eyes to pray, I saw my babies' faces. All I wanted to do was hug BJ and Cam and tell them again and again how much I loved them. I couldn't even begin to fathom what the survivors and victims' families must be going through.

After those devastating back-to-back personal losses, I was blindsided again in August by the "surprise" announcement that incumbent District 22 Senator Joel Lourie wasn't seeking reelection and had basically handpicked his successor. As I headed to the airport to catch my flight to our national legislative conference in Seattle, I decided to go ahead and announce my intention to run for Senate District 22 after a newspaper reporter for *The State* in Columbia, South Carolina, told me she had spoken with the incumbent and was led to believe I wasn't interested in running for the seat. I was genuinely surprised by his decision, as well as the impending announcement and vacancy, so I simply asked for a day or two to think about it before making a public statement. That wasn't gonna happen since the reporter advised that she was about to publish the story online at midnight with or without my statement.

* * *

By September, things were finally starting to settle down. Tuesday, September 29, felt somewhat like a typical day. This was only my third or fourth time visiting Radhika Patel's hair salon in Columbia. At the time, her salon was a small space on the second level of a red brick building in the Spring Valley area.

As God would have it, we were the only two there. While I sat in her chair waiting for her to complete the final step with a flat iron to give me a silk press, she leaned down and asked, "Are you okay?"

I smiled and simply said, "Yes, I'm good."

I felt fine and couldn't understand why she seemed perplexed.

"I just sense that your heart is heavy. Are you worried about something?"

A day or two before, I had just taken Cam to the doctor where we were told that he would need surgery to repair his knee after tearing his LCL for the second time during a high school football game. Radhika had no way of knowing about Cam's injury or the fact that the orthopedic surgeon told us he had to order specialized surgical instruments to perform the surgery. If it didn't go exactly right, we were told, Cam would never walk straight again.

She put the flat iron down and asked, "Do you mind if I pray for you?"

"No, I don't mind at all," I quickly replied.

Radhika knelt at my feet and began to pray out loud—a bold, beautiful, heart-wrenching prayer—as she worked her way up. By the time she laid her hand on my heart and moved on to my head, I struggled to hold back the tears and could feel the pressure I had become so accustomed to, easing. I wondered why she prayed so fervently for my heart and my head and lingered there. Some 30 minutes later, for the first time in a long time, I felt totally at ease.

Maybe it *was* stress. I tried to let it go, but it wouldn't let *me* go.

* * *

By the time I drove to Dr. Marion's office on October 2, I still felt a little wobbly when I walked in. He wasn't there that day, so I agreed to see the physician's assistant who cut right to the chase and told me I didn't look or act like I was having a stroke. Yet all of my symptoms suggested that a stroke was precisely what was happening. He then told me an ambulance was en route to transport me to the hospital.

"Wait!" I exclaimed, as pride and fear took over. "My best friend said she'll take me."

When Millie arrived, it was a whole ordeal. Dr. Marion's office made her sign me out. Even that didn't deter me. After getting into Millie's car to head to the ER, I suggested that we stop by Chick-fil-A so I could get a sandwich and an ice-cold Dr. Pepper. (Lord only knows how long I'd be in the ER.) Millie found a

CFA drive through on the way. By the time we got to the ER, I couldn't walk. Dr. Marion's office must have alerted them, as they quickly wheeled me to the back and began to perform every test imaginable.

The ER docs and nurses were treating me as if I were having a real, life-threatening medical emergency. A nurse kept asking me basic questions like, "Where do you live? How old are you? How many children do you have? What are their names?"

When she handed me a cookie and asked me to try to chew and swallow it, I laughed and told her that I had just devoured a whole Chick-fil-A sandwich and a Dr. Pepper with no problems. She smiled and politely, but firmly, asked me to chew and swallow the cookie.

What in the world was happening? Was this a real, life-threatening medical emergency that was obvious to everybody, except me?

As the test results began to come in, the neurologist looked very concerned and calmly broke the news.

"Ms. McLeod, you've had a stroke."

"A *stroke?*" I said, thinking she must be mistaken.

"Yes," she assured me. "*Not* a mini-stroke. *Not* a TIA. A full-blown stroke."

I broke down and cried. How could I have had a stroke? I was barely 47 years old. The gravity of the situation hit me as I watched Millie call Tracey, Erica, BJ, and Cam to give them the news. Knowing how worried they would be upset me even more. I asked the neurologist to show me what the stroke looked like because honestly, I just couldn't believe it.

And there it was on the screen—a small, discolored area on my brain that provided irrefutable evidence of the medical trauma I had endured. Every irresponsible, prideful, and reckless move I made that day came rushing back. But for God's grace, this could've gone so differently. There I was, dealing with a stroke

I never saw coming. But God did. And it was obvious once I thought about it. Somehow Radhika did too. By early that Sunday morning, I was begging the hospital to release me and praying the media wouldn't find out. Since I was already an "announced" Senate candidate, there were some who couldn't wait to expose even the slightest hint of weakness or infirmity. It was then that I realized the historic flood would be a storm of epic proportions, for my constituents *and* for me.

Just three days after being released from the hospital, I attended our legislative delegation's briefing on the flood using Cam's crutches—another bad idea that caused more questions than I was prepared to answer. Because I was running for the Senate seat, all eyes were on me, scrutinizing my every move.

The South Carolina Democratic Party (SCDP) establishment didn't want me. I was way too vocal and independent. Neither did incumbent District 22 Senator Joel Lourie. His brother, Neal, was my Republican opponent's "campaign chair." With the tragic murder of Forest Acres police officer Greg Alia, who was shot and killed in the line of duty in the Senate district just two days before, and so much of my House and Senate districts under water after the flood, I *had* to walk again.

The following week, I started physical therapy. Relearning how to walk independently, keep my balance, and not drag my left leg was humbling and much harder to do than I had ever imagined. Heels were out of the question for the foreseeable future. And of course, I was still a bit hard-headed and naive about the days ahead. It would take at least a year of extensive physical therapy, patience, and prayer for me to even begin to regain a significant amount of mobility.

Meanwhile, *The State*'s editorial board weighed in and joined the Democratic District 22 Senator and his family to endorse and support my Republican opponent. The only thing that surprised me was that the editorial board's endorsement of my opponent became one of the best endorsements I **never** had. They said my opponent, "moderate" Republican Susan Brill, would preserve the status quo and that the newspaper couldn't endorse me because the S.C. Senate wasn't ready for someone like me, who:

- could explain the state's major challenges far better than Ms. Brill
- had shown tenacity that is often lacking in our legislators, who are too often willing to work quietly behind the scenes or even ignore problems rather than calling out colleagues
- was one of the few African-American legislators to demand changes to correct leadership failures at the Richland County Election Commission and clean up a toxic, hostile work environment at the Richland County Recreation Commission

The editorial went on to say, "But being this outspoken is a double-edged sword ... we worry about how effective Ms. McLeod would be as a Democrat in an overwhelmingly Republican State Senate ... At a different time in the history of the Senate, we might prefer Ms. McLeod's approach ..."

Perhaps the editorial board had forgotten that the incumbent Senator Joel Lourie was also a Democrat in an overwhelmingly Republican State Senate.

Much of what the editorial referenced was about what happened after I won the House District 79 seat five years before and challenged members of my own party because I believed they chose to protect themselves instead of their constituents during the state's redistricting process. Fighting a redistricting plan that benefited both parties instead of the people Democrats and Republicans purported to serve, earned me a front-page, top-fold article with a salaciously misleading headline suggesting that I didn't want any more Black people in my district.

So yeah, I was constantly at odds with my own majority-Democratic legislative delegation because I insisted that the SCDP fight for my swing district when incumbent legislators on both sides of the aisle packed it with Black voters during the redistricting process. Not long after that, I was also the only member of my delegation to demand transparency and accountability for Democrat and Republican voters who were disenfranchised when the Richland County Election Commission failed to deploy enough working voting machines to polling places during the 2012 Presidential Election. Those fights were more than I bargained for and soon fueled my desire to leave public office. Some SCDP operatives heard me speak candidly about my frustrations with the S.C. Democratic Party.

My stress level only increased a few months later when a video went viral of a female Spring Valley High School student in Richland School District Two who was violently dragged out of her desk and slammed to the floor by a Richland County School Resource Officer (SRO) for no apparent or justifiable reason. When the calls and texts started pouring in, I didn't realize that this young lady's story would birth one of my biggest legislative contributions and become an integral part of my political legacy.

I was barely out of law school in 1996 when I discovered that my home state was number one in the nation for women who are murdered by men and could hardly believe any school resource officer in my county and school district would treat a female student that way. The first thing I did was call my sheriff to ask if he had seen the video. He told me he had.

"Is it real," I asked.

He assured me it was and then asked me to do the impossible and not respond on social media or make any public statements until I had seen everything.

"Did she have a weapon?"

"No."

"Did she threaten to harm anybody?"

"No."

"Is there another video? Did I miss something?"

Again, his answer was, "No."

With that, I had everything I needed.

Democratic members of our Richland County legislative delegation began to call me with lots of unsolicited advice like, "Hey Rep, you know you're not gonna win the Senate seat if you continue to press this. Sticking your nose into school board issues is the best way to lose your election."

For me, it was never about winning or losing an election. I'm a mom first. And as a community leader, I didn't have the luxury of just protecting and advocating for *my* sons. It was my responsibility to protect all students in my district and community, especially after discovering a South Carolina law that allowed the officer to be called into the classroom, although no crime was committed.

Holding those responsible, accountable would help ensure that what happened to this student never happens again. That could easily have been one of my babies. And although I didn't know the young lady who was violently ejected from her desk at Spring Valley High School, she was one of "my babies" too.

The harder I pressed, the more I learned. A state law known as "Disturbing Schools," had been on the books for decades. After researching, I discovered its original intent was to keep South Carolina students, teachers, administrators and staff members safe from outside agitators on school grounds. Yet, this law had morphed into something so sinister. By the time this young lady became its latest victim in 2015, more than 30,000 South Carolina students had been arrested at school, many for non-criminal misbehavior and sent directly into the school-to-prison pipeline, also known as the South Carolina Department of Juvenile Justice.

Sadly, but not surprisingly, most of the students who were impacted looked like me. And once in, many of them never had the advocacy, resources, or support to get out of the system.

As the events continued to unfold and news quickly spread about my position on this issue, some colleagues and community members began to vilify the student and suggest that she was somehow responsible for what happened to her. None of them seemed to wonder about or care why no video footage or witness accounts captured a disruptive, defiant, or dangerous student, or why a law enforcement officer was called into the classroom to deal with a nonviolent, nonthreatening, noncriminal incident.

I was the only one asking questions, and some of them couldn't be answered publicly.

For example: "Could this student have a learning disability or special needs that would warrant additional consideration or special accommodations from the school district?"

Of course, her teachers and administrators knew the answers. We just didn't.

Regardless, there was no justification for the way the school resource officer treated her. Under South Carolina law, if she were his daughter, sister, girlfriend, wife, or *dog*, he would've been arrested and put in jail. Instead, he was hailed as a hero by some and never criminally charged.

Sheriff Leon Lott did fire him from his job and gave me his word, even before I introduced legislation to change this law, that Richland County sheriff's deputies would no longer arrest students at school for disturbing schools if they weren't engaged in criminal activities on school grounds.

He also offered to help me amend the law so that no more South Carolina students would be sent into the school-to-prison pipeline from their classrooms for "disturbing schools." Sheriff Lott kept his promise.

While still in the House, I introduced a bill to change the Disturbing Schools Law. On the day the House subcommittee convened on my bill, the South Carolina Sheriffs' Association shared a letter with the Republican majority on the committee asking them not to move the legislation forward.

During that meeting, one officer from a different county lamented, "Please don't take this tool out of our toolboxes."

"To what tool are you referring?" I asked.

"The power to arrest," he replied.

So instead of protecting us, this officer saw the power to arrest young Black boys and girls as an essential tool in his toolbox.

As a former lobbyist, it was enlightening to be a legislator and discover that some lobbyists and lobbying organizations, particularly those that leaned Republican or overtly pandered to the Republican majority, wielded more power and influence than I did. The Sheriffs' Association's lobbying efforts kept my bill from advancing to the House floor. And my only thought was, *they better hope I don't get elected to the Senate.*

When I shared my frustrations with Dr. Masolwa, my pastor at the time, his comments changed my entire perspective. He said, "Mia, you're always trying to figure out what your ministry is. *This* is your ministry! God has placed you in this seat because you're a strong advocate for the people who is not afraid to speak up. Most elected officials don't have the courage to do that."

He was right. That's why I was constantly fighting with the South Carolina Democratic Party. On the flip side, Republicans wanted to pick up the seat to help their party get to a supermajority in both chambers sooner, which would mean they would have enough votes to pass bills and override the governor's vetoes without Democrats' help or support.

So there I was, heading into a new year, trying to navigate my new normal: weekly doctor's office visits; daily physical therapy sessions; House and Senate districts devastated by the historic flood; and constituents, in both districts, who needed a strong advocate to help them access the resources and support available to them at state and federal levels.

BJ and Cam were legitimately concerned. So were my sisters, Tracey and Erica, and my brother, Jimmy. Every time I allowed myself to think about how differently this health scare could've gone, fear crept back in. God had so much more for me to do and yet doubt and insecurity seemed to be paralyzing me. In those moments, I realized that everything Mama and Daddy told me was true. I just needed to trust God … even if I wasn't sure where He was taking me.

Not long after I announced my intention to run for Senate District 22 in 2015, *The State* did another "story," plastering my name and face on the newspaper's front page, top fold, to suggest that I used my legislative position to secure a contract with the City of Columbia. If they had bothered to do their research, they would've known that city council had legally exempted any contracts at or under $50,000 from the procurement, or competitive bidding process.

What the newspaper conveniently left out was that I had represented the City of Columbia long before I ever ran for office and my professional work with the city was legal, ethical, well-documented, and fully disclosed on my state ethics reports and theirs. Ironically, my Republican and Democratic colleagues, who were awarded much larger contracts from other government entities while they served in the legislature, didn't make the front page. In fact, numerous other lawmakers whose contracts were six or seven figures were barely acknowledged on a subsequent page of the article. No pictures. No fanfare. And not even a hint of impropriety.

Even *after* I won the Senate seat pretty handily against Republican Susan Brill, who was endorsed by *The State*, it seems the newspaper wasn't done and reached back out to city officials to ask if the city would continue to contract with my firm, once I was sworn in.

Since I'm damn good at my job and unable to live on a base annual legislative salary of $10,400, I don't have a problem finding paying work. What I do have a problem with is media outlets that create "stories" to suggest that my clients are contracting with my firm *because* I happen to serve in the legislature. Legislators and government officials must disclose whether they are employed by, contracting with, related to, in business with, or otherwise affiliated with any individual or entity that has budget or policy issues that come before the South Carolina legislature. Since the city and I fully disclosed the professional work for which my firm was contracted, our contractual relationship was legally and ethically compliant under South Carolina law. Public records could've easily been obtained to verify that.

If *The State* really wanted to stir up some "good trouble," perhaps it should've headed to a county courthouse when court was in session because in my home state, legislators who happen to also practice law, elect South Carolina judges ... the same judges those lawyer-legislators appear before in court on behalf of their clients.

Last time I checked, South Carolina is one of only two states in the country where legislators elect judges. Yet, so-called legislative watchdogs rarely, if ever, show up in South Carolina courtrooms to monitor how clients of lawyer-legislators fare during court proceedings or whether there appears to be any undue influence on the judges these lawyer-legislators elect. For the rest of us who don't practice law and happen to serve in the legislature, it would be nice to receive the same deference and work under the same professional standards as our colleagues. All working professionals who serve in the S.C. General Assembly should be required to adhere to the same legal and ethical codes of conduct. Period.

Mama and Daddy always told us that we can't do what everybody else does and they were right.

As a freshman senator, I chose to push past the double standard so that I could continue to focus on the people I served. My first order of business for the 2017 legislative session was to reintroduce my Disturbing Schools Bill. I spent countless hours working through the key components of the bill with my Republican colleagues, the S.C. Sheriffs' Association and Sheriff Lott. We had subcommittee meetings on it and managed to get it passed out of the Senate subcommittee with a favorable report. By the time we debated it on the Senate floor, my Disturbing Schools Bill had strong bipartisan sponsorship and support and passed the S.C. Senate and S.C. House overwhelmingly in 2018!

Today, South Carolina students can only be arrested on school grounds if they engage in criminal activity at school, are suspended or expelled and return to school to harm others, or communicate a threat.

Yet, even as we celebrated that hard-fought victory in 2018, I still struggled with deeply personal losses from the year before. My Aunt Barbara was diagnosed with ovarian cancer, and I traveled to Michigan as much as I could to support her. It was difficult to juggle so many life challenges. Yet, I believed my service was making a difference in people's lives, so I kept fighting.

Losing Aunt Barbara, Mama's baby sister who was like a second mom, and my first cousin, Jeffrey, who was like a brother, in the same year was devastating for my family and me. Thanksgiving dinners and other family gatherings would never be the same. My big sister Tracey, who survived Stage IV breast cancer

20 years before, faced a recurrence of breast cancer that year. I remember leaving the Senate floor to go with her to every oncology appointment and thinking about the courage she and Mama had shown when both were diagnosed with cancer in 1997 and underwent extensive rounds of chemo and radiation. On May 28, 2018, after I knew Tracey was healed and had recovered, I decided to go ahead and have that outpatient knee surgery I had been putting off. It was Memorial Day and Cam was home after completing his sophomore year at Colorado State. My orthopedic surgeon told me I'd have to make time for outpatient physical therapy and should be back at work in about a week, so it seemed like the perfect time.

The surgery went well and by all accounts was uneventful until two days later when my leg was still swollen and the pain seemed to be getting more intense. I assumed it was what the nurses warned me about once the pain meds wore off.

When I went to my first outpatient physical therapy session the pain was worse. As the therapist removed the gauze to assess whether we could start therapy that day, he quickly realized my leg was still too swollen. I sent my orthopedic surgeon a text in the middle of the night on the following Sunday and told him. He advised me to come to his office first thing Monday morning. Fortunately, there was no fluid to drain and no signs of infection, so they wheeled me next door to the ER for IV fluids to ward off any Sickle Cell complications that might make a bad situation worse. By then, I was frustrated that it was taking forever for them to see me. The pain was excruciating, and I just wanted to go home. Thank God, I didn't. The doctor explained that I had developed a post-surgical blood clot in my leg (deep vein thrombosis or DVT) that had already traveled to my lungs (pulmonary embolism or PE). I didn't even go to the ER until June 4, a whole week after the knee surgery. This was my first orthopedic surgery, and I didn't realize Sickle Cell Anemia put me at higher risk for blood clots with any orthopedic surgery.

After a series of burning heparin shots in my belly, they rolled me up to the ICU to begin my extended hospital stint.

I could see the fear in my family's eyes, even though they tried not to show it. When Uncle Gary looked at my left leg, which had swollen to about four times its normal size, he took a deep breath and said, "So this is it ... right? We're not running anymore." I nodded in agreement but was still in shock trying to figure out how things had gotten so bad, so fast.

Weeks later, I was grateful to finally be able to go home. I developed pneumonia just before my release, which further complicated things and forced me to stay several more days. Yet, I was still thankful to have survived what so many people don't.

Realizing that I needed a walker just to stand or take a step was a sobering moment for me. I've always been so independent. This time was different. A home health nurse came a few times each week to take my vitals, check my leg, and provide physical therapy. It would be a long, grueling recovery process. My left leg was still about three times the size of my right. I could do very little for myself. Tracey had literally just beaten breast cancer for the second time and stayed with me for weeks until I was strong enough to take showers without her help. For the remainder of 2018, I was confined to my house and committed to physical therapy and rest.

Being at home meant God finally had a captive audience. He forced me to "Be still ..." something even a stroke couldn't do three years before.

* * *

Soon, I became engrossed in Brett Kavanaugh's contentious United States Supreme Court confirmation hearing and was forced to reckon with my own rape during the summer of 1986.

It was a traumatic experience that I had shared with absolutely no one and thought I had successfully repressed. It wasn't until I watched those hearings that my own trauma was triggered and I was forced to confront it. As I wrestled with whether to publicly disclose what happened to me over three decades before, I also had to think about the fact that no one in my immediate family knew. Not my sons. Not my siblings. Not even my mom and dad who were no longer living.

Like Kavanaugh's accuser, Christine Blasey Ford, I struggled to remember the exact date, time, and location of the assault. But I've never forgotten the pain, hurt, guilt, shame, and fear I felt in that moment and many moments since.

And no, I never reported it.

Daddy had finally allowed me to go on the date and would have killed him ... literally. That's why I couldn't risk telling anybody. After the way they treated Anita Hill, the law professor who courageously testified that then U.S. Supreme Court nominee Clarence Thomas had sexually harassed her when he was her supervisor, I knew I had made the right decision.

So while my ability to remember every detail of the assault may have been sketchy, the identity of the person who assaulted me wasn't. As U.S. Senator Lindsey Graham made a mockery of the Kavanaugh hearings with his own partisan, political sideshow—blaming Democrats for masterminding the allegations to destroy Kavanaugh's family and derail his Supreme Court nomination—what God was telling me to do became painfully obvious.

I had to challenge Lindsey Graham.

Telling BJ, Cam, Tracey, Erica and Jimmy, that I was raped during the summer of 1986, was almost as scary as the thought of running for statewide office. For the rest of 2018 and well into 2019, I tried to "talk God out of it." Seemed like the harder I prayed, the clearer He was. I knew I had to run against Senator Lindsey Graham in 2020. The question was, "How?" I was still on crutches and anticipating at least one more knee surgery.

As I prepped for the second knee surgery in 2019, I had lots of time and even more reasons to second guess what God told me. For five straight days, I drove across town, about 40 minutes each way, so that a nurse could inject a blood-thinning medication called Lovenox into my stomach to prevent blood clots leading up to the surgery. Clinching my fists as the medicine burned my belly, I thought, *Surely I've misunderstood. God knows I need to be 100 percent healthy and mobile to campaign statewide.*

I was on crutches for so long that my sorority sister, Myra, had them blinged out for me with beautiful pink and green rhinestones that were sure to turn heads and start conversations. Although super cute, the crutches weren't showpieces. I needed them. Meanwhile, I wondered how I could continue physical therapy, serve in the S.C. Senate, and hobble around the state on crutches to beat Lindsey Graham?

Just the thought of it overwhelmed me so much that I found myself meditating on my circumstances instead of what God told me to do. By that time, Radhika had become my pastor. She kept reminding me that "God doesn't give instruction without provision." Although I had come a long way in terms of my healing since the surgeries, blood clots, and pneumonia, I still had such a long way to go to regain full strength and mobility. How could God expect me to run against Lindsey Graham when I still needed physical therapy and crutches just to get around?

Jaime Harrison, a South Carolina native and former S.C. Democratic Party chair, had already announced. Even though it was obvious that the S.C. Democratic Party establishment's machine was behind him, that didn't really concern me. I like Jamie and was surprised when he announced that he was running. If the people of South Carolina put my voting record and accomplishments up against his in a primary, there was no doubt in my mind I would win. So while my own thoughts and fears about my limited mobility continued to paralyze me, God had a plan that none of us could have foreseen. It was a very timely and powerful reminder that "His thoughts are not our thoughts. Neither are His ways our ways ..."

Each personal and political battle I've faced has taught me more about how to adequately arm myself against the physical, spiritual, mental, and emotional adversaries that are constantly trying to take me out. From confronting life-threatening health issues to surviving a myriad of political attacks from the right and the left, I know what it takes to look fear squarely in the face and do it anyway—even if I have to do it alone. And yes, even if I have to do it afraid.

Daddy's girl, Bennettsville, S.C.

My family (clockwise): Daddy, Tracey, Jimmy, me, Erica, Mama

Mama and Daddy

CHAPTER ONE
Looks Can Be Deceiving

The thing you fear most has no power. Your fear of it is what has the power. Facing the truth really will set you free.
—Oprah Winfrey

Choosing to confront fear and learn from it is one of the best decisions I've ever made. Never was that more clear than at the beginning of the pandemic. As we celebrated the promises of a new year in January of 2020, the pandemic seemed like a distant threat for those who weren't traveling internationally, so I thought it would probably be a while before COVID-19 hit South Carolina.

My firstborn had just celebrated his 26th birthday and purchased his first home, a two-story, new build in a rapidly growing area that was perfect for young professionals. Just after returning from a speaking engagement at my godparents' church in Richmond, Virginia, and enjoying BJ's housewarming, the pandemic was declared by the World Health Organization.

Googling information about COVID-19 and its implications quickly became part of my daily routine. I remember questioning S.C. Republican Majority Leader Massey on the Senate floor about whether the pandemic would affect us and how. He was extremely dismissive, even suggesting that we go on with our lives and "do what we've been doing," as if my questions were meant to evoke fear and concern when there was no need for either.

As the news was breaking, Governor Henry McMaster insisted he would still attend a parade in the upstate the following weekend. Although I was deeply concerned, a part of me wondered if I *was* overreacting. Did the governor and the majority leader have information that we didn't? Why were their actions not aligned with the advice and guidance of experts? Shouldn't we, as government leaders, take every recommended precaution to protect the lives and livelihoods of our constituents?

Why did it take at least two open letters from me to shame the governor into temporarily shutting down businesses until we could assess the risks associated with this virus and determine the best course of action, based on the science, to help keep South Carolinians safe?

On March 25, I woke up to the news that my friend and former colleague Jack West had died from complications of COVID-19. Son of former South Carolina Governor John C. West, Jack was well known and loved by many. He was one of the first to die in South Carolina and it was obvious that the Republican majority wanted to keep that heartbreaking news under wraps. When I first heard he was sick, I thought, "Jack hasn't been out of the country lately, so it can't be COVID-19." I called his bestie and business partner, Ron Fulmer. I've adored these two "grumpy old men" since we worked side-by-side on the City of Columbia's government relations team years before I ever even thought about serving in the South Carolina House or Senate.

Jack was a Democrat. Ron was a former Republican lawmaker, who served in the House. Anytime Millie and I were around the two of them, we were gonna learn *and* laugh ... a lot!

Ron was brutally honest about Jack's prognosis. Yet, he seemed hopeful. I continued to pray for Jack, as well as Ron and their families. It was tough to think about Jack being on a ventilator.

The news of Jack's passing seemed surreal. He was so funny and full of life. And just like that, my buddy who stopped by my Senate office just to make me laugh or introduce me to one of his clients was gone.

Even after it became blatantly obvious that COVID-19 was killing South Carolinians at an alarming rate, the Republican majority didn't seem concerned. Reluctantly, Republican House and Senate leaders temporarily suspended the legislative session so that we could assess the threat, determine next steps, and chart a path forward.

Governor McMaster's daily press conferences seemed to have morphed into an opportunity to discourage masks, end temporary closures, reopen schools prematurely and force our state's working poor back to work. By cutting the $600 federal pandemic unemployment benefit, the governor forced the state's lowest wage earners to return to their $7.25 an hour jobs for "slave wages" with no mandatory COVID-19 safety protocols. Many South Carolinians couldn't survive physically or financially.

Once I decided I wasn't running for the U.S. Senate in 2020, I tried to focus on my reelection to the State Senate. After serving six years in the S.C. House and four in the S.C. Senate, I was prepared to campaign and win, even during a pandemic. What I didn't realize at the time was that my reelection bid to the Senate would be a little bittersweet because I didn't do what God told me to and run against Senator Lindsey Graham.

After deciding that my limited mobility made it practically impossible to run a strong statewide campaign against Lindsey, I met Jaime Harrison for lunch to let him know. Jaime had already announced his intention to run against Lindsey and asked for my support. When he first asked, I told him I couldn't commit because I was still trying to decide whether I would run against Lindsey Graham myself. He told me he understood.

Still, several establishment Dems reached out to ask, "Do you have a problem with Jaime?"

I didn't. It was never about Jaime. It was always about what God told *me* to do.

Meanwhile, a Democratic congressman from a different state reached out to let me know that, like Jaime, he was super close to our Sixth District Congressman Jim Clyburn and that Jaime had the congressman's full support. That news came as no surprise. However, his call did. He went on to say, "If Jim thought the U.S. Senate seat was winnable, *he'd* be running for it."

He asked if there was any way I would consider getting behind Jaime. The more he talked, the more I realized Jaime's run was about elevating his profile for his next move, rather than actually winning the Senate seat. That hit me hard. I still hoped Jaime would work like hell to win.

Lord knows, *anybody* would be better for South Carolina than Lindsey Graham.

I believed I couldn't run statewide on crutches. Yet, this restlessness in my spirit just wouldn't go away. When Jaime and I met for lunch, I told him I decided not to run against Lindsey and would support him. He seemed relieved about my decision and grateful to have my support.

Turns out, 2020 was the year I'd face one of my biggest reelection opponents—another "moderate" Republican whose last name happened to be Blatt. Lee Blatt was a descendant of Solomon Blatt, one of South Carolina's longest serving House speakers, who at one time was a die-hard segregationist. Blatt's name still carries a lot of political weight in our state. He served as speaker of the S.C. House for decades, including the year I was born. Some 37 years after Blatt's tenure as House speaker, I was elected to the S.C. House, and my legislative office was in the "Blatt Building."

In the weeks leading up to the 2020 General Election, I was doing what I always do—hosting town halls and community forums to engage and enlighten voters about the issues and challenges our district and community were facing. Because of COVID-19, my team and I had to do things very differently. Instead of in-person events, Zoom and Facebook Live were quickly becoming a thing, so I hosted my first virtual town hall series on COVID-19 via Zoom and livestreamed it on Facebook.

Our virtual town hall series was a hit and had significant engagement because people in and beyond my Senate district were hungry for timely, accurate information that allowed them to hear directly from the experts, so that they could safely navigate the pandemic.

By the time my birthday rolled around in August, COVID-19 was impacting every aspect of our lives. My campaign team suggested that a virtual birthday fundraiser could help me raise money as we tried to figure out how to continue to engage voters in meaningful ways. A few elected officials submitted videos for the virtual fundraiser, including Congressman Clyburn. He talked about how close he and Daddy were and said something in the video I never knew.

Daddy was the one who helped him get his start in politics.

That news warmed my heart because everybody who knows me knows how much of a "Daddy's girl" I was. It was Daddy who connected me with Congressman Clyburn in 1991 when he was working at the South Carolina Human Affairs Commission. By the time Daddy urged me to volunteer on his initial campaign for Congress in 1992, I had just started law school and was excited to make phone calls, stuff envelopes, and volunteer at his campaign events to help him become our state's newest member of Congress.

Fundraising for my reelection to the Senate was going pretty well. Yet, it seemed insignificant considering the challenges facing

South Carolinians during the pandemic. As I worked around the clock from my home office to help those who lived in Senate District 22 and those who didn't, I was reminded that when people know you care and will fight for them, they won't hesitate to reach out and ask for help. Phone calls and emails started coming in from all over South Carolina—from the Upstate, Lowcountry, Pee Dee and Midlands, which was the region of our state that I represented.

Many were unemployed because of the pandemic and couldn't get a live person on the phone at the South Carolina Department of Employment and Workforce (SCDEW) to answer questions about the application process for unemployment benefits. Others had school-aged children and were understandably concerned about the very real possibility of schools and workplaces reopening prematurely, since exposures and deaths across South Carolina were consistently on the rise.

Still, others were living with chronic health conditions like I was. And because the Republican majority politicized the pandemic, people needed help accessing accurate information about the virus to safely navigate their environments. Too often, it was hard to break through the partisan rhetoric and misinformation that was deliberately circulated to minimize and confuse.

After Labor Day, District 22 constituents and community members were starting to call me daily to express concerns that my republican opponent had big campaign signs with the name BLATT and hardly any other identifiers, except the Senate district number. From his signage, nobody could tell whether he was a Democrat or Republican, male or female—let alone anything about his platform.

What he did have was lots of money to self-fund his campaign, as well as resources and support from the Republican caucus. So, while I was serving my constituents and other South

Carolinians from home, my opponent was increasing his name recognition throughout the district with prominently placed campaign signage from Blythewood to Forest Acres and beyond. I kept reminding myself that signs don't vote and that I just needed to keep working hard and raising money.

When my phone rang early the next morning, it was Kelly, my sorority sister and constituent. Before I could even finish saying, "Good morning," she hit me with, "Blatt's got signs at both ends of my street in Wildewood and I don't see any big signs of yours in my area. What do we need to do to help you get more signs?"

I could hear the concern in her voice and assured her that we were waiting on a batch of our big signs to come in. She asked if we needed campaign contributions. I told her we did and asked if she could host a virtual fundraiser or help engage donors in her network. She promised to help. Minutes after we hung up, my phone rang again.

This time, a constituent and supporter from my church called to tell me that Lee Blatt had just left her house. Thinking I must've misunderstood, I said, "I'm sorry. Didn't hear you. Can you repeat that?"

"I *said*, your opponent just left my house. I was outside doing some yardwork and out of nowhere, this guy walks up my driveway and introduces himself. He said he was running for Senate District 22, so to be sure, I asked him who he was running against and he said, 'Mia McLeod.' I didn't hesitate to let him know that my family and I support *you*. He didn't stick around after that. I just couldn't believe he was actually walking the neighborhood during a pandemic when people are advised to stay home to limit physical contact."

That phone call concerned me much more than Kelly's. If my opponent was going door-to-door campaigning, how would that impact my ability to connect with voters, since my doctors were adamant that I work from home to limit my risk of exposure to COVID-19? What about Senate District 22 constituents who didn't already know me or weren't familiar with my work and the fights I'd led over the years?

Those types of phone calls quickly became a daily occurrence, and I hoped that constituents and community members who knew and supported me, continued to do so and shared their reasons with family members, friends, colleagues, neighbors, and others in their networks. Donald Trump was on the ballot again and nobody seemed to be sure how the pandemic was going to affect this election, since there was no precedent for the challenges we were facing.

Before long, anti-Lindsey money started to pour into Jaime's campaign from all over the country! Jaime's TV ads were saturating media markets in every geographic region of South Carolina and beyond. Even friends and relatives in other states were calling me to ask about his chances and whether they should support him. I reached out to Jaime to let him know that my godparents in Virginia and other relatives and friends around the country would be sending him campaign contributions. He seemed excited about the outpouring of support, so I thought he would put the influx of money to good use.

In the days and months leading up to the general election, I communicated with Jaime more regularly to help him connect with other Democrats and a few Republicans who expressed interest in supporting his campaign. As media outlets reported that more than $130 million had flowed into Jaime's campaign, he admitted that he too, was shocked. It was obvious that regardless who won the U.S. Senate race, S.C. Democrats would finally have access to some of the financial resources needed to build and strengthen the party's infrastructure. I was elated about the SCDP's ability to reach, enlighten, engage, and mobilize voters.

My home mailbox and post office box were inundated with mail from the S.C. Democratic Party about Jaime's historic campaign. "Jaime for U.S. Senate" ads ran day and night on local, state, and national media outlets. So, when Jaime told me he wasn't doing any get-out-the-vote (GOTV) efforts because of the pandemic, I was surprised. With that much money, I just knew he and his team were gonna find innovative ways to engage and mobilize voters, especially since they had the resources.

And when credible SCDP sources lamented that the majority of the anti-Lindsey campaign funds that seemed to flow effortlessly into Jaime's campaign, flowed right back out to pay Washington, D.C., consultants who knew very little about South Carolina, I was floored.

Around the same time, several House members vented openly about their frustrations. Instead of campaign contributions, some House Dems who had opposition were pissed that the Harrison campaign purchased yard signs for them instead.

As we got closer to election day, I was still pulling and praying for Jaime to win ... just less optimistic that he would, as rumors spread within the Democratic community about intentionally inflated poll numbers and less voter engagement on the ground.

My sons and their friends weren't the least bit excited or engaged by Jaime's U.S. Senate race, although I convinced them to vote for him. Most of his support seemed to be anti-Lindsey, not pro-Jaime. So much wasn't adding up. I could've kicked myself for not having the courage to do what God told me to do. Still, there was no use wallowing in self-pity or regret.

Before we knew it, election night was here. The returns would soon tell me everything I needed to know about my race ... and his.

It was getting close to 7 p.m. and the polls were about to close. I was immersed in my own race as the returns began to trickle in, but I noticed that Jaime appeared to be losing to Lindsey Graham. After all the votes were tallied, Jaime lost by a double-digit margin. And that was just the beginning of the revelations God had for me.

What happened on November 3, 2020, seemed to have surprised pollsters, political pundits, candidates, and incumbents, statewide and nationally, across the political spectrum. Joe Biden and Kamala Harris defeated Donald Trump and Mike Pence to win the U.S. presidency as well as the majority of Electoral College and popular votes. Georgia was the only Southern state to break Trump's stronghold in the region. It was Georgia and Arizona that helped seal the win for the Biden/Harris ticket.

In South Carolina, God answered my prayers with the most affirming, decisive victory I've ever had over a Republican opponent. I beat Lee Blatt by over 24 points without knocking on doors or leaving my house. That same year, the S.C. Senate Democratic Caucus lost three of its well-known, long-serving members: Vincent Sheheen, a lawyer and S.C. Democratic Party favorite who had previously run twice for governor and was defeated both times by Nikki Haley; Glenn Reese, a Krispy Kreme mogul who had always won in his SCGOP county of Spartanburg; and Floyd Nicholson, a former mayor, city council member, teacher and Greenwood coach who had been successful with voters on both sides of the political aisle in his majority Republican counties.

Not only had I defeated my Republican opponent by a record margin, but my Senate district outperformed every other Democratic Senate race that year. Still, losing three members of the Senate Democratic Caucus was a devastating blow for the 16 of us who were reelected.

In January of 2021, we returned to a very different Senate, one where the Republican majority unapologetically acted as if it had already secured its soon-to-be supermajority, flexing its newfound power and control with rule and procedural changes that didn't require our approval. What better way to remind us that the SCGOP no longer needed our voices or votes to prioritize and pass legislation that would further marginalize, disenfranchise, and oppress the minority.

On the morning after my reelection to the Senate, I was excited and grateful that Senate District 22 voters decided to send me back to the State House for four more years. Yet, I still couldn't shake that nagging feeling that God was showing me something bigger. Then it hit me.

The U.S. Senate race wasn't Jaime's to win. It was mine.

I promised God I would trust Him from that day forward, no matter what. And it wasn't long before He tested me on that promise.

* * *

During the holiday break in the midst of the pandemic, South Carolina Senate Democratic Minority Leader Brad Hutto asked me if I would deliver the Democrats' State of the State Response to Governor McMaster's annual address in January of 2021. As the governor's most vocal critic about his mishandling of the pandemic, of course I accepted. Around the same time, God began to talk to me about doing more.

All of my frustration was directed toward Governor McMaster.

And for good reason.

Although I wasn't sure what God was leading me to do at that point, I knew I was committed to being obedient this time. And because I'm an introvert who tries to avoid cameras, delivering the State of the State Response was going to be extremely uncomfortable for me. I knew I had to do it though and was determined to give it my absolute best. Besides, I looked forward to exposing the fact that the governor was politicizing the pandemic. My response had to show how his actions and inactions were harming the people of South Carolina.

As I began to think about what I would say and the impact I hoped my response would have, I received a call from a fairly new caucus member on the morning of December 28. It was my Senate Dems colleague Dick Harpootlian. I had no idea why Dick was calling, so I answered and we spoke briefly about the holidays before he said he had something to ask me.

Not thinking it would be anything crazy, I said, "Cool ... what's up?"

"I've talked to Brad and he told me he asked you to do the State of the State Response, so I'm calling to ask you for a favor."

I said, "Okay, what do you need?"

Dick paused for a moment, "Would you be willing to let Joe Cunningham do it?"

This time, I was the one who paused, "Ummm ... do *what?*" I asked, thinking I must've misunderstood his question.

"Deliver the State of the State Response," he blurted.

My raw reaction was an emphatic, "NO!!" which was much nicer than the emphatic "HELL NO!!" that actually came to mind.

Dick obviously didn't expect me to respond so quickly and decisively, because he then attempted to explain why he asked me, starting with, "Do you know who Joe Cunningham is?"

I said, "He's the guy who won the 1st Congressional District seat in Charleston and couldn't even get reelected to a second term, right?"

"Ahhh right, but here's why I think you should consider letting him do the State of the State Response. And you don't have to give me an answer now. Just take a few days and think ..."

Before he could finish, I interrupted and said, "I've already given you an answer, Dick, and it's NO! I don't need to think about it. Next question."

"Yes, Joe lost his reelection, but he's probably gonna run for governor and it would give him a chance to get his name and face out there. Plus, nobody gives a shit about anything we have to say. I bet you can't even tell me who gave the Democratic Response last year, or hell, the last few years. People are tired of seeing and hearing from us. They don't give a fuck about which one of us is talking. They just don't wanna hear from legislators. This guy is good-looking and he'll have women lined up to support him."

By the time he went there, he was talking to himself. I was *so* deeply offended on *so* many levels. To put it bluntly, I was done. *Done* done.

That phone call disrupted my morning and my peace … and I was determined to get both back. The new year came in quietly, as I prayed for protection from COVID-19 for my family, my constituents and their families, my community, and for me. Seemed a little strange to still feel as vulnerable as we did in March of 2020 when the pandemic was first declared. I think most of us were finally coming to terms with the fact that we had to fend for and protect ourselves as the governor and Republican majority did less and less to protect us.

The closer we got to January 13, the more nervous I was about having to venture out of my house to record the State of the State Response, especially since I would be in the presence of other people—some I'd know; others I wouldn't—for the first time since the pandemic began.

Will I be able to social distance while I'm recording? I thought. Will the podium and microphone be sanitized? Would any of the folks at SCETV or on my team be COVID-positive but asymptomatic?

Just the thought of it was starting to freak me out.

When I walked into SCETV on that Monday, January 11, I knew I had to keep my composure and not give in to the what-ifs, so I prayed and tried to let go of the stress and anxiety I was feeling. My team—Lauren, Trav, and Meghan—met me there. After a few moments, we were escorted down the halls and into the recording room. The cameras, audiovisual equipment and teleprompter were soon ready to roll. We did one quick practice run and before long, it was time for take one!

Breathe Mia, I thought, as I took a deep breath in and exhaled audibly. From that moment, there was no doubt God was with me. I was calm, confident, and no longer anxious.

If I killed it on the first take, we could get outta there and back to the safety and comfort of our homes. That was the plan. Well, at least that was *my* plan. Of course it didn't happen that way.

Take one was going perfectly until something didn't sound right. I had spent so much time drafting, proofing, and editing my response, I could almost feel even the slightest deviation. And sure enough, the semifinal version had inadvertently been loaded into the teleprompter. Must've been an oversight, since I sent the final draft to SCETV in advance, as requested. It was just enough to get my nerves going again, so I took another deep breath and exhaled. *No big deal*, I thought. This was just the first take. Lauren and Meghan offered to load the correct version, and in just a few minutes, we were ready to roll again.

Take two was going really well ... until things went left—at the same spot. How could the semi-final draft be back on the teleprompter after my team had just carefully reloaded the correct version? Surprisingly, I was still calm and determined not to let these little hiccups disturb my peace. My team tried again to load the correct version into SCETV's system, and this time, the studio director was there to ensure there would be no more issues.

Take three was underway and I convinced myself that "the third time was the charm."

Wrong.

This time, the correct version was displayed, but the teleprompter was arbitrarily deleting some of the words and sentences. *What in the world is happening?* I thought. The SCETV staff did a little more troubleshooting, fixed the problem, and we were on to take four.

By that point, all of us were kind of looking at each other in disbelief. As I started to deliver the response for the fourth, and hopefully final time, it was going exceptionally well until I got to the beginning of the last paragraph. The teleprompter screen went totally blank and would not come back on. The SCETV staff again apologized profusely. This time, I could tell that they were even more perplexed. There was no logical reason or explanation for the outage. The SCETV crew verified that everything was fully charged and in good operating condition. None of the indicators were showing signs of distress or power failure. The operating systems were working normally.

That's when I knew it was just the enemy trying to disturb my peace. I had a choice to make. Was I going to trust God or bow to the chaos and confusion that seemed to be wreaking havoc all around me? Looks can be deceiving, so in true Isaiah 54:17 fashion, I reminded myself of God's promises and shook off everything that was coming for my confidence and my peace ... knowing that it wouldn't prosper.

"Annnnnnd ... we're back," the staff shouted.

Whew, I thought.

A few minutes later, the teleprompter was up and running again, finally! Why it blacked out was still a mystery, but at least they got it restarted. This was turning into quite a lengthy and eventful experience. The camera guy assured me that I was delivering the response better than most. He seemed baffled by the challenges and genuinely sorry they were happening. As I made my way through the majority of the response for the fifth time, the teleprompter scrolled toward the final paragraph, the screen went dark again, and this time, couldn't be revived.

I wanted to scream.

Yet, all I could do was chuckle, look up toward heaven, shake my head, and think, *"I see you, God. I know you've got this and I trust You."*

His supernatural warmth enveloped me. The studio director said we would have to take a break so her engineers could troubleshoot whatever was causing these issues.

Everyone in the room was concerned. The SCETV staff asked if we wanted to shut it down for the day and reschedule for tomorrow. I said, "Absolutely not!"

They knew that I had been standing on my feet all that time and asked if I wanted to sit down while they performed the system checks. I genuinely thanked them and politely declined. Although my legs and feet were tired, for me to sit down would've felt like I was cowering in the face of adversity. *God is way too good for me to not continue to stand boldly on His Word in this moment,* I thought. *No, I'm fine right here at this podium. And no matter how long it takes, I'm gonna stand right here until I've done what I came here to do.*

I could tell they didn't really understand why I refused to sit. And that's okay. They didn't have to.

After a pretty long break, the engineers were able to restore power to the teleprompter, and it was time for take six. In my excitement and haste, I'm the one who messed up this time. The teleprompter didn't. It was my first real faux pas of the day, so I tried to give myself some grace. Regardless, we were gonna have to do yet another take. Ugh. I could feel my stress level rising, so I asked everyone to give me a minute. They graciously agreed.

I closed my eyes and prayed silently, standing right there at the podium. When I opened them, I knew in my spirit that this one was it, so I told them I was ready to roll.

Take seven went perfectly! Everybody looked at each other with big eyes, as if they were afraid someone forgot to hit the record button or something. While they were looking around, I was looking up saying, *thank you* to the one who reminded me to just "Be still and know."

The guys who operated the cameras told me that my response delivery was the absolute best they had ever seen. Although it was hard for me to believe when they first said it, I knew God was with me. What they had actually witnessed was His strength and excellence on display, not mine.

They asked if I wanted to see the video before I left, in case I didn't like it and wanted to re-record. At first, I said yes because I'm my harshest critic. If it wasn't absolutely perfect, I would definitely want a do-over.

As I walked toward the monitor to see the video, something in my spirit said, *so you're done trusting God now?* Instantly, I made a quick U-turn and headed toward the door. I couldn't believe the words that were actually coming out of my mouth. I told them I would wait to see the response when it aired on Wednesday. The studio director smiled and said she would send me an encrypted copy a little sooner, which was very thoughtful and kind. By then it would still be too late to redo it if I didn't like it.

When I watched the video at home on my laptop, I cried. Everything that happened on Monday seemed like a bad dream. Yet, it really did happen. And the camera guy was right; my delivery was as close to perfect as I had ever seen. My words were clear; my voice, strong. Hair and makeup, flawless. And what was even more shocking was that I had done both myself because all the salons were closed.

It was like I was watching someone else. I knew in my heart that for the first time I was actually seeing myself the way God sees me. It was His strength and courage on full display.

When the response aired after the governor's State of the State Address, I was still taken aback by how flawless my delivery and appearance were. Nobody would ever look at it and believe we encountered the obstacles we did. It literally felt like we were under siege almost the entire time we were trying to record.

Like Scripture says, "When you pass through the waters, I will be with you; and through the rivers, they shall not overwhelm you; when you walk through the fire you shall not be burned, and the flame shall not consume you."

After it aired, my phone started ringing right away. *Obviously, people do listen to legislators.* I heard from folks all over the state and some from out of state, commending me on the substance and delivery of my response. Even God has a sense of humor because Dick sent me this text the following morning:

Mia, you knocked it out of the park last night. I was wrong.
You were much better than Joe would have been.
Occasionally I am wrong and I am glad I was this time.
–Dick

Delivering the State of the State Response

LESSON ONE: *Fear Is a Friend*

Most people think fear is a dark, frightening, crippling, debilitating giant of an enemy that is out to paralyze, embarrass, humiliate, or ultimately destroy us and any semblance of confidence we may have thought we had. Those types of thoughts aren't grounded in reality, they're grounded in fear. And although they may feel real, those assumptions couldn't be further from the truth.

Actually, fear is not our foe. It's a motivator, facilitator, catalyst, or vehicle that grips all of us at some point in our lives. Where we allow that vehicle to take us is up to us. For me, fear represents the unknown, the what-ifs, and those dreaded feelings that whisper: *What if I'm not good enough? What if I suck at this and fail? What if everybody sees it? What if I can't recover from it?*

When we let fear drive, the results are similar to what they would be if we take our hands off the steering wheel while driving a car. We've voluntarily given up power and control with regard to our speed and direction. And just like driving a vehicle recklessly, the outcome can be catastrophic, hurting ourselves and others in the process.

Over the years, I've learned to ask myself: *Why am I feeling this way? What am I afraid of? What did fear come to teach me? Do the opinions of those who may be offended or upset with me really matter? Am I more concerned about what they think than what God thinks? If I give in to this fear, can I look myself in the mirror? Will my action or inaction keep me awake at night?*

My faith reminds me that I'm already equipped to overpower and overcome any adversity. Only if I choose to, though. Fortunately, I've come to realize that fear is **not** my enemy.

We must acknowledge our fear and decide whether we'll stand up and face it or stand down and cower in the face of it. As I've heard Christian author Joyce Meyer say many times, "You can be pitiful or powerful, but you can't be both." In other words, we get to choose. Each time we face our fears, we get to decide whether we'll be the victim or the victor. When I think about the fears I've had to overcome, the Sickle Cell diagnosis during my freshman year at USC would be near the top of my list. Not only did I have to digest what my doctors, well-meaning family members, friends, and later my bosses and colleagues said about it, but I also had to admit to myself that for years, I've allowed the opinions of others to influence—and sometimes limit me.

Just after I was diagnosed with Sickle Cell, my doctor in Bennettsville told me that if I wanted to have children, I had better have them by the time I was 30 years old. While I didn't think his medical guidance made a huge impression on me at the time, the impact of his words on my decisions are obvious to me now. I got married at the age of 25 while in law school, gave birth to my first son while I was a second-year law student and my second son one month after my 30th birthday. Thankfully, both of my babies were healthy. Yet, both pregnancies were high-risk, and I experienced complications during and after both deliveries.

When I started my professional career, the Sickle Cell diagnosis was still so new to me. It hadn't impacted my work or my ability to work. I just didn't know what to expect, so I reluctantly shared the diagnosis with department leaders and later regretted doing so, after one of them used that information to limit my opportunities to contribute to the team, under the guise that he was "looking out for me."

After several life-threatening medical challenges, I'd be lying if I said I wasn't afraid. When thoughts of dying young overwhelm me, I remember Daddy's words of wisdom: "Those who are afraid to die are also afraid to live." And, "In all of my years in the funeral business, I've never seen a death certificate that read, 'Cause of Death—nothing.'"

Those examples reflect the extent to which fear had become the driving force in my life. Each time my doctors, bosses, or colleagues weighed in with solicited or unsolicited opinions and advice, I allowed those outside influences to fuel my fears.

Yes, Dick's call made me mad. It also made me fearful. Once I stopped focusing on the assumptions and predictions of others and started thinking about all of the amazing things God allows me to do in spite of the challenges I face, I knew I was on to something.

CHAPTER TWO
Ante Up

If you think courage is expensive, try cowardice.
—Mia McLeod

Even after delivering a successful State of the State Response, I still wondered whether I had made an unforgivable mistake by not running against Lindsey Graham. Would I continue to lead with courage in the State Senate?

So many unanswered questions. I needed time to process it all. Yet, God was still pressing me to do more. At first, I wasn't sure what more was. By then, my left leg was a little better and I reluctantly put my crutches down to practice walking without assistance. Taking that first step took me back to my younger days when my parents refused to let us use anything as a crutch.

Not even me. Not even Sickle Cell.

If they had been alive in 2020, there's no doubt they would've been right there, cheering me on, holding me accountable, and telling me to do what God told me to do.

Even when other people encouraged me to run against Lindsey, I was still focused on my limited mobility and thought I knew what was best. How could I talk about the goodness of God and all of the major storms He had brought me through, hobbling around on crutches? How could I survive all of that and still chicken out when He told me to do something the world considered impossible? Did I *really* trust Him? Why was my faith wavering?

After days and nights of tormenting myself with questions like that, I decided to focus on the future instead of wallowing in the past.

That's when I clearly discerned what He was leading me to do next. And it was a doozy. Yet I was determined to do it, no matter what. He sent me another opportunity to test my will, my word, and my faith. This time, I wasn't about to let Him down.

Governor McMaster had to go. It was obvious he wasn't fit to govern us through a pandemic. I never even wanted to run for the House or Senate—let alone governor. Yet, that was exactly what God was telling me to do. Barely off crutches and not even back in kitten heels yet, I caught my eyes rolling at just the *thought* of traveling around the state in flats. Ugh. Clearly, I was distracted by the superficial. Even that wasn't going to make me repeat the mistakes I made in 2020. And there I was again, begging God to show me that running for governor was **not** what He was telling me to do.

Instead, He sent me confirmation. I received a text message from a high school classmate that took me back to text messages we exchanged the year before in 2020.

Nancy Bethea Hatchett and I have known each other since we were kids. Both of us grew up in Bennettsville and always enjoyed laughing, talking, joking, and cutting up in school, but lost touch after graduating high school. I didn't realize Nancy was a nurse and lived in Columbia until I saw her at the hospital years ago while visiting my sister Tracey. We were so excited to reconnect and exchange phone numbers. Still, we only texted each other a few times here and there.

In February of 2020, I was in Richmond, Virginia, with my godparents, Mary and Woodrow Jackson, speaking at Riverview Baptist Church's Black History Month program. Just after delivering the keynote speech, I left the pulpit to take my seat on a panel. The panelists were seated at a long table at the front of the church. Each of us had microphones. Just before the panel discussion began, I reached down into my bag to check the time on my cell phone and make sure it was on vibrate. As soon as I picked up my phone, it was vibrating and I saw that the time was 4:30 p.m. There was a text message from Nancy coming through. All I could see in the preview window was, "Hi Mia, how are you? I dreamt of you and your mother last night. In the dream your ..."

Of course, I clicked on the text to finish reading it because I was curious about Nancy's dream, especially since she mentioned Mama. She had never mentioned a dream to me before and wasn't particularly close to my mom, so I was intrigued. The last time I had gotten a text from Nancy before that, was in 2019, after a classmate's funeral. So, to get a text from her almost a year later was unusual, and I had to know why.

Hi Mia, how are you? I dreamt of you and your mother last night. In the dream, your mother was sitting in the audience at an event for you, and she was beautiful. Her hair was very black, her face plump, and she had on the prettiest peachy, salmon-colored lipstick. We hugged. She was sitting at the table with others I couldn't see, but she looked sooo happy. Then, I escorted a woman and a man. The woman was kinda rude to me but not the man ... I told you about the woman's rudeness and that I wasn't gonna host anymore and I woke up. It seemed so real ...

After reading Nancy's text, I struggled to focus on the panel discussion that had already started. Although I was in Virginia, no one but my family knew that. I rarely post about my speaking events on social media beforehand and hadn't, so Nancy had no way of knowing I was there to speak at my godparents' church.

The woman she described was probably my godmother. She's sweet as can be and still just as feisty as ever! I could see her coming across as rude to someone who doesn't know her. My godfather is very reserved and mild-mannered and sounded a lot like the gentleman Nancy described in her dream. As I looked out into the audience, I realized that the pews were practically full because the event was well-attended.

Interestingly enough, not one person was seated in the front row. Both front rows on the sides and the larger one in the middle were empty, which was so odd. It was like I could feel Mama sitting right there on that middle pew, front row, as I re-read Nancy's text.

"Oh. My. God. Nancy!!!" I texted. "I'm in Richmond, Virginia, RIGHT NOW and just finished speaking at an event! I'm sitting on a panel now and just looked at the time on my phone when I saw your text. That's crazy and you got me looking out into the audience now because I know my mom is here with me. Lord, have mercy."

"Mia, she's there and God wanted you to know it!!" said Nancy. "I wasn't going to text you and something kept saying, *Let her know your dream!* I truly believe that God lets us know so many things. Your mother is proud of you!! She was glowing and beaming and hugging her was sooo real. I could feel her."

"Yes, He does!!!"

"It was like that when my mom passed. I hugged her in a dream and kissed her forehead. It was so real that I bumped my forehead on the wall in the kiss. I dreamt once that my dad was in the backyard and there was a snake. I called home immediately and my mom said, 'Nathaniel just killed a snake.' Your mother was so beautiful in my dream, Mia, as she was in life, but so plump and radiant ... it was so real. I told (my husband) Bennie this morning as soon as I woke up.

God is good and your mom is watching you."

Before the program was over, we texted again.

"Girl!!! I needed that reminder today and it's sooo real because I'm here at my godparents' church and you mentioned seeing a woman and a man in the dream. My godmother is sweet, but feisty, so she was probably the one you thought was rude. This is unbelievable! Has to be God!"

"Has to be because you were nowhere on my mind as I'm sure I wasn't on yours. I don't mean that in a bad way, but it's the truth. Yeah, that feisty woman was rude to me, and you were wearing black, and you leaned down to me as I was telling you how rude she was. For some reason in the dream I started telling her my credentials and educational background. It was a trip, but it sure felt REAL!! To hear you say where you are now and tie it all together is like ... WOW!!

Be safe, enjoy, and have fun. I'm glad that God let me see your mother and give her a hug. And glad that He kept it on my mind all day to tell you. I love you and God loves us best and gives us just what we need when we need it. I had NO IDEA where you were and that you were speaking. This is just wow!"

"And I'm wearing a black dress."

"Oh, wait now!! You better quit! My momma used to tell me when I was growing up not to dream about her because they'd be too real. You gotta send me a picture of you and the inside of where you are. I remember seeing burgundy and some ivory in the dream. It wasn't very sunny or well-lit or bright. It seemed like your mom was the brightest, most glowing part of the dream. She just lit everything up."

I didn't see Nancy's last text until later that night, so I sent her photos I had taken earlier that day with my godparents inside their church. Everything she described from her dream was right there, me in a black dress and black boots with my godparents in a dimly lit burgundy and ivory sanctuary.

I was speechless.

So, I really had to just sit with that for a minute. My mom passed away in 1999, the day after her 61st birthday. I held her hand and watched her take her last breath. And although I think about her every day, this dream of Nancy's hit differently. Was her spirit there in Richmond with me because she knew I was going to struggle with what God was telling me to do next? Was she beaming with pride because I had already made the decision to trust and obey Him, no matter what? Nancy's text message was all the confirmation I needed.

I was so grateful that she shared her dream with me because it took me back to a time when I watched Mama and Tracey face cancer diagnoses within the same year, lose their hair, handle rounds of chemo and radiation with smiles on their faces and gratitude in their hearts. That kind of strength and courage was the fuel I needed to keep moving forward in faith, trusting, and believing God would give me the courage to be obedient this time, realizing I can do nothing in my own strength. Yet, I can do *all* things in His.

I started sharing my thoughts and intentions with close friends and family, even reached out to political folks I trusted, like Trav, my former Senate campaign manager. If I was really gonna run, Trav would have to help me assemble my team. He was chair of the S.C. Democratic Party at the time, so I knew he couldn't be on the team. He would still be my go-to guy for campaign advice, guidance, and referrals.

Anton Gunn, Amelia "Millie" McKie, Kayla Mallett, Tracey and Erica, BJ and Cam, and Radhika, were my original kitchen cabinet members because they knew why I served and were very familiar with the fights I had taken on. In addition to always having my back, I could count on them to give me honest feedback I could trust.

One thing was certain. This was far more than just a statewide gubernatorial race. And I was far more than just a Black woman running. I was the only gubernatorial candidate in the race who had never lost a House or Senate election—the only one who had served and was still serving in the S.C. legislature at the time and the only one who had years of state government experience in the executive and legislative branches.

Over the years, I've watched those in power use inadequate qualifications and experience against women and people of color —especially in the South where we are often intentionally discredited, undermined, and eliminated from many competitive political spaces. Perhaps that's why it was 2016 before Columbia elected a Black woman to represent the capital city in the S.C. Senate and 2022 before South Carolina had a Black woman run for governor. I wouldn't just be an *aptly* qualified candidate. I would be the *only* qualified candidate in the race. Just didn't realize that qualifications no longer seemed to matter for the first Black woman to occupy that space.

As I continued to serve in the S.C. Senate and began to get things in place to run for governor, some were pushing me to speed things up since there were rumors that Joe Cunningham would be announcing his gubernatorial bid soon. Can't say that I was overly concerned about the one-term congressman—a Kentucky native who lived in Charleston and had never worked or served in state government. Didn't think his announcement or candidacy would have much of an impact on mine. Perhaps in another state, that might've been the case.

But this is South Carolina.

After he announced, I was still trying to assemble my team. It was obvious that the Cunningham campaign was raising money and getting a solid lead on fundraising. So, although I didn't feel we were ready to announce, I deferred to the advice of the campaign experts and announced anyway.

On June 3, 2021, I was super proud to launch my gubernatorial campaign from the home of civil rights icon, family friend, and one of my biggest political "sheroes," Modjeska Monteith Simkins. Launching from her house was Kayla's idea because she saw the similarities in our fights and the courage each of us had shown, although decades apart. The fact that Kayla had no idea I actually knew and loved Ms. Modjeska made her recommendation all the more significant. My kitchen cabinet's first major decision about where to launch our campaign was unanimous!

Standing on Ms. Modjeska's steps on that hot, sunny day was indescribable. It warmed my heart to see so many young Black girls and boys, women and men, who came to witness and share in our historical moment. I wasn't running to make history, though. I was running to make a difference. Still, the opportunity for my candidacy to inspire a younger generation of Black and female leaders was never lost on me. And I wasn't the only one to inspire others that day.

Margaret Seidler and her husband Bob drove two hours from Charleston to Columbia to stand with me and it meant so much. In 2020, Margaret, a white woman, reached out to our funeral home via email to say that she had been researching her ancestry and discovered a connection between her family and mine—the Morris Family. We didn't know each other and she had no idea who would receive or answer her email.

Because Daddy had always been our family historian, I knew he would've wanted me to respond and to listen. So, I called Margaret at the number she included in her email and intentionally tried to put my own thoughts, feelings, and fears aside to hear what she had to say. I was eager to learn more about our families' connection. We talked for a couple of hours that day. Honoring Daddy's memory meant I needed to hear everything Margaret was willing to share about her research, so we continued to talk each time she had an update.

Margaret touched on some information I already knew. Joseph W. Morris was my great-great grandfather. Daddy found information that suggested he was born free in Charleston. Because of the deeper dive Margaret's genealogist did on her behalf, our family was invited to participate in a Zoom call with Margaret, her genealogist, and other families. That call provided much more information and insight about my great-great grandparents Joseph and Lizzy Perry Morris and their children.

Through Margaret's research, I learned that Joseph W. Morris was considered a "nominal" slave because he was purchased by his parents and enslaved by them to keep him out of the traditional slave trade. That's why Daddy thought his great-grandfather was born free. Other members of the Morris Family were enslaved in the traditional sense. When Margaret later shared with me that her ancestors actually enslaved mine, it was a sobering moment. I wasn't sure how to feel, and Margaret suggested that I take the time I needed to really digest that. She was devastated by the pain her uncle caused our family and the accompanying shame that his actions brought on her family's name and legacy. Yet, Margaret was just as happy as I was to learn that even in the face of unimaginable hardships and adversity, my ancestors were able to rise above it and thrive.

In fact, my great-great grandfather, Joseph W. Morris, went on to graduate from Howard University in 1875 and then enroll at the University of South Carolina Law School, the same law school where I earned my Juris Doctor well over a century later. S.C. Supreme Court Justice Franklin Moses, Sr., supported and mentored him. By 1876, he was elected commissioner of Charleston Public Schools and nominated to serve in the S.C. Legislature, an opportunity he declined so that he could finish his studies. He graduated with distinction in 1876, began practicing law, and later became president of Allen University. Professor Joseph W.

Morris was influential in politics and education at a time when the freedom he enjoyed and the levels of education, experience, and elevation he achieved were extremely rare for Black people.

It was because of Margaret's research and resolve to find out and share as much as she could about her family's connection to the Morris Family that I also learned I am at least a seventh-generation South Carolinian! What Margaret's findings gave me when I needed it most was detailed confirmation of my family's many contributions to our state, a reminder that I come from "good stock," as Daddy used to say. More importantly, her findings confirmed for me that the strength, courage, resilience, and tenacity I've shown is not by accident or chance. It's actually in my DNA. Those qualities are authentic depictions of who I am and who my ancestors were.

It took a tremendous amount of courage for Margaret to reach out after she discovered that our ancestors were connected through the slave trade. She's not responsible for who her ancestors were or what they did. I love her and Bob for who *they* are and what they're actively and intentionally doing to acknowledge the sins of the past so that we can begin to move forward. Words can't even begin to describe how grateful I am that God brought her into my life, just when and how He did.

If Daddy were alive, he'd be talking Margaret's ears off about all of their new discoveries and revelations. For me, this journey has been one that tests my faith like few things have. I knew I would need spiritual guidance to remind me that "this battle is His," not mine.

* * *

By 2021, Radhika wasn't just my pastor. I believe God sent her into my life in 2015 for all the right reasons. Having a front row seat on her journey to purpose as I attempted to navigate my own, allowed me to see what active faith and trust in God looks like. As I witnessed certain aspects of Radhika's "walk with God," I was inspired to open my mind, my heart, and take Him at His Word. That's easier said than done. Seeing her faith in action, at levels I could only aspire to reach, blessed and empowered me. I've learned and grown so much spiritually under her tutelage. Faith leaders who practice what they preach, are vulnerable enough to openly admit their mistakes, consistently seek God's guidance, acknowledge when they miss the mark, and do their best to submit themselves to God's Word and will over their own … are a rarity these days.

* * *

June 3 came quickly and Ms. Modjeska's house was full of supporters, campaign team members, and the media. Pastor Radhika was there to pray with us beforehand and open us up in prayer after we gathered outside on the front steps. As I walked up to the podium in my flats, and looked around at so many familiar faces who were there to cheer me on and witness this historical moment, it was sobering to know that once again I was blazing a trail—this time as the first Black woman to ever run for governor of South Carolina. Memories of all the times I sat with Ms. Modjeska and Daddy at her house, sometimes right there on her front porch, were so vivid. My great-great grandfather and other Morris family members were resting eternally in Randolph Cemetery, right across from us at Elmwood Avenue and I-126. Oh, how I wished Daddy, Mama, and Ms. Modjeska could've lived to see this moment! I knew how proud they would be.

With courage and gratitude, I stepped up to the podium and into the annals of South Carolina history:

Good morning!

Thanks to all of you for taking time out of your day to be here. For those of you who may not know why we chose to be here at the home of the late civil rights activist Modjeska Monteith Simkins, it's because I used to visit Ms. Modjeska here with my dad when I was a college student at the University of South Carolina. The two of them would sit and talk for hours sometimes about the struggles and challenges facing people of color when it came to equity in education and healthcare. She fearlessly and unapologetically fought for racial equality and advanced the causes of working people and those who were underrepresented so that they too would have a voice and reason to hope for a brighter South Carolina. I had no idea then that Ms. Modjeska's causes would one day become my own.

I'm State Senator Mia McLeod and I'm a fifth-generation (I later discovered that I'm seventh-generation.) South Carolinian. Born and raised here and I've never left, in spite of the fact that the state of my hometown county is indicative of the true state of our state under Governor McMaster's failed leadership.

When my great grandfather moved our family from Columbia to Bennettsville in 1914 to start our family business, I believe it was because he saw the promise and dared to do something different. That's why ours is one of South Carolina's oldest Black, family-owned funeral homes that's still in business ... 107 years later.

For generations, my family has chosen to stay here in South Carolina because when you love our state as much as we do, you're able to look beyond her challenges to see her possibilities and fight like hell to help her reach her true potential.

Sadly, because of desertion and neglect, we're losing so many of our best and brightest to neighboring states that offer higher paying jobs, opportunities for a better quality of life, and leadership that actually cares about and caters to the needs of ALL of the people. That's something South Carolina hasn't had in decades of Republican governors, who care only about their base and have no real connection to or compassion for the rest of us.

So, when my boys, both recent college graduates, tell me that this state … our state … under Republican control … doesn't represent their interests or value their voices … it's heartbreaking. And I know I'm not alone.

That's why I ran for office and it's why I've taken the fights straight to those in power … even when it meant pissing off members of my own party. I've been fighting the status quo for over 10 years now, and I'm still fighting … taking on the fights that no one else will … even when I have to fight alone.

Now, more than ever … having the courage to lead matters. The past year has been **hard**. When we needed leadership, we got cowardice. When we should've been united, Republicans politicized everything to divide us.
For those who believe like Gov. McMaster and others, that South Carolinians should just shut up and get back to their $7.25/hour jobs, I challenge them to try to live on those wages.

And while many South Carolina Dems continue to work hard to solve problems in our rural, underserved parts of the state, the governor is turning away federal unemployment dollars that folks across South Carolina desperately need … proving once again that he's concerned with only one problem—getting himself reelected.

Time and time again … these so-called leaders are still clinging to their good-ole days, when the privilege and power of a few, trumped the rights and freedoms of many. Yet here we are. It shouldn't be **US** versus **THEM** or **ME** versus **YOU**. We get to decide today, **who** we are and **how** we plan to move forward.

Year after year … gubernatorial election after gubernatorial election, S.C. Democrats have done the same old things, the same old ways, and gotten our butts kicked.

The future is now. We've gotta reject the notion that South Carolina is always gonna be a divided red state. With your help, I look forward to building a UNIFIED state, where the majority and the minority matter.

All too often, we've seen the self-serving good-ole boys wield power with no courage … abandoning what they know is right for that which is easy, safe, and politically expedient. When it's time for them to stand up and fight for us … **ALL** of us … we get excuses, like:
'It's not the right time to raise the minimum wage.'

Well, if not now … **when**? Change is scary. I get it. But we must remember that 'God has not given us a spirit of fear … but of power, love, and a sound mind.'

I believe in a South Carolina where the governor has the courage to lead ... the compassion to feel empathy for others ... a connection to the people **she** represents ... the character to do the right thing simply because it's the right thing ... and the conviction to stand ... even if she has to stand alone.

A South Carolina where **EVERY**body thrives. Where folks earn wages they can actually live on. Where there's equal pay for equal work. Where Medicaid is expanded to ensure that all of our state's most vulnerable have access to affordable healthcare ... a struggle I know all too well. Where students get a quality education regardless of where they live. Where addiction and mental health issues are treated in hospitals, **not** jail cells. Where rural S.C. counties are no longer the forgotten corridors of shame and neglect. Where our best and brightest **from** here ... **stay** here.

That's the South Carolina we deserve. And there's an army of excited, everyday people who've been waiting to build a better, stronger state.

Scripture reminds me that "we walk by faith, not by sight." So, if you believe as I do, that together ... we can build a better, stronger South Carolina ... a South Carolina that all of us can be part of ... a South Carolina that all of us can be proud of ... then, this ... **this** is our moment!
But only if we have the courage to seize it! South Carolina is ready for a leader who has the courage to lead and the guts to govern! If you're ready for her too ... go to MiaforSC.com and let's get to work!!

After answering questions from the media and making my rounds to personally thank everyone who came, I was excited to be on *The Roland Martin Show*—a show that focuses on issues of interest to Black America. I had often tuned in to Roland Martin during his earlier days at CNN and looked forward to being his guest to share my vision for South Carolina. Afterward, I completed my first official round of fundraising calls to raise money for the gubernatorial campaign. It would be the first of many long, grueling days and nights.

Another nine months would pass before I could officially file to run for governor. When I announced my gubernatorial run on June 3, I didn't realize the South Carolina Senate would still be in session for practically the rest of June, forcing me to juggle the demands of the Senate with those of my new position as a statewide gubernatorial candidate.

In the days and weeks after launching my statewide campaign, I traveled to Greenville, Spartanburg, and York counties in the Upstate, my hometown of Marlboro County in the Pee Dee and Charleston County in the Lowcountry. All of that was before returning to Columbia for the legislative session during the week of June 21 and discovering that Governor McMaster had vetoed all of my budget requests.

Navigating the politics of the pandemic was still a daily challenge for so many South Carolinians. The phone calls were starting to ease up a bit, although people in my Senate district and across the state continued to suffer. Everything related to COVID-19 was being politicized. Meanwhile, I struggled to find a healthy balance between serving in the Senate, campaigning statewide for governor, making time for fundraising calls, interviewing folks for key positions on the gubernatorial campaign team, and taking care of myself to ward off any significant health challenges.

Although I came home extra late and beyond exhausted most nights, I was still in a pretty good headspace ... learning more about myself and others and the true cost of leading with courage, especially in times of crisis. Little did I realize, it was time for me to ante up.

2021 gubernatorial launch at the home of Modjeska Simkins

With my godparents, Woodrow and Mary Jackson, after speaking at their church in Richmond, Va.

LESSON TWO: *Courage Costs*

Courage costs. And many times, we haven't really thought through what that looks and feels like. When we take "the road less traveled," we often feel isolated and ostracized. It can be lonely and uncomfortable, causing us to look for an alternate route or some way to reach our destination without subjecting ourselves to the inevitable storms that makes the journey seem so treacherous. Having courage on the front end gives us the strength to stay the course so we aren't compelled to take shortcuts. When we proceed with courage, we get to experience the kind of personal growth and development that ultimately transforms us.

Most people think that achieving success in politics requires compromise.

What it really requires is courage. I admit, it's not an easy path. Truth is ... it's a lonely one. Doing the hard thing is *never* easy but *always* worth it. Warming a seat while refusing to take a stand isn't courageous. Neither is flip-flopping on tough issues or going along to get along. Yet, I've served with Republicans and Democrats who do just that. Courage is expensive. It requires us to be fully committed because when we aren't, the people who depend on us are the ones who pay the most. Each time we embrace the status quo and don't speak up when we should, the costs increase exponentially.

The Cost of Not Knowing

The cost of not knowing that public policy impacts everything we do ... and more specifically, *how* it impacts everything we do, is huge. Trusting politicians, especially those we elect and don't hold accountable, is like giving a stranger our proxy to make the best decisions for us and never checking their voting record to make sure that they are, in fact, doing that. It's like putting our lives and futures into someone else's hands—someone who knows nothing about us—and may not even care. Blindly trusting our elected officials to do what's right or best for us is a passive and problematic approach. Yet, it happens every single day.

In 2017, when my sister Tracey's cancer returned, I was a freshman in the S.C. Senate and by then, Mama and Daddy were deceased. I remember leaving the State House to go with her to every medical appointment. Her oncologist, Dr. Butler, and her surgeon, Dr. Parker, believed the best course of treatment was a double mastectomy. Of course, she agonized over the removal of both breasts, and be-cause she had just lost her best friend to breast cancer, Tracey opted not to have reconstructive surgery, which she believed contributed to her best friend's death. It took her weeks to make a final decision.

Tracey fought back tears as she told Dr. Parker she would go ahead and have both breasts removed and that she did not want the reconstructive surgery. All of us were relieved that she had made the right decision for her and could begin to move forward with the treatment her doc-tors prescribed. Dr. Parker spoke with Tracey again about her history of breast cancer, coupled with our family's medical history and how each of those factored into her personalized treatment plan. He reassured her that her prognosis was good and that he expected her to make a full recovery.

Before we left the examination room, the nurse entered and told us that she had some bad news for Tracey concerning her insurance coverage. Tracey had recently retired from state government after dedicating her life to serving others—especially young people whose mistakes landed them at the S.C. Department of Juvenile Justice— where she had spent the majority of her career.

We walked with the nurse to her office and closed the door to talk privately. The nurse looked heartbroken as she informed Tracey that despite her doctors' orders, her state health insurance plan would only cover the cost to remove one breast. Her out-of-pocket cost for removing the other breast would be almost $30,000. I couldn't believe what I was hearing, so I asked the nurse how the state health insurance plan could deny coverage for critical, life-saving medical treatment like this? She dropped her head and softly whispered, "They do it every day."

As I grabbed my phone and walked outside to call my legislative contact at the State Health Plan, I took a deep breath and exhaled to gather my emotions first. After explaining my sister's diagnosis, prognosis, and asking how BlueCross BlueShield (BCBS) and the South Carolina Public Employee Benefit Authority (PEBA) could override her doctors' orders, I walked back into the nurse's office to wait for a call back. Tracey's nurse was on the phone, so I sat in the chair next to my sister, still reeling from what we had just heard.

When the nurse hung up the phone, she looked at me, perplexed. "Did you just call somebody?" she asked. Before I could answer, she said, "I just got a call from the state health insurance plan." Then, with a nervous smile and a look of shock, she said, "They reversed their decision! That has *never* happened before!" Tracey looked at me and, with tears rolling down her face, reached out to give me a hug.

The nurse sounded confused and relieved and said, "I don't know who you are or what you do, but you just helped your sister and eight other women who were denied the same surgery today."

Everything in me wanted to celebrate because I was so grateful that Tracey would be able to get the life-saving medical treatment she desperately needed and deserved. Thank God I was there with her to hear and see what was happening firsthand. Yet, in spite of my gratitude and relief for Tracey and the other women whose lives were positively impacted, I couldn't even allow myself to bask in the moment because my first thought was, *Who's gonna be here tomorrow?*

The next day, I looked at PEBA's board of directors and realized that *none* of the board members who were working with BCBS to make these life-altering—and sometimes, life-ending—decisions for insured South Carolinians like my sister Tracey, were doctors, nurses, or health-care practitioners. The majority of them were lawyers and business-people—political appointees—who had no business being consulted or engaged in insured patient's medical details, let alone empowered to override doctors' orders.

Both of us learned so much from that experience. It's not enough to simply know that public policy impacts us. We need to know *how* and to what extent it impacts us. That requires us to learn as much as we can about the people we vote into office—where they stand and how they vote on the issues that matter to us. Ultimately, we should know whether we can trust them to make rational, responsible decisions when it comes to their appointment powers. Will they appoint caring, compassionate people whose education, skills, and experience are relevant and add value to these processes?

Like it or not, politics impacts all of us. So, when I hear friends, neighbors, and constituents say things like, "I don't do politics," I usually reply, "Well then, politics will do you."

And when I share this personal story about my sister Tracey, they get it.

The Cost of Not Listening

NOT listening to that "still, small voice" that told me to run against Lindsey Graham in 2020 is probably my biggest political regret. If only I had remembered the phrase, "She doesn't know what she doesn't know." I still may not have known that a global pandemic was imminent. However, I would've been able to trust that God knew.

Funny how He gives us a glimpse of the future in a word, a picture, or a phrase that we'll need to recall later when doubt and fear creep into our minds. "Not knowing what

I didn't know" in 2014 and 2015 was very different from "not knowing what I didn't know" in 2020. The lesson, though, was the same. God was teaching me to not rely on or be distracted by what I see, how I feel, or what I *think* I know. If I had done that in 2020 and simply trusted Him—based on what He revealed to me four or five years before during an FBI probe that involved my client—I would've run against Lindsey Graham like he told me to.

And I'm confident I would've won.

Years ago, while I was serving in the S.C. House and running for the Senate, I represented a business client who was being investigated by the feds for some of his business dealings.

Unbeknownst to either of us, all of my phone conversations with my client were being monitored and wiretapped by the FBI. When I was notified that the FBI wanted to interview me, I called my friend Reggie Lloyd who happens to be a former U.S. Attorney. Reggie immediately advised me not to go into the interview without legal representation.

I laughed because I knew I didn't have any information about my client's business affairs that would interest the FBI, so I didn't think I needed a lawyer. Because Reggie insisted and couldn't represent me himself, he reached out to James Smith, a legislative colleague, to make sure I had representation. I wasn't afraid because I hadn't done anything wrong, but I'll admit that it was a little intimidating that the FBI wanted to interview me.

The first interview went well. James and I drove out to their offices and met with an agent. After I answered a few brief questions, the agent told me he didn't think they would need to interview me again. I was relieved and thought, *See, Reggie, told you I didn't need legal representation.* Weeks later, however, the FBI notified me that agents did, in fact, want to interview me a second time. Now, I'm concerned. I had already told them everything I knew, which wasn't much. So, why did they need to interview me again?

When I walked into the second interview, it was a drastically different environment. FBI agents were seated around the table with blank stares. After giving me a vague explanation about why they wanted to speak with me again, they began to play excerpts of my phone conversations with my client. One of the first audio recordings was of me talking with my client about a meeting I had just had in Dekalb County, Georgia, for a different client.

Now, I'm really nervous and fear is starting to creep in— not because I had done anything wrong. I hadn't. There was just something about hearing my voice on tape when I had no idea I was being recorded that made me feel extremely vulnerable and, since I'm being completely honest, violated.

Next, the agents played another audio clip of me talking to my client about what I ate for lunch. I thought, *You guys can't be serious. Where is this going?* What the agents didn't know is that I may not *look* like I love to eat, but I do! My friends tease me all the time about being a foodie. When my client said lunch was on him and sent me to his restaurant in Atlanta, I called him on my way back to South Carolina to tell him how amazing the mac and cheese and collard greens were. Here's the thing, I'm also a country girl, who knows good mac and cheese and collard greens when I taste 'em. Besides, I was genuinely surprised that they tasted so much better than the mac and cheese and collard greens at the same restaurant in Columbia where I live.

The agent who was asking the questions about that clip looked me up and down, as if to say, *You're going on and on about mac and cheese and collard greens and you don't look like you eat that much.* After the third or fourth replay, she was like, "Sooo, what are we really talking about here?"

By then, I literally felt sick to my stomach.

I could tell that the agents were trying to decode our conversation, as if my references to mac and cheese and collard greens had a totally different meaning that only my client and I understood.

James was concerned about where the agents' line of questioning was going. What did my meeting in Atlanta for a totally different client have to do with my client who was the subject of the FBI investigation?

Since my fears were in overdrive at this point, I admit that when the details of my conversation with my client that day started coming back to me, I was even more concerned about how many times he used the N-word.

He and I were introduced by a mutual friend years ago. We served on boards together and had some mutual social and business acquaintances. I adored his wife and children and had often been around them at social and political gatherings. When we spoke via phone, our conversations centered around business, our families, and, if time permitted, we sometimes vented about the challenges we faced with regard to the politics at play in the spaces each of us occupied.

This was one of those conversations.

As I braced myself for the next audio clip of that same conversation, the bigger concern for me wasn't *whether* I used the N-word on that call. It was *how many times* I used the N-word on that call. Code switching is natural for me when I'm talking to another Black person I'm comfortable with. However, that practice and those conversations are strictly offline and private. As I gazed around the room that day, there was only one other person of color in it. Hearing our offline conversation in an open forum was devastating.

While wrestling with all of the thoughts, feelings, and fears in my head, one of the agents asked a question about the type of work I did in Dekalb County, which seemed unrelated to their investigation and was totally out of left field. By then, I was so eager to move on from the mac and cheese and collard greens audio clip that it didn't even matter.

I had already started to answer when James intervened and advised me to pause until he was sure about why that question was posed. I remember the agent saying to James that the question was relevant because, "She doesn't know what she doesn't know."

Wait. What??!

I proceeded to answer the question and never forgot what the agent said. When she explained that the procurement director I met with in Georgia for a different client had just been indicted, I was shocked.

Not knowing what I don't know has caused me to be much more focused and intentional about trusting God to cover and protect me in every situation like He had obviously done in this one.

When we choose to listen to that "still, small voice" and make the best, most informed decision possible, we tend to become less fearful about the things we don't know and more intentional about doing the right thing ... even if we have to do it alone. And yes, even if we have to do it afraid. Knowing who and whose I am has been life-changing for me. We can't possibly know everything about everything. It's in those moments of uncertainty that we must muster the courage to listen to wise counsel, trust God's divine guidance, and move forward in faith anyway.

The Cost of Not Acting

The cost of not acting is by far one of the most dangerous. Here are a few critical areas where South Carolina's inaction has hurt the people of our state the most.

Redistricting – I was a freshman in the S.C. House of Representatives when the S.C. Legislature began its redistricting process. I couldn't wait to roll up my sleeves and get started, eager to learn all I could about it. It didn't take long to realize that as a new member of the House, my input could be extremely valuable, especially since I was the only Democrat who had just won in a swing district. My responsibility to voters was to ensure that they had fair and equitable representation. Ideally, that's the way the redistricting process *should* work.

Sadly, that's not the way the redistricting process works in South Carolina.

Because I had just won in a swing district, I didn't expect or ask that my district lines change drastically during the redistricting process. Yet, they did. The S.C. Republican Party was in control and "packed" it with Black voters, although I never asked the SCGOP to do that. When I pressed them as to why, some of my Republican colleagues insisted that the Dems asked them to or that they did it for me. I may have been new to the House, but I knew the SCGOP wasn't doing anything for me.

That led me to do some research on my own. I soon discovered that a critical component of the GOP's national strategy was to "pack" or "blacken" swing districts like mine for three reasons: to further marginalize the voices of the minority; to divide districts along racial lines, so that when voters see a "D" by a candidate's name, they can safely assume that candidate is Black; and to create a permanent Republican-majority stronghold.

That's when I shared my findings with our House Democratic Caucus and state Democratic Party. I was confident that, like me, they would want to fight the SCGOP's redistricting plan.

Turns out, I was wrong.

At the time, I believed my position as a representative in the 124-member House would actually carry some weight and that my ability to speak on behalf of the tens of thousands of people I represented would too.

Wrong.

The House Democratic Caucus lawyered up, so I assumed we were preparing for a fight.

Wrong again.

When our House Dems Caucus lawyers recommended that we fight the SCGOP's redistricting plan, Caucus and SCDP leaders decided not to, even though they knew what Republicans were attempting to do. It wasn't until a few of my more seasoned Caucus colleagues pulled me aside that I realized what was happening.

They basically said, "I know you wanna fight these Republicans because you don't like what they're doing to your district, but lil' girl you just got here. We like our districts just the way they are—safe—so we only have to worry about a primary. You'll be alright. Just leave it alone. Don't go changing those maps because we don't want the SCGOP going back and messing with our districts."

Fortunately, I was able to join a civil lawsuit as a private citizen to try to convince the courts that the SCGOP's race-based gerrymandering, or redistricting plan, was indeed unconstitutional. Unfortunately, the deck was already stacked against us, *by* us. With no help or reinforcement from the Democratic Caucus or State Democratic Party, the SCGOP's race-based redistricting plan was ultimately enforced. Just as I predicted, Democrats' refusal to act cost us everything on the GOP's list and more. It barely took the SCGOP a decade to get that "permanent Republican-majority stronghold." In 2022, the SCDP lost eight House seats, giving the SCGOP a supermajority in the S.C House. And the SCGOP's supermajority in the S.C. Senate was just one seat away.

COVID-19 – In the first quarter of 2020, the pandemic was confirmed in South Carolina. By April, it had spread to all 46 counties. Initially, the Republican governor and the Republican Senate majority leader were intentionally minimizing the threat and suggesting that we continue to go about business as usual. When the number of new, confirmed cases began to skyrocket, they implemented a temporary shutdown of business and government offices, only to ease up on safety protocols as soon as they got pushback from their base.

Meanwhile, the Republican majority still refused to expand Medicaid or do anything to increase access to quality healthcare in South Carolina, so the racial and socioeconomic disparities that already existed continued to be exacerbated by the pandemic. In addition, Governor McMaster and the Republican majority came up with a new designation for low-income workers. All of a sudden, they were deemed "essential" employees and forced back to work even sooner, knowing that conditions were not safe. Not long after that, schools were reopened prematurely so that parents could be forced back to work.

Consequently, South Carolina saw unprecedented numbers of COVID-19 exposures and deaths with significant disparities for people of color and the working poor. By 2022, we were informed that the then S.C. Department of Health and Environmental Control would no longer report the daily or weekly numbers of deaths and exposures, so we were forced to look up the numbers on our own. South Carolina's government leaders refused to act, inform, or protect us, long before they stopped publishing the numbers. Sadly, during the height of the pandemic, our state had at least 2 million COVID-19 exposures and 20,000 deaths because state government leaders played politics with people's lives.

Race – In 2015, just weeks before my friend and colleague Senator Clementa Pinckney and eight of his parishioners were tragically gunned down at Mother Emanuel Church, I hosted a town hall series on race and its impact on our communities. I'll never forget the final town hall of the series at First Northeast Baptist Church, which happened to be my church at the time. None of us could have imagined that just three and a half weeks later the unthinkable would happen right here in our home state.

WIS-TV news anchor Judi Gatson graciously agreed to moderate our panel discussion. One of the panelists, a University of South Carolina professor, said something I had never heard a white person say before when each panelist was asked to share a little about themselves before we delved into the complexities of race.

He introduced himself by candidly acknowledging that the reason he had a "seat at the table," in rooms his qualifications alone wouldn't have allowed him to enter was because of the color of his skin and the privilege that was inherently associated with it.

That was definitely a mic-drop moment and the very first time I had ever heard a white person publicly acknowledge privilege in that way. I remember borrowing one of my favorite lines from the movie *Jerry Maguire* to say to him in the presence of our town hall guests:

"You had me at hello!"

The impact that his acknowledgement had on our ability to then proceed with an honest, thoughtful, productive conversation about race and its true implications was indescribable.

Acknowledging that racism exists and has far-reaching implications is the first step toward racial reconciliation and healing. Not the *only* step. Just the first. And it's a big one. I remember how encouraged and hopeful I was because of that simple, unusual gesture and how quickly that hope dissipated four weeks later at the murderer's first court appearance.

Let me be clear. Forgiveness is a fundamental principle of Christianity and, in my opinion, one of God's most powerful. So when several family members of Ethel Lee Lance, Tywanza Sanders, DePayne Middleton-Doctor, Cynthia Marie Graham Hurd, Susie Jackson, Sharonda Coleman-Singleton, Myra Thompson, Reverend Daniel L. Simmons, Sr., and my friend and colleague, Senator Clementa Pinckney pushed past their unimaginable grief two days after the murders and expressed forgiveness and mercy toward their loved ones' killer. I was both captivated and devastated.

Captivated by their selflessness and strength. Devastated that such a powerful display of grace could cost us everything.

The sheer ability of family members to express forgiveness so soon after this senseless, unconscionable act, sent shockwaves around the world. Like many others, I watched and wept as loved ones of the slain displayed the kind of unwavering faith, undeniable courage, supernatural strength, and restraint that most can't even begin to fathom.

Since the enslavement of our ancestors, Black people, especially those of us who were born and raised in the South, have been expected to turn the other cheek, forgive our oppressors, and love those who hate, hurt, kill, or attempt to destroy us. That expectation almost always remains intact, even when there's no accountability for first time or repeat offenders. Those of us who live by faith believe and understand that we must forgive others, just as God forgives us. We also understand that forgiveness is a process. And although we know what forgiveness is, it's equally important to clarify what it isn't.

Forgiveness isn't relinquishing, waiving, or forfeiting the desire or expectation that perpetrators will be held accountable, that layers of oppressive systems will be assessed, reformed, and dismantled, or that public policymakers will introduce legislation and pass laws that adequately address and resolve the issues.

I believe family members of the slain who expressed forgiveness following the Mother Emanuel Massacre were simply acknowledging to God and themselves that they would ultimately begin their painstaking individual journeys toward forgiveness because that's what God requires of those of us who believe in Him. As believers, we know that His love is far greater than any hatred we're forced to endure on this earth. Forgiveness is a decision and the first step we can take toward our own healing.

What I wasn't prepared for was the notion that these family members' public expressions of forgiveness somehow suggested that they were willing to forego the long overdue, critical conversations and actions that ultimately precede public policy reforms and facilitate significant systemic changes. Yet, somehow, the grace family members showed on June 19, 2015, led to a seemingly collective "pass" for Governor Haley, state legislators, congressional members, the media, and many others. That "pass" conveniently implied that if family members directly impacted by this heinous, senseless act of race-based hate can forgive and move on, so can the rest of us.

And that's exactly what the state of South Carolina has done—moved on.

Guns – South Carolinians are still feeling the impact of the General Assembly's refusal to pass common-sense gun laws to help keep South Carolina residents safe and hold those who recklessly and callously kill law-abiding citizens accountable.

In light of the escalation of gun violence in South Carolina and across the nation, including mass shootings and the murders of unarmed Black men and women, common-sense gun reforms were very much a part of our town hall discussions.

I still hoped and prayed that South Carolina's elected leaders would finally take some action.

While removing the Confederate flag from atop the State House was a long overdue symbolic gesture, even that didn't come down easily. It was removed under duress and would still be flying high today if the business community hadn't put pressure on then Governor Haley to bring it down or face devastating economic boycotts and other forms of protests. For some of our state's leaders, it was never about the lives that were lost, only about the money that could be.

I sat directly behind Governor Haley at the prayer vigil after the Mother Emanuel Massacre and cringed as she spoke about why we shouldn't "politicize" this tragedy by making it about guns.

As the world watched, efforts to close the Charleston loophole and require background checks for firearm sales were squashed by the Republican majority.

I'm writing this memoir almost a decade after one of the most heinous hate crimes in recent history, and South Carolina is one of only two states in the nation that still doesn't have a hate crimes law. My Senate colleagues, including some who served with Senator Pinckney, have kept us from even debating the Hate Crimes Bill on the Senate floor for three consecutive years.

Yet, if you ask them about the Mother Emanuel Massacre, they're quick to express fond memories of their fallen colleague and the grace that family members showed the killer.

What happens when there aren't any significant public policy changes after such a tragic stimulus?

Nothing.

Nine years later in 2024, the S.C. Republican Party finally took action that revealed a blatant disregard for the lives that have already been lost because of senseless acts of gun violence in our state. With a Republican majority stronghold in both legislative chambers, the SCGOP passed a permitless carry bill that now puts guns in the hands of 18-year-olds, enabling them to carry openly in our state without a Concealed Weapons Permit or training.

That's precisely the kind of "action" we don't want or need. It's reckless, wrong, and will lead to many more senseless murders in South Carolina.

When our elected officials don't count the cost and lead with courage, the people they represent pay the price. The escalating costs of **not knowing**, **not listening**, and **not acting** continues to wreak havoc on all of us.

CHAPTER THREE
Pruning Ain't Pleasant

Behold I have refined you, but not as silver; I have tried and chosen you in the furnace of affliction.
—Isaiah 48:10

It was January 2020, and Aspen was a winter wonderland. I was there as part of the prestigious Rodel Fellowship—a national public leadership fellowship for elected officials. After another knee surgery, it was tough trying to get acclimated to the high altitude that can be especially troublesome for Sickle Cell warriors. Needless to say, I was the only member of our cohort who was on crutches ... cute, blinged-out crutches ... but crutches nonetheless, that were absolutely no match for the thick ice and snow that was everywhere.

My daily challenge was to get to and from the seminars without busting my ass. It was treacherous. The Rodel Fellowship team and my cohorts went above and beyond to ensure that I got everywhere I needed to be, safely.

At the conclusion of the seminar, we were asked to write a one-page letter to ourselves.

The assignment quickly became a distant memory because I had much bigger challenges to think about. When I returned to the comfortable temperatures and weather conditions of my home state, I couldn't have imagined that a pandemic was lying in wait and our lives would be divinely disrupted a little over a month later. Even when I received an envelope in the mail, I assumed it was just a thoughtful check-in note from Kathleen Godfrey, a brilliant, beautiful soul who was one of the driving forces behind the fellowship.

I had just won my November 2020 reelection to the S.C. Senate handily against Lee Blatt, a well-funded Republican with significant name recognition, and didn't have time to open the letter until the election was over.

After finally coming to terms with the fact that I wasn't running against Lindsey Graham like God told me to, my letter seemed perfectly timed, because I was in the process of trying to forgive myself. It's amazing how God knows exactly where we are and gives us exactly what we need, exactly when we need it. The letter was a huge reminder that I was right where I was supposed to be at that moment.

It was as if God had given me the words in advance that would ultimately provide the clarity and courage I needed to finally realize that what He has called me to do is so much bigger than me. And I can accomplish all of it in His Strength ... not my own.

As I re-read the letter for what seemed like the 10th time, I could feel God wrapping His arms around me, reassuring me that everything was going to be okay. For the first time since 2019, I was coming to the realization that He wasn't mad at me. That letter was an inflection point, something for me to sit with and meditate on for a minute.

Although I felt that Governor McMaster wasn't doing what he could to help *all* of the people of South Carolina during the height of the pandemic, it wasn't until the Senate minority leader asked me to deliver the Democrats' State of the State Response that I realized God was preparing me for yet another battle. I just didn't know there would be a lot more than one. Still, I was determined to trust and obey Him this time ... no matter what.

A few months after delivering the State of the State Response,

I dealt with yet another incident in my area that had gone viral. On April 13, 2021, in The Summit—a diverse neighborhood in the heart of my district and not far from my home—a young Black man was walking down the public sidewalk when he was accosted by a white male homeowner who was physically much larger than he was. Video footage shows the homeowner walked out of his house and shoved, berated, and threatened the young man for no apparent reason. As I watched the video in horror, and listened to the homeowner repeatedly scream at him that he didn't belong there and threaten to harm him if he didn't leave immediately, it didn't take long for me to conclude that this young man's "crime" was simply "walking while Black" in a neighborhood that the white homeowner considered "his."

On the heels of the tragic, senseless murder of Ahmaud Arbery in Georgia and countless other unarmed Black men before and after George Floyd, who were gunned down or choked out solely because of the color of their skin, it was extremely difficult to watch. Eyewitness accounts confirmed that this calm, unassuming young man was simply walking down the sidewalk alone, minding his own business. Yet, he was blatantly bullied by a man who physically towered over him, like he was an intruder, trespasser, or enemy.

As a proud mom of two amazing sons, I often wrestled with the very real possibility that they might one day face this same kind of vitriol.

The next day, I went to the well of the Senate to share this young man's story with my colleagues. Even I wasn't prepared for my raw, emotional reaction to what was happening around the country and in our own backyards. I'm sure my colleagues weren't either.

Exhausted, frustrated, and exasperated, the letter I wrote to myself soon became "my charge..." a divine reminder that our pain has a purpose that is bigger than us.

Dear Mia,

The struggle is real and sometimes you get a little discouraged, but stay the course. The Rodel Fellowship has equipped you with the leadership skills and network of support that will be invaluable to you now and in the years to come.

Stay focused. Stay engaged. Stay connected. More than ever before, recognize that God has you in this space during this season of your life for very specific reasons.

When life gets hardest, "Be still and know" that He covers you and you are able to do ALL things in His strength, not your own.

Wherever you are right now when this letter reaches you, know that it is not by chance.

His timing and His will are perfect. Even when it seems you're losing the battle, choose to focus on the war. The causes for which you are fighting are BIGGER than you ...

Love always,
Mia

It wasn't the only letter that would have a huge impact on my historic run for governor. Shortly after my announcement on June 3, 2021, God was about to start the uncomfortable, painful process of pruning people out of my life. Some I considered friends. Others, I had even supported in the past. To say, it "hurt like hell..." would be an understatement.

On June 26, a few members of my campaign team and I headed to Horry County for a big Democratic Party event. Horry County is on the South Carolina coast and most well-known for Myrtle Beach. As we drove toward the small city of Loris, they briefed me about the event and told me that my gubernatorial primary opponent would be there as well. I looked forward to meeting and talking with Horry County Dems because the Myrtle Beach area is in the part of South Carolina we call the Pee Dee.

I'm a Pee Dee girl and couldn't wait to share my vision for a better, stronger South Carolina in an area that suffers because of gross systemic disparities along racial and socioeconomic lines.

A day or two before, I had given final approval of a letter written by my fundraiser. I've always been a straight shooter and my constituents and supporters really seemed to appreciate that because it's such a rarity in politics today. The letter captured my voice and the essence of the message I wanted to convey. One of the big themes of my platform centered around a commonly used definition of insanity, which is universally described as "doing the same things and expecting a different result." I even personalized the letter for the S.C. Democratic Party by saying, "The definition of insanity is doing the same thing *year after year ... election after election* ... and expecting a different result."

Here's an excerpt of the letter:

It's an old platitude and we've all heard it. "The definition of insanity is doing the same thing over and over again and expecting a different result."

And yet, time after time ... gubernatorial election after gubernatorial election ... we keep running the same type of candidate.

√ Male
√ Lawyer
√ Republican-lite
√ Loses in November

Leading with the truth is critical for me. Scared Democrats are the main reasons I wanted to leave the S.C. Democratic Party back in 2016. And since Trav talked me out of it then, I was confident that after all of the long, candid conversations we'd had about why S.C. Dems continue to lose elections, Trav would put an end to the "insanity" if he became the SCDP chair. I've never been a "party person." So, I made an exception to attend at least two State Democratic Party conventions—just to "second" his nomination for S.C. Democratic Party chair—which he won both times.

Sadly, the insanity continued.

In South Carolina, nobody wants to talk about race or gender. Yet, they're the biggest elephants in the room. Obviously, I was a different gubernatorial candidate—the first Black woman to ever run for the office and the only announced candidate in the race who was actually qualified. I wasn't gonna allow anyone to lump me into this space like my race, gender, and experience weren't relevant. They've been relevant all my life, often to close doors in my face.

Just after I announced I was running for governor, there was an effort underfoot to try to force me to blend in with my white male opponent by doing things the same old scared, cookie-cutter, insane, Republican-lite way—just to undermine the fact that Democrats would finally have a real choice on their 2022 primary ballots.

One of the first conversations I remember having about the letter was with my former legislative colleague Mandy Powers Norrell, who was very supportive and had recently become a beloved member of my "kitchen cabinet." Mandy and James Smith ran for governor and lieutenant governor respectively in 2018. She told me to call James because she thought he had issues with the letter we sent out "about white men." I insisted that my fundraising letter made no reference to race and told her I would call him on my way to the Horry County event.

I had always considered James a friend. We helped and supported each other when we served together in the S.C. House. We rode together in a colleague's SUV to attend the prayer vigil in Charleston on the morning after the Mother Emanuel Massacre. James represented me pro bono when my client was the target of an FBI probe and I was subpoenaed to interview as a witness in the case. I supported him when he ran for governor three years before. And I'd be lying to myself and to him if I said I was surprised when he lost.

Someone had to speak the truth about why S.C. Democrats hadn't won a statewide gubernatorial race in almost 20 years. My letter wasn't meant to criticize him or Vincent Sheheen, who had run twice for governor against Nikki Haley and lost both times. And although James and Vincent may have been surprised by their back-to-back losses ... nobody else was.

I supported both of them each time they ran. At the time, I thought we were fighting for the same things. They were the SCDP's golden boys and despite the fact that Black women are considered the backbone of the S.C. Democratic Party—often working behind the scenes to validate and elevate white candidates in our communities—that level of support is rarely reciprocated.

My fundraising letter was never intended to throw shade at either of them. It was simply drafted to acknowledge a failed strategy that the S.C. Democratic Party seemed desperate to keep using ad nauseum and to let S.C. Democrats know they had a real opportunity to choose a different kind of candidate in 2022 and break that cycle.

What I wasn't prepared for were the reactions I got from James and Trav. On the evening of June 25, 2021, I received a text message from James and a screenshot of my fundraising letter. He didn't say he had a problem with it or why he sent me the screenshot. Obviously, I knew what my letter said.

At the time, I didn't realize that James, Trav, and others had somehow subconsciously inserted a word that wasn't there. All of them saw "white" before male in the checklist. The word "white" could easily have been included because it was accurate. Ironically, I didn't use race as a distinguishing factor because I didn't need to, since the "male" and "Republican-lite" references sufficed. Joe Cunningham, my gubernatorial opponent, checked all of those boxes and I wanted donors to know that if we kept doing the same things, we'd keep getting the same results we'd gotten for the last 20 years.

Because I still couldn't understand why James was offended by the truth, I asked Mandy again if she thought I should call him. I just wasn't sure what to say and didn't want to offend him any more than I already had. Mandy said she thought it would be good for me to hear directly from James why he was offended. And she was right. That call led to an enlightening conversation that ultimately changed my relationship with James and the S.C. Democratic Party establishment.

On the morning of June 26, I called James and he answered. I could tell immediately that his tone was different, almost curt.

"Hey James!" I said. "Can you talk? I'm calling about your text because you didn't say whether you had a problem with the fundraising letter, sooo … do you?"

"No, I don't have a problem with the letter," he said. "I have a problem with your team. I just think it was in very poor taste and not a good reflection of you and your leadership."

"Why do you think that?"

"Because Mia, you couldn't have been okay with them sending a letter like that out, right?"

"Yes, I approved the letter, James, and nothing in it was directed toward you. Nothing in it was false or embellished either. I just thought the SCDP needed to acknowledge the truth about why Democrats continue to lose elections in our state."

"You need to fire all of 'em!" he said, abruptly. "I don't know who's on your team, but all of 'em need to go. I mean, look at this letter … and look at where you launched your campaign … from an old rundown house. I mean, what the hell was that about? I'm your friend and I want you to win. This letter and your launch just weren't a good look for you."

Whoa. Wait. Flag on the play!!

If James felt blindsided and betrayed by my fundraising letter, he had just paid me back tenfold. His true feelings about me and my launch were detailed and personal, hitting me much harder than a general fundraising letter ever could've hit him. I'm not even sure how long it took me to regain my composure and respond. I didn't have the words. He spoke for a few more seconds and then … dead silence.

"Are you still there?" James said.

"Ummm … yeah, I'm here, James. Sooo are you saying you don't know why I launched my campaign from Modjeska Simkins' house on Marion Street?"

"That's exactly what I'm saying. Doesn't matter anyway now. Just wasn't a good look."

By the time he was done unloading his real thoughts and feelings, I was wayyyy more offended than he was.

One of the things I had been most proud of about my launch was that I got to kick off my historical run for governor of South

Carolina from a historical site that was personally significant to me. It was where Ms. Modjeska had actually lived. I had many fond memories of her and a strong personal connection to her, her home, and her work. The causes she courageously championed ultimately became my causes when I was elected to the S.C. House and Senate.

For a minute, I was lost in the irony of it all. I had been serving for a little over a decade and every single one of my fights to disrupt the status quo had also been Ms. Modjeska's fights during the Civil Rights Movement.

When Daddy first took me to her house, I was in high school. And later, when I became a student at the University of South Carolina, we always went to see her when he picked me up or brought me back to school, since I didn't have a car. Her legacy is one that all South Carolinians need to know about. It's one that S.C. democratic legislators, in particular, should be extremely proud of.

For James to have served in the S.C. House for over 20 years and to appear to not know who she was, where she lived, or what she was about, was even more disheartening. Her portrait sits prominently in the S.C. State House. James' law firm was just a few blocks away from her Marion Street home, which is an old house that my great-grandparents used to live next door to. And it's definitely not rundown. It's a historical landmark that has been preserved since her death. How could he not know why my decision to launch from her home was so personal, so intentional?

He was right about one thing. "Doesn't matter anyway now," because I would never be able to unhear what he said. All I could do was hurry up and end the call before I said some really ugly, even harsher truths.

"Thanks for telling me how you really feel," I said. "We're almost at this event in Horry County. I'm not gonna fire my team. I stand by the letter and it's obvious that you are offended. I was hoping we could have a candid conversation and we have. I just didn't know you felt this way about who I am and what I'm doing."

As our honest exchange came to an end, he told me there was no way he'd be able to support me after that letter and that Vincent couldn't either. Apparently, the two of them had already talked about it. For me, all that meant was neither of them ever intended to support me anyway and my letter gave them the justification they needed.

Daddy used to tell me, "Some people will act like they love you as long as you stay in your place."

"What's my place, Daddy?"

"You'll understand what I mean when that time comes, baby."

Although I didn't understand it then, Daddy was right because this was beginning to feel like, "that time."

When we left the event in Horry County, I was physically and emotionally exhausted. The conversation with James kept replaying in my head like a broken record and I just wanted to disengage from it all. On the way back, I spoke with my fundraiser, Will. Trav had recommended that we hire Will again, since he was the one Trav hired in 2016 to help me fundraise for my initial S.C. Senate bid.

Will also happened to be the white guy who penned the original draft of the fundraising letter. And since we only had a skeletal team in place, I proofed, edited, and approved it. I couldn't wait to share with him the highlights of my conversation with James earlier that day.

And to my surprise, Will wasn't blindsided like I was. In fact, his immediate response was, "Well ... Trav already chewed my ass about it too, sooo ..."

I interrupted, "Why would Trav be upset about the letter?"

"That's what I was thinking too, but he gave me an earful," he said. "You need to call him."

Reluctantly, I went ahead and called Trav, since we still had at least another hour to go on the road back to Columbia. And after talking to Will, I really wanted to hear Trav's thoughts.

"Well hello, Senator McLeod," he answered.

I cut right to the chase and told Trav that Will said he had a problem with the fundraising letter.

"He's correct," he said. "I've talked to him about that."

Then, I proceeded to tell him about the conversation I had with James earlier. Trav didn't seem surprised either.

"Well Senator, you sent a fundraising letter out to potential donors that specifically went after 'white' men," he said. "I just don't think that was smart."

I took a deep breath.

"Trav … I sent a fundraising letter out about why Democrats need to do things differently if we ever wanna win again in this state. Why are y'all so focused on 'white' men when the letter doesn't say 'white' anywhere in it?"

"It absolutely does say 'white,' Senator. You're calling out 'white' men in your letter."

"Where, Trav? Where does it say, 'white' male? Did you bother to read the letter before you went off on Will?"

"I did read it, Senator, a few times … actually."

"Then show me where it says, 'white' male, Trav."

By then, I was probably more agitated than he was.

"Hold on … let me get it. So while I'm getting the letter, you're telling me Will sent something out without your knowledge or approval?"

"No, I'm telling you … Will drafted the letter and, of course, I read it and tweaked it before approving it. I just don't understand why you and James keep insisting that it had the word 'white' in it.

"Here's why," he said confidently as he proceeded to read it aloud to me over the phone. When he got to the checklist, he stopped abruptly and said, "Wait a minute … I could've sworn that the checklist had 'white' male … not just male. Where did I see that?"

"I don't know, Trav. Where did you see it?"

As he kept searching for a version of the letter that didn't exist, it hit me. Maybe James, Vincent, Trav, and other white males had seen the word "white" because they knew every item in the checklist applied to them too … not just my opponent. They read the letter based on its truth and were obviously offended by it.

How could one missing word be the *only* word each of them saw?

What Daddy told me many years ago, about how I'd be treated if I ever got out of "my place," was true. My help and support of their campaigns over the years was expected and welcomed. Yet, stepping out from behind the scenes to run for the highest office in the state myself, and being critical of the SCDP's losing strategy, wasn't.

Yeah … I had definitely gotten "out of my place," alright. And Daddy must've known that at some point, I would.

Right then, my plate was much too full to dwell on the fundraising letter or the fallout from it. The implications and revelations would become more and more obvious as the months progressed. Campaign fundraising and events around the state quickly began to consume every moment of my days and nights that weren't already filled by the demands of the Senate. I couldn't believe we were that busy and still had almost a year to go before I could officially file to run for governor.

The campaign trail was grueling. Yet, I was determined to see this new "divine assignment" through to the end.

* * *

By late June, I was thinking about reaching out to Stacy Abrams in Georgia. We shared some obvious similarities. Stacey is a Black woman who served in the Georgia House of Representatives and ran for governor of Georgia. In fact, she was the first Black woman to become Georgia's Democratic gubernatorial nominee. I had recently learned that she and Vice President Kamala Harris were also Rodel Fellows. There was one more thing Stacey and I had in common. During her first run for governor of Georgia, she wrote about the fact that she had amassed hundreds of thousands of dollars in student loan debt and openly lamented about how overwhelming it was to tackle that debt while juggling household financial responsibilities, serving in the Georgia legislature, and running for statewide office.

I know that pain all too well, since Brian and I consolidated our student loans in the early '90s and realized after we divorced, that neither death nor divorce would relieve us of that joint obligation. My parents paid for my undergraduate tuition at USC, and the cost of law school was on me. Brian had undergraduate and graduate school student loans. When we got married, we were law school and graduate school students. It seemed like a good idea at the time to streamline our post graduate student loan payments. However, it didn't take long for $88,000 in principal to morph into a $1,100-monthly payment, which we paid on time every month for well over a decade.

After a series of family medical challenges—including around-the-clock home health care and support for Daddy when a routine colonoscopy perforated his colon and put him in the intensive care unit for months—Brian and I began to struggle to pay our mounting student loan debt.

By then, our firstborn was a toddler. After two high-risk pregnancies with complications, it took some time for us to get back on our feet financially. Brian was a special education teacher. Even with a law degree, I was only making $60,000 annually when we divorced and I left state government in 2003 to start my own public affairs firm. Neither of us are strangers to hard work. Although both of us spent the majority of our careers in the public sector, our consolidated student loans didn't qualify for public service loan forgiveness programs.

In 2010, I was earning a robust six-figure income as a consultant and returned to state government as an elected official, with a $10,400 annual "salary." I had money saved and thought I could handle it because my business was doing pretty well. After I was elected to the S.C. House of Representatives and the State Ethics Commission directed me to sever all professional and financial ties to my business partner and the majority of my firm's clientele, things became extremely difficult for me financially. Add to that, then Representative Nikki Haley's failure to disclose on her ethics reports in 2007 and 2008 the corporate clients she did consulting work for while serving in the S.C. House, which led some corporations to stop contracting with S.C. legislators who were actively serving.

The stress of struggling to earn a living while I served, continued to impact every aspect of my life—especially my financial and physical health. And all of this was happening *before* the pandemic hit. With fewer business opportunities, less income to cover rising costs, and a consolidated student loan with compounded interest that continued to accrue daily, I often had to remind myself that God's plan is always bigger than ours.

By 2021, our consolidated student loan debt had practically quadrupled and the monthly payment was so high that neither of us could afford to pay it, individually, or collectively. The only pandemic relief available to us was a few more forbearances and deferments, leading to an even higher balance.

When Stacey Abrams wrote about her painful experience with mounting student loan debt, she was basically describing mine too, and I was grateful to know I wasn't alone. Although our shared experiences gave me hope, it was short lived because every effort to get any meaningful relief was denied, simply because our loans were consolidated.

On one of my countless calls with our student loan provider, I learned that because the divorce rate is so high, student loans can't be consolidated anymore. That's great news for those who might make the same mistake we did, but useless for us since they still refuse to separate our loans or allow us to pay a reasonable monthly amount.

A recent study revealed that women hold 66 percent of all student loan debt, with Black women having the highest average. No wonder it takes us longer on average to pay it off. As I get closer to retirement age, the decision to consolidate our student loans in our 20s has been the bane of my existence for practically 30 years now.

Stacey and I didn't really know each other. We had briefly interacted at legislative conferences. I had her cell number and looked forward to reaching out to talk with her about her experience as a gubernatorial candidate in a neighboring state. Plus, I was excited to learn more about her and her game-changing work in Georgia after losing her gubernatorial bid to Republican Brian Kemp. I dialed her number and she didn't answer. When I heard her voice on the outgoing greeting, I knew I still had a valid number for her, so I assumed she was busy and left her a voicemail message.

Later, Trav and I were talking and I mentioned to him that I had reached out to Stacey. He agreed that the two of us should reconnect and offered to help. I reminded him that I had already left a voicemail message on her cell phone and that she hadn't responded.

Unlike me, Trav was able to reach her on his first attempt. As soon as he reached out, Stacey and I had a call scheduled. Obviously, serving as SCDP chair carried some weight, so I tried not to take it personally. I admit that I was feeling some kinda way about needing a middle man just to facilitate a telephone conversation with her. No time to be in my feelings though. I shook it off and was still just as excited about our upcoming call.

When Stacey and I spoke, neither of us was at a loss for words and the conversation flowed effortlessly. She shared a few insights about her journey and the challenges she encountered. In response to specific questions I asked, she offered advice. Some I could use, some I couldn't. Nevertheless, I believed she understood the unique challenges I faced as the first Black woman to run for governor of South Carolina and I was grateful for the opportunity to reconnect and have that conversation.

Overwhelmed and determined to fill key campaign positions as soon as possible, I continued to ask Trav to help me find the right campaign manager, preferably someone who previously worked with Black women or men who ran statewide. I also went back to my list of folks who supported me in previous House and Senate races. One of those supporters was former S.C. Governor Jim Hodges.

Reaching out to my former boss was easy because he was our state's last Democratic governor and had appointed me to serve as director of the State Office of Victim Assistance (SOVA) within his Office of Executive Policies & Programs.

When I initially spoke with Governor Hodges about my gubernatorial run to ask for his advice, he shared with me that because of his position with his firm, he wasn't able to get involved in the primary, which I assured him I understood. He suggested that I reach out to the national Democratic Governors Association (DGA) and attend some of the organization's events to establish a rapport with DGA leaders and members.

His advice was a bit surprising, since he knew I was serving in the State Senate during a pandemic while raising money *and* campaigning statewide. But he had served as governor once and I hadn't yet, so I thanked him and tried to figure out how to do what he advised.

After we hung up, I started doing a little research on the DGA to prepare to reach out to them. The more I read, the more I wondered why the DGA hadn't reached out to *me*. Was the organization even interested in establishing a rapport with *me*? After all, I was a state senator who had never lost a House or Senate race—even in swing districts—with a proven track record in every space I had occupied. So why was I constantly feeling like I had to chase these national organizations just to get their attention and then grovel for their support?

It was becoming increasingly obvious that my opponent already had a relationship with the DGA and the organization seemed to have been quietly backing him. Of course, he had time to attend their events and conferences. I remember how I felt when someone sent me a screenshot of a photo he took with Stacey Abrams at a DGA conference that year. It hurt. Then, I thought, "people ask us to take pictures with them all the time. She probably has no idea he's my opponent."

The S.C. Democratic Party establishment is notorious for low-key hand-picking, and supporting statewide primary candidates who wouldn't challenge the status quo. Now that I'm much more aware of how the SCDP operates, I can't help but think that my opponent's presence and photo ops at the DGA conference that year were intentional. The Old Guard on both sides of the political aisle wants candidates it can control. And while the Republican Party certainly has its faults, fear of exercising its power doesn't seem to be one of them.

Conversely, the South Carolina Democratic Party establishment has been scared of its own shadow for decades. Even when the party does have the ability to exercise actual power, it usually lacks the courage to use it. I know many S.C. Dems who are actively engaged in party politics and consider the SCDP "weak" since no individual or organization can truly represent the people if they're afraid to speak up and stand up.

Party loyalty that puts self above service and comfort above courage is never going to make sense to me—especially when there are so many injustices and inequities that demand our individual and collective attention. "Playing the game" and refusing to challenge the status quo are not winning strategies, which is precisely why the SCDP keeps losing.

Over the years, I've talked to many Democrats in South Carolina and across the nation who have quietly quit the Democratic Party for those very reasons.

I took one last look at the photo of Stacey Abrams with my opponent and hoped it would make me want to learn more since the DGA, Democratic National Committee (DNC), and other national organizations work closely with the SCDP. I couldn't help but wonder which types of candidates the organization usually promotes or supports. Didn't take long to discover that Stacey seemed to be the only Black female gubernatorial candidate the DGA had promoted, although the 2021 announced gubernatorial candidates and 2022 gubernatorial primaries had an unprecedented number of qualified Black women vying for governor in multiple states across the nation.

And while the DGA claimed it didn't get involved in statewide primaries, that wasn't the case in mine. The DGA, DNC, SCDP, and other organizations all sang the same tune publicly, almost in unison, that their organizations stand down and don't get involved in primaries. Yet behind the scenes, anyone who looked closely enough could see that what they were saying simply wasn't true. Each of these organizations seemed to favor white male democratic candidates and typically turned a blind eye to the challenges of Black women who were vying for statewide offices.

At that time, Stacey seemed to be the only exception.

Imagine my surprise when someone forwarded me a fundraiser flyer for Georgia gubernatorial candidate Stacey Abrams. The flyer indicated that her fundraising event was planned for

April 23, 2022, less than two months before my gubernatorial primary in Richland County—the county I live in and represent. Stacey's campaign coffers were bursting at the seams. So why would she come into *my* county and state to solicit campaign contributions for her Georgia statewide run two months before my gubernatorial primary?

I sucked it up and asked my team to find me a few minutes between campaign events to at least stop by, albeit uninvited. When my team called back and said the SCDP advised that no one would be admitted to Stacy's fundraiser without a campaign donation, I was done.

I was elected to the S.C. House in a swing district in 2010, after defeating a well-known Tea Party candidate in the general election. As a first-time candidate with no name recognition, it wasn't really surprising that I didn't have the SCDP's help or support. That was the year S.C. Senator Vincent Sheheen first ran for governor, and like me, was serving in the S.C. Senate at the same time.

A few colleagues who served with him shared that in 2010 and 2014 the SCDP and Senate Democratic Caucus provided Vincent's gubernatorial campaigns with fundraising help and support, a dedicated Caucus staffer, and Caucus-backed legislation to ensure that he had some legislative wins to tout on the campaign trail. That level of support was never offered to me.

Both of us had served in the S.C. House and Senate. I had experience in the executive branch for Democratic and Republican administrations prior to being elected.

Even with the state party's help and support, he lost both times to Nikki Haley, the second time by a much wider margin than the first. When James Smith and Mandy Powers Norrell ran for governor and lieutenant governor respectively in 2018, the SCDP was all in for them as well. In fact, it was Mandy who reminded me that by the time the SCDP held its Democratic Convention in 2018, she and James had already had at least two SCDP-sponsored, televised debates. She was blown away by the obvious disparities compared to my gubernatorial campaign.

The Party couldn't say it was because James and Mandy ran unopposed. They had Democratic Primary opposition just like I did. By the time Marguerite Willis and my legislative colleague, Senator John Scott, entered the gubernatorial primary later that year, I had already publicly pledged my support to James and Mandy. Although I didn't know Marguerite well, I was serving with John in the S.C. Senate in 2018. He was upset with me for not changing course to support him as Marguerite's running mate for lieutenant governor and tried his best to convince me that James worked against me behind the scenes when I first ran for the Senate in 2016.

In 2020, the same year Vincent lost his reelection bid to the S.C. Senate and two other S.C. Senate Democrats met the same fate in their districts, I received more votes in my Senate reelection bid than any other S.C. Democratic legislative candidate or incumbent. Because of the pandemic, I wasn't able to campaign as I normally would. Yet, I still beat a strong Republican opponent in the general election by the widest margin of victory.

None of that seemed to matter in my statewide gubernatorial race, though. The party has its favorites, and because I've always had an independent mind and voice, I'm not one of them. I get it.

Besides, I was already convinced that the SCDP *wanted* to lose, since the party seemed to relish being the perpetual underdog. If Republicans continued to be in charge, the SCDP could launch endless digital attacks and keep doing things the same old "insane," scared, cookie-cutter, Republican-lite way to pull on the heartstrings of Democratic donors who desperately wanted change. Then ... take a page straight outta the GOP playbook by promising that change was finally within Democrats' reach *if* donors could just send a donation by midnight.

As fall approached, I hoped things might begin to slow down a little. Our close-knit family had been through a lot over the last four years. I was looking forward to spending time with Mama's side of the family at Thanksgiving, which had always been our tradition. Great food, fun and fellowship! Uncle Sonny, Mama's only living brother, had already lost his baby sister and nephew in 2017. By 2021, he was grappling with the loss of his only brother, Larry, and his wife, Janis.

As I sat with Uncle Sonny in their Burlington, N.C., home after Aunt Janis' funeral, he was still smiling and thinking about others, in spite of his own sadness and grief. Before I left, he made a special point to put a check in my hand for my gubernatorial campaign and tell me how proud he was of me.

After all of that, we decided not to put our elders and immune-compromised family members at risk by gathering for Thanksgiving that year. Although Aunt Janis' funeral was a sad occasion, I was still grateful to see and spend some quality time with all of them.

Because we don't normally get together for Christmas, I wasn't surprised when I learned that Uncle Sonny was heading to Myrtle Beach, S.C. with his sons and grandkids. I figured they wanted to get away for a few days. The COVID-19 numbers were still ridiculously high here in South Carolina. That wasn't surprising either since the governor and SCGOP leaders had politicized mask wearing and vaccines and had already stopped publishing the number of daily exposures and deaths. Then, my cousins called to tell me they were back in Burlington because Uncle Sonny contracted COVID-19 while visiting Myrtle Beach and had been admitted to the hospital in North Carolina. And just like that, our Jeffries family patriarch, life of the party, and Mama's oldest and only living brother succumbed to complications of COVID-19. My heart was hurting. With so much pain, it was tough to keep going.

P Pay Period: 01/10/2023 through 01/10/2023
C Check Date: 01/10/2023

Name: MIA S MCLEOD
Agency: A010-LEG DEPT-THE SENATE

Personnel No: 1007655

	Earnings	Deductions	Taxes	Net Pay
C Current:	10,400.00 −	5,540.56 −	1,467.31 =	3,392.13
Y YTD:	10,400.00 −	5,540.56 −	1,467.31 =	3,392.13

E Earnings	Hours	Current	YTD
L Legislators Salary		10,400.00	10,400.00
T Total Earnings		10,400.00	10,400.00

Deductions	Current	YTD
3407 Ben-GARS EE Pre-tax	2,464.00	2,464.00
3622 GA-Health-SHP EE Pre-t	1,172.16	1,172.16
3623 GA-Opt Life Pre-tax	172.80	172.80
3662 GA MoneyPlus ADM Fee A	27.84	27.84
3664 GA-Med Spending ASI	1,500.00	1,500.00
2306 GA-State Parking Facil	120.00	120.00
3655 GA-SL/TD Post-tax	83.76	83.76
Total Deductions	5,540.56	5,540.56

I Imputed Income			138.00	138.00		

T Taxes	Tax Type	Status	EXMT AddlAmt	Cur Tax	YTD Tax	Cur Txbl Earn	YTD Txbl Earn
Fe Federal	Withholding	Head Househd		656.97	656.97	5,201.20	5,201.20
Fe Federal	Social Security			475.24	475.24	7,665.20	7,665.20
Fe Federal	Medicare			111.15	111.15	7,665.20	7,665.20
Sc South Carolina	Withholding		01	223.95	223.95	5,201.20	5,201.20
T Total Taxes				1,467.31	1,467.31		

P Payment	Account	Type	Amount
F FIRST CITIZENS BANK	083218	Checking	3,392.13

*** MESSAGES ***

2023 Senate pay stub

LESSON THREE: *Pain Has a Purpose*

When it comes to afflictions, not many are as qualified to speak about the myriad of challenges I've faced, overcome and chosen to share honestly, transparently, even publicly.

Sickle Cell. Rape. Stroke. DVT. PE. Deaths. Divorce. Debt. Betrayal. Rejection.

Every aspect of my life has been wrought with pain—physically, spiritually, mentally, emotionally and financially. These "afflictions" have, at times, impacted my health, my faith, my quality of life, my relationships, my family, my financial stability, my public service, my self-confidence. Everything.

And yet, I've come to realize that none of the adversity I've faced has been by chance because I've emerged from each "fiery furnace ..." better, stronger, wiser, more courageous, more confident, more clear, more resilient, more tenacious, more resolute, and more prepared for what's next. Guess that's what Scripture means when it says, "It was good that I was afflicted ..."

No matter how bad it seems, our pain has a purpose. It's not purgatory. It's certainly not punishment. It's actually preparation for our next level. God's Word says, "Our latter days will be greater than our former." The reason we must persevere through some pain on our pathway to purpose is because pain is what prepares us to step boldly into the amazing things that await us on the other side of it.

When I ran for governor, I was a state senator and the first

Black woman to ever file to run for the office. Although I had always run as a Democrat and won races for the S.C. House and Senate, I didn't have the support of the S.C. establishment Democrats when I announced my run in 2021 and officially filed for the office in 2022. If I had let that stop me from running, it would've taken me longer to discover my inner strength. Although extremely painful, if God hadn't exposed the hearts and motives of others or pruned people out of my life, I may not have been able to discern who I could truly depend on and trust.

Don't get it twisted. The kind of pain I've endured in my life sucks. And yet, I truly believe I'm the fearless warrior I am today because of it. The journey can be lonely, uncomfortable, and unpredictable at times. Instead of trying to avert the pain, I've learned to press through, understanding that there is a bigger purpose at play. They say, "What doesn't kill us makes us stronger." The fact that we're still here, still standing means we're stronger now than we've ever been and nothing can stop us, but us.

Setbacks are simply setups for the next chapter or new season. I try to think of them as stepping stones—opportunities for growth and transformation. Without pain we may never experience the fullness of who we are created and destined to be.

CHAPTER FOUR
I Never Lose

Blessed is the one who finds wisdom, and the one who gains understanding, for she is more profitable than silver and yields better returns than gold. She is more precious than rubies and nothing you desire can compare with her.
—Proverbs 3:13-15

Daddy used to say, "Who does the problem solver go to when the problem solver has a problem?" Then he'd smile and point his index finger up toward heaven. Funny how Daddy's words of wisdom came to mind like a flash of lightning just when I needed reassurance that God was right there with me and everything was gonna be okay. Truth is, as we got closer to the day I could officially file to run for governor, everything wasn't okay. I wasn't okay.

The campaign trail was grueling, probably because the Senate demanded so much of my time. And because my primary opponent served one two-year term in Congress and decided to announce right after losing his congressional reelection bid, Will, my finance director, insisted that I go ahead and announce in 2021 —a whole year early—even though we knew we weren't ready.

In spite of my reluctance, my opponent was raking in every fundraising dollar he could before I announced. And although he couldn't even oust Nancy Mace, a super weak Republican challenger with nominal name recognition at the time, the media's love fest with Joe Cunningham was beyond baffling and border-line creepy. I was starting to think they must've been on his pay-roll when he tweeted about bird poop on his car one morning and it instantly became "breaking news."

I happen to live and serve in one of our state's largest media markets. The press "camps out" at the State House each day the legislature is in session. Yet, rarely did any media outlets cover my work in the S.C. Senate after I announced my run for gover-nor. Bet if I had missed major votes or been at the center of any-thing scandalous, they would've run it back like a game-changing Super Bowl play.

And although I was the gubernatorial candidate in the race who was actively serving, the only way people in and around my Senate district knew about the work I was doing was when I told them. Meanwhile, I was still working hard, fighting for well over 110,000 people in my Senate district like I had always done, cam-paigning around the state, and struggling to squeeze fundraising call time into an already jam-packed schedule. Even when the media did occasionally cover our campaign, the stories always led with our fundraising numbers, which would've been fine if they were comparing apples to apples.

Yet, even lazy, biased media coverage wasn't going to keep me from doing what God told me to do this time. Besides, my team was small in number and mighty in fortitude. They worked around the clock to make sure we were everywhere we needed to be because they believed in the causes and the candidate. If I had to run statewide again, I'd want Heidi Johnson Young, Beth Young, Mayra Rivera Vasquez, Courtney Thomas and Chris DeVries with me every step of the way. By that time, Lauren Harper, an invalu-able member of Team Mia for SC since my earlier days in the S.C. House and Senate, had recently moved on to a new opportunity. And I missed her terribly.

Our gubernatorial campaign interns, Mariam El Geneidy, Dominique Praylow, Hannah Williams, and Maricellyn "Rissy" McDonald, stepped up and were ready and willing to do what needed to be done on day one. Our entire team understood what we were up against. They always did more than what was expected and always had my back.

Most nights I'd get home at 10 or 11 p.m., shower, inhale a quick bite to eat, check Senate and campaign emails, and record videos for upcoming events in different parts of the state that I wouldn't be able to physically attend. It was usually close to 1 or 2 a.m. before I was able to lie down for a few hours, only to get up and do it all over again the next day.

I remember how excited I was to be asked to participate in the 2022 South Carolina Prayer Breakfast on Wednesday, March 16, which also happened to be the official filing day for the gubernatorial race. I knew God was up to something when event organizers asked me to read Ezekiel 37, the "Valley of Dry Bones," from the Old Testament.

Every word of that Scripture may have ministered to the hundreds of people who filled the convention center on that rainy early morning. Yet somehow, God chose it specifically *for* me to minister *to* me. As I read it aloud, I could feel God reviving the "dry bones" in my own life. He was reminding me of His power that is at work within us, showing me that even situations that look dead can be revived by simply trusting Him, believing His Word, waiting patiently with expectation, and yielding to His divine timing.

Being asked to read Ezekiel 37 on the very day I would officially make history as the first Black woman to run for governor of South Carolina—the very day I would publicly affirm my obedience by answering the call of God on my life—was not by chance or coincidence. As I read Ezekiel 37 on that historical day,

I could feel God's presence in ways I hadn't before. And with His presence came His "peace that surpasses all understanding."

When my family and our team arrived at the S.C. Election Commission later that morning to pay the filing fee and formally submit my application to run for governor, many friends and supporters were there, including some who had traveled from my hometown of Bennettsville. Others had driven from Charleston and different parts of our state. God's peace was still with me and I was so grateful to be able to take it all in, knowing that this was an unprecedented moment in time. If only Mama and Daddy could've been there to see it!

After filing and taking a little time to celebrate with everyone, I had to cut it short because the Senate convened at 1 p.m. on that Wednesday and the time was 1:15 pm, so I was already late. Didn't wanna give the media or my opponent any ammunition to use against me.

The days and months after filing were even busier than the days before. By April of 2022, I was speaking at the African Methodist Episcopal Church's annual conference in Florence, then heading to Marion for campaign speaking engagements and then on to Charleston for more of the same. Engaging voters in meaningful ways and answering the questions other candidates didn't want to answer or couldn't, was what I enjoyed most about the campaign trail. As we traveled across the state, voters expressed excitement about my candidacy. I looked forward to debating Joe Cunningham and was elated that our first debate was already in the works.

So, when the S.C. Democratic Party's Black Caucus stepped up to sponsor our first televised debate on SCETV, I was surprised to get a call from Trav, who was the SCDP chair at the time. He advised me to not participate and suggested that I wait and participate in a later SCDP debate.

He seemed disappointed that I was adamant about participating. How could I not? When I asked Trav why he was advising me to not participate in the only televised debate that had been scheduled, he replied, "It just won't be a good look for you, Senator."

Trav was alluding to an article that had been written about allegations against a member of the SCDP's Black Caucus. I reminded him that articles are written all the time, and at that point, I had no reason to be overly concerned, since the allegations were against one member of the SCDP's Black Caucus, not the Caucus itself. When I decided to participate anyway, Trav claimed to know more than had been released publicly and told me it would be "problematic" for me if I proceeded. Still, I wasn't moved.

Trav called me at least two more times, asking me to not participate in the SCDP's Black Caucus debate. With each call, our conversations got more heated and it became increasingly obvious that Trav was frustrated because I wouldn't listen. Still, nothing he said changed my mind, especially since he kept pleading with me to *only* participate in the SCDP's debate.

This is the SCDP's Black Caucus debate, so what's the difference?

Ironically, the SCDP, to my knowledge, hadn't planned or scheduled a debate at that point. Trav mentioned that the SCDP wanted to host a debate during the SCDP Convention week, which was days before the Primary.

"Why wait?" I said. "We could have a second one then too."

I just couldn't help but wonder why Trav was dragging his feet.

Mandy had already told me that when she was James' running mate in 2018, the SCDP hosted at least two televised debates for them *before* the SCDP Convention. I vaguely remembered that and recalled receiving information about the candidates from the SCDP in 2018 when they ran for governor and lieutenant governor respectively. Obviously, the SCDP hosted more than one televised debate during the 2018 democratic gubernatorial primary.

Trav's insistence that I bow out of the SCDP's Black Caucus debate seemed unusual—even for him. And it felt like a slap in the face when I learned that he was the one who asked SCETV to scrap our only televised debate. Everybody who knew me knew that Trav wasn't just my friend and closest political adviser. He was more like a brother. Anytime I heard Democrats or Republicans questioning his motives or bashing him, I'm the one who always came to his defense. And just like siblings, we disagreed a lot so I had no reason to think this time would be any different.

Unfortunately, I was wrong. This time *was* different.

When Trav blatantly disregarded everything I had shared with him about why the SCDP's Black Caucus debate was so important and took it upon himself to cancel it—knowing it was our only scheduled televised debate—I felt blindsided and betrayed. What hurt more was learning that he did it under the guise that the SCDP's Black Caucus debate wasn't a party-sanctioned event.

Were the televised debates the SCDP hosted during the 2018 democratic gubernatorial primary considered "party-sanctioned" events? I had never heard that phrase before. Likewise, SCDP officials who were extremely engaged at the Party level admitted that they had never heard the term "party-sanctioned" used before. It made me wonder all the more why it was being used then. In 2018, both gubernatorial candidates were white.

In 2022, for the first time in South Carolina's sordid history, a Black woman was running in the statewide gubernatorial primary … against a white man.

My team and I wondered if Congressman Clyburn, South Carolina's longest-serving and highest-ranking SCDP leader, would be willing to push the SCDP to reconsider and allow the SCDP's Black Caucus debate to move forward. A televised debate would help get the word out about the statewide primary as well, which we assumed he would want since he faced primary opposition and would also be on the ballot. I called him on his cell phone and left a brief voicemail message asking him to return my call. I never heard back.

Trav called my team to let them know that although the SCDP's Black Caucus debate had been canceled, he was working to bring Vice President Harris to the SCDP's Blue Palmetto Dinner, as if that was supposed to somehow make up for canceling our only televised debate.

Later, my team told me Trav reached back out to let them know he had scheduled an SCDP televised debate at SCETV. When they told me the SCDP's "party-sanctioned debate" was actually scheduled for Friday at 5 p.m—the same night as the SCDP's Blue Palmetto Dinner featuring Vice President Harris and the same hour that early voting for our gubernatorial primary closed—I couldn't believe it.

I wondered why Trav would schedule our one and only televised debate on any Friday at 5 p.m. when nobody would be paying attention. And why would he intentionally wait until the very hour that early voting closed in South Carolina?"

I had been begging him for weeks to schedule a televised debate. I even posted a video to challenge my opponent because it was obvious to everyone who was paying attention that he didn't want one. Since we didn't have a televised debate scheduled, I agreed to participate in church town halls in the Upstate for people who wanted to hear directly from us. In fact, I was scheduled to be in Greenville at one of those churches on that Friday evening.

My opponent was obviously aware and had already advised the church's event planners weeks in advance that he had a conflict. It was also no coincidence that it was the very date Trav was trying to convince me to agree to weeks before. Each time

I insisted on participating in the SCDP's Black Caucus debate, which would've also been held at SCETV weeks before the SCDP Convention, it was a problem.

So, when my opponent posted a tweet weeks *after* my video message to him, challenging me to a televised debate—as if *he* were the one leading the debate challenge—asking me to join *him* on Friday afternoon right *before* the SCDP's Blue Palmetto Dinner and, not coincidentally, right *after* early voting in South Carolina was officially closed—I knew.

The fix was in.

Joe Cunningham and the SCDP were obviously on the same page. I was the one who wasn't. Even though I was seeing and experiencing their plan in real time, it was still hard to believe that someone I considered a brother could betray my trust the way Trav had. And it wasn't just about me. The SCDP's actions ultimately betrayed the people of South Carolina.

On June 5, five days before the SCDP Convention and nine days before my gubernatorial primary, I worshipped at Bibleway Church of Atlas Road during the 8 a.m. service and at Brookland Baptist Church in West Columbia during the 11 a.m. service. Serving in the S.C. Senate and traveling the state to introduce myself left very little time to campaign in Richland County, the county I live in and represent.

I had no reason to believe that the S.C. Democratic Party wouldn't do what they had done in previous statewide elections and send mailers to registered Democratic voters letting them know who the candidates were and when the statewide primary was. After all, this was also the first time in South Carolina's history that four Black women were vying for statewide seats.

Since Democratic Party leaders often express that Black women are the "backbone" of the Democratic Party, how could the SCDP not engage and inform the electorate in a race that was so consequential? With four Black women running statewide, voters needed and deserved to see who we were and what we were about. That's the S.C. Democratic Party's job.

How could the Party exploit its own base by doing absolutely nothing? Not one mailer. Not one phone call. Not one substantive, televised debate. Not one TV ad. Nothing.

At 11:55 am on June 5, when Dr. Charles Jackson was finishing up his sermon at Brookland Baptist and the church service was practically over, my opponent and his entourage strolled in and walked down front, as if his unreasonably late entrance wasn't disrespectful enough. And as many Black pastors do, Dr. Jackson graciously recognized him again, since he wasn't there when his name was initially called earlier during the service.

My intern Dominique was with me during the 11 a.m. church service and we walked over to the church's banquet hall afterward. I approached a table where three older Black women were sitting, introduced myself as Senator Mia McLeod, and told them I was running for governor. Before I could say another word, one of the ladies closest to us looked confused and said, "Wait. What did you say you're running for?"

I smiled, told her my name again and said, "I'm running for governor."

Still perplexed, she paused for a moment and the other two ladies did too. "I know your face," she said. "You represent this area, don't you?"

"I do represent Richland County and have for the last 12 years."

"I knew it! Just had to put the face with the name. You're a fighter. My husband and I have always supported you."

After a few more seconds, she went right back to the conversation we were having before she recognized me and blurted, "When? When are you running for governor?"

It was hard to see past the genuine concern on her face.

"A little over a week from Tuesday," I said. "The statewide gubernatorial primary is on June 14 and early voting has already started."

"This year? You're running for governor this year?!" she exclaimed, almost as if she didn't believe me.

I told her I was. I could tell that something was horribly wrong because of the way she looked at the other two ladies and then back at me. She was clearly devastated and seemed to be fighting back tears when she asked, "How come the Democratic Party didn't tell us that?! We live here in Richland County and the Democratic Party always sends us something in the mail to let us know who's running. We didn't get anything from them this time! And we've already voted early."

She dropped her head almost as if she was ashamed and said, "I saw that there were people running for governor on my ballot, but I didn't think I knew any of 'em, so I didn't vote for anybody in that race. I definitely would've voted for you! Oh my God ... what can I do to help you win?"

The tears in her eyes were even more poignant than her words. I looked at Dominique and leaned over to the woman to console her, not realizing that I probably needed to be consoled too because *that* was the moment I knew we were in trouble right here in Richland County.

When I told her I appreciated her support and that she would only be able to help me win in November if I won the Democratic Primary, she promised me that she and her friends at the table would do whatever I needed them to do to help. I hugged and thanked them, as all of us fought back tears. Still, I couldn't help but wonder whether the SCDP had already accomplished what it set out to do. The state party knew that my opponent was funded by out-of-state donors with deep pockets, many of whom were affiliated with national organizations.

In fact, I learned during the final weeks and months of the campaign that the SCDP expected to benefit from Joe's big dollar out-of-state donors because he was the one national Democratic organizations were low-key supporting. When I got the news that the money my opponent was raising would likely go toward a co-ordinated general election campaign with the SCDP if he was, in fact, the Democratic nominee, I didn't wanna believe it.

And, by intentionally not publicizing the statewide guberna-torial primary or sending Democratic voters information about the candidates or our platforms, most SCDP voters would suffer the same fate that the woman I met after church did—voting blindly or perhaps not voting at all.

Could that be what the South Carolina Democratic Party wanted?

If that was indeed the master plan and everything went accord-ingly, my opponent would be the Democratic nominee and the SCDP would likely gain access to some of that coordinated cam-paign money. As concerning as it was, I had to let it go. Besides, the SCDP Convention and our only televised debate were quickly approaching. My team and I were upset about the fact that early voting would be closed by the time we took the stage on June 10, while Democrats from all over South Carolina were en route to or already at the convention center for the SCDP's Blue Palmet-to Dinner.

In the early afternoon of June 6, I was speaking to a group of Democrats on Zoom when I received a call from a Santee, South Carolina, phone number that I didn't recognize. Because I couldn't answer, the caller went to voicemail and called again while I was still speaking on Zoom. When I finished my Zoom call and mentioned to some of my team members that I had missed a couple of calls from Santee, they immediately thought it must be Congressman Clyburn calling me back to offer his assistance with all of the challenges we were facing with the SCDP. I didn't think so since I had Congressman Clyburn's personal cell phone number and he had mine. Yet, I immediately felt a slight sense of relief that *somebody* might be able to get the SCDP to do *something* to share critical information about the upcoming statewide primary with Democratic voters.

And if anybody could do that, everyone on my team agreed— it would be Congressman Clyburn.

While Heidi and I were on the phone, I noticed that I had a voicemail message from the unknown phone number. When we hung up, I listened to the voicemail. It wasn't Congressman Clyburn. It was his longtime friend and staffer John Rickenbacker. His voicemail sounded a bit urgent.

"Yes, umm Senator McLeod, umm … Mia … John Rickenbacker. I work with Congressman Clyburn. Please give me a call … when you get a chance. It's Monday, around 1:24 p.m. I texted you my cell number so you could see it. Um … please give me a call whenever you can. I need to talk with you. Thank you so much. God bless. Bye-bye."

I immediately returned his call but was not at all prepared for what he was about to tell me. He started by letting me know that the congressman sent "sample ballots" to Democratic voters in his 6th Congressional District. The "sample ballots" I've seen have the names and sometimes the photos of the preferred candidates with the boxes next to the names and faces they want voters to choose, checked.

I wasn't surprised by that since some of my House and Senate colleagues send sample ballots to Black Democratic voters in their districts too. It's an Old-Guard practice that I don't like because if we arm voters with essential information about the candidates—who they are, which seats they're vying for, and what they stand for—voters would then be empowered to make their own informed decisions about who might best represent their interests. SCDP establishment Dems were sending these ballots long before I was elected and I was sure they'd be sending them long after I left office.

I didn't know why Mr. Rickenbacker felt the need to share that with me, so I continued to listen. He seemed a little uneasy about what he wanted to say. When he finally got to it, I understood why.

He told me that the congressman wanted me to know that some of his sample ballots might have Joe Cunningham's name on them. When he said that, I was genuinely confused. So, I asked, "Why would any of Congressman Clyburn's sample ballots have my opponent's name on them?"

He sighed and then paused for a few seconds. "Ummm ... Jim can't really control what goes to some areas ... not all of them."

Still confused, I asked, "Sooo ... are you saying Congressman Clyburn can't control what's printed on *his* sample ballots*?*"

He seemed to slow down so that he could choose his words carefully.

"I'm just saying that he may distribute them one way, but there may be changes made afterward.

"Sooo, who would (have the audacity to) change Congressman Clyburn's sample ballots? County party chairs? I don't understand."

"I'm not sure. The Congressman just wanted you to know that some of his sample ballots may have your opponent's name on them ... ummm ... in case you get any calls or happen to see some with his name on it."

I could tell he was eager to end the conversation, so I thanked him for letting me know and tried to process what I had just heard.

When we hung up, I called my team to share with them what Mr. Rickenbacker had just told me.

As we discussed what was disclosed on that phone call, they figured out even before I did that the intel we had previously received about the national organizations' strategy to ensure that my opponent was the Democratic gubernatorial nominee was obviously on point. And that phone call put us on notice. The SCDP establishment Dems seemed to be executing their plan to influence the outcome of our statewide gubernatorial primary.

Even as I think back to that day and that phone call ... I'm speechless.

It was undoubtedly the most perplexing and enlightening conversation I had during the year I campaigned statewide. I so wish Daddy had lived to witness the actions of the man he had encouraged and supported.

Choosing not to help or support me is one thing and certainly the congressman's prerogative. Intentionally trying to harm me is another.

Still, there was no time to wallow. The next day was June 7, and it was going to be a long one. I was campaigning at opposite ends of the state—first in Florence County and later in McCormick County. Little did I know then, that yet another Democratic "leader" was plotting to sabotage my campaign. This time, it was S.C. House Minority Leader Todd Rutherford. I knew he wasn't happy about a decision I made the year before. So, when people started calling and sending me clips of him standing at a podium in the second-floor lobby of the State House to endorse my opponent, I wasn't surprised. And if he had simply done that, there would be nothing memorable or eventful about his press conference. Unfortunately, he chose to make it an indictment of me instead of an endorsement of my opponent.

In 2021, I refused to sign off on his wife's magistrate appointment when the nominating senator, Darrell Jackson, forwarded the appointment paperwork to my office for my signature. When my Senate colleague told me that the House Minority Leader was upset with me for not signing and to look for a call from him, that didn't surprise me either. I returned the House Minority Leader's call the next day, the day after I delivered the State of the State Response, knowing exactly what he wanted to discuss. It was important that Todd heard directly from me why I wouldn't sign off on his wife's magistrate appointment.

What I didn't expect was his reaction. He immediately became enraged ... cursing, yelling, screaming, and threatening me, which seemed bizarre and way over the top, since signing or not signing my name is my prerogative. And as disrespectful as he was, I managed to keep my cool and tried to explain to him that he could proceed with his wife's appointment and I wouldn't stand in his or his wife's way.

In other words, I didn't plan to stop it. I just wasn't comfortable endorsing it.

In South Carolina, state senators get to nominate magistrate judges and the governor then appoints the nominees. Our staff advised me that his wife's nomination could still be submitted to the governor and that she could still be appointed, even if one senator declines to sign off on or support the nomination.

Yet, none of that seemed to matter. For reasons unknown to me, Senator Jackson later decided not to submit her application to the governor. And in true Old Guard fashion, he and Todd continued to work together as if nothing ever happened.

So, after ignoring the petty, bullying tactics Todd used to try to get my attention for a year and a half, he decided to drag my name and character through the mud under the guise that this latest bullying stunt was an "endorsement" of my opponent.

Here's the thing—I've never *started* a fight. But I've never run from one either.

Unfortunately, he came for me on a day when I had some time to take it all in and respond in kind. I was in the passenger seat of Dominique's car leaving Florence County to head to my next speaking engagement in McCormick County. When I watched the clip of his press conference and heard the lies he told about me, I felt I had to respond with the truth. So, I simply said what I said in two back-to-back Tweets and moved on.

I don't harbor hatred in my heart for anyone. Hate is way too heavy. Doesn't mean others don't harbor hatred in theirs for me. I don't get to control that. What I do control is my response to it. It didn't take long for me to discover that speaking the truth is still considered "hate speech" for those who aren't ready to hear, acknowledge, or receive it.

Our brief "beef" set Twitter ablaze. House and Senate colleagues were calling and texting me. Well-meaning friends and supporters were too. Everybody had an opinion. Some thought I was way too harsh. Others were glad somebody … anybody, finally stood up to him. People who didn't really know either of us thought I was mad because he "endorsed" my opponent. If they had simply listened to what he said, instead of just reading the headlines, they would've realized that his "endorsement" was just a ruse to get media attention.

If he had actually endorsed my opponent, I would've been fine with that. I responded the way I did because I was straight tired of being vilified and trashed for over 16 months, just for doing the right thing.

Some SCDP loyalists discreetly reached out to tell me that they knew Todd's actions were vindictive and that his comments about me were lies, totally misrepresenting who I am. They just wished I had taken "the high road" by not responding. Every time I heard that, I understood why Democrats in South Carolina had gotten their butts kicked for the last 20-plus years. So, an SCDP "leader" could publicly assassinate my character without consequence and I should just keep taking the high road by not countering his lies with the truth?

They knew the truth and were afraid to speak it, which meant they would neither defend me nor hold my offenders accountable. Yet, they couldn't wait to tell me I should've taken the high road and turned the other cheek the moment I defended myself?

Please miss me with that.

Perhaps I wouldn't have felt obligated to respond if another SCDP leader had. Yet, these guys *never* came to my defense, especially when I was attacked by male Democratic Party "leaders." And since that was the case about 99 percent of the time, I think it's safe to say that no SCDP "leader" or "loyalist" has ever publicly defended me or any other strong Black women against our male Democratic attackers. Without even trying, I had already thought of at least two other Black female Democrats who had been politically attacked by Black male SCDP "leaders." As usual, their bad behavior was met with the same good ol' cowardly crickets.

At that point, I was done with all the state party's crap.

The truth isn't always pretty or palatable. It *is* always liberating, though. And on June 7—exactly one week before my gubernatorial primary after the brief "Twitter beef"—I felt more free than I had in 12 years of being affiliated with a party that is scared of its own shadow and would rather fight me than the self-serving politicians who are the true enemies of the people we represent.

When I arrived at SCETV on Friday, June 10, for what the SCDP promoted as a gubernatorial debate during the party's convention weekend, I wasn't surprised at all to find that it wasn't even a real debate. It was just an hour-long Q&A, obviously for show, with no time or opportunity to really address the issues in a substantive, meaningful way, or challenge the responses of our opponents.

Since the SCDP intentionally scheduled this one televised event that would put us on the stage together for the first time at 5 p.m.

on a Friday afternoon when nobody would be watching and early voting had closed, it was clear that we would simply be going through the motions. I felt like I was participating in a sham. All I could do was let it go and remind myself that the statewide primary was only four days away.

As I walked into the convention center after the Q&A, Millie had just finished taking pictures with our sorority sister, Vice President Harris. She thought I must've taken pictures with Kamala before going to SCETV. I hadn't because I wasn't advised or invited. I already had plenty of photos with Kamala. That wasn't my issue. What bothered me was that the vice president was visiting Richland County—the County I live in and represent— and I wasn't even able to greet and welcome her.

As one of only two Black female senators in the state at the time and the first and only Black woman to represent Richland County, the county of our state's Capitol, in the S.C. Senate ... well, I gotta admit ... it *did* sting a little.

When I told Millie that the SCDP made sure I was "busy" at SCETV when Kamala arrived and didn't invite me to welcome her to my county, she couldn't believe it. After all, I had traveled to Greenville on crutches to meet Kamala at the airport the first time she visited South Carolina and stayed with her the entire day for multiple events in Greenville and Columbia. Kamala and her sister, Mya, and I talked, laughed, and bonded on that first trip.

When she was running for president, I attended almost all of her South Carolina events and enjoyed helping her connect with colleagues, sorority sisters, and others who could broaden her base of support all over our state. I was honored to be her table guest at our sorority's annual Pink Ice Gala too.

While running statewide, I didn't have time to connect with Kamala or Mya, like I did before. As the first Black woman to serve as our nation's vice president, I knew she would understand what

I was up against and I looked forward to hearing her speak at the Blue Palmetto Dinner. With a historic four women running for statewide seats, I was certain that she would proudly highlight our historical progress in her remarks.

Imagine how shocked and disappointed I was when Vice President Harris didn't even mention the statewide primary or acknowledge the fact that an unprecedented four Black women were vying for statewide offices in just four days. When she highlighted the November election and mentioned the importance of voting in *that* election, I realized the SCDP was at it again. And it was intentional.

There are no words to adequately describe how invisible the SCDP's actions made me feel. I didn't think the S.C. Democratic Party could stoop any lower than it already had. This felt like the ultimate betrayal.

The next day was more of the same. The SCDP went out of its way to highlight my opponent. His intro video and music at the convention played perfectly. They just happened to have "technical difficulties" with mine. I've never been one to sweat the small stuff and I wasn't about to start. The S.C. Democratic Party definitely wasn't worth it. In three days, I could finally be done with them. And quite frankly, I couldn't wait! I gave my convention speech to a cheering crowd and exited the SCDP Convention stage for the very last time.

On Tuesday, June 14, I woke up feeling amazing! Election day had finally come and I was excited because I kept my promise to God! I ran hard, gave it my all—even when I didn't want to or feel like it—and learned so much about myself and others in the process. Campaigning statewide while continuing to serve in the Senate, tested my faith, my courage, and my patience in ways I hadn't been tested before. I was super proud of my team and the race we ran. If I won, my fight would continue because my biggest opponent for the last 12 years wasn't the SCGOP. It was the SCDP. Just the thought of fighting the state party establishment for four more years was exhausting.

If I didn't win the Primary, I would accept God's will and be equally grateful for the lessons because there were many. As the polls closed at 7 p.m., Pastor Radhika picked me up from my house and we made our way downtown to our watch party.

When the results began to come in, Joe was in the lead. As it became obvious that the majority of precincts had reported, I gave my concession speech and called Joe to congratulate him. Of course, it wasn't the result we wanted. However, God's peace was still with me and I had no regrets.

It was then that I fully understood what Nelson Mandela meant when he said, "I never lose. I either win or I learn."

After I was done speaking, I enjoyed the rest of the evening mingling and talking with supporters until a little after midnight. The next day, I was back in the Senate for session—tired and relieved that our statewide campaign for governor had come to an end.

So many South Carolinians on both sides of the political aisle told me they appreciated me for stepping up.

Several SCDP members asked me to run as Joe Cunningham's running mate and seemed a bit agitated that I wouldn't even consider it. It wasn't until I spoke with one or two who acted as if I owed them or the state party an explanation, that I realized how misinformed some S.C. Democratic Party loyalists were. Their argument was that my opponent and I would be so much stronger together on one ticket.

Fortunately, I didn't need to win the gubernatorial primary or become Joe Cunningham's running mate to inspire change.

Respectfully, what even well-meaning Dems didn't realize was that the SCDP had already gotten everything it was gonna get out of me. I wasn't about to validate or lend credibility to the state party's preferred candidate, especially when he represented everything I had been fighting against for the last 12 years.

Grateful to continue representing the people of Senate District 22, I looked forward to some quiet time to rest, relax, and digest everything that happened on the campaign trail. There was a lot to unpack and I needed the time and space to do it.

After thanking my family, team, supporters, friends, and colleagues, I longed to really disconnect from all things political. Having at least 30 days without social media or local, state, and national news felt like a great start. I didn't want to take political phone calls or answer political emails and text messages. Realizing that was a tall order, I gave myself a little grace and kept going until I just couldn't anymore. Letting go of all of the weight I carried during the gubernatorial campaign wasn't gonna be easy. The time I needed was necessary, not optional.

At the end of the 30 days, I still wasn't ready to re-engage so I graced myself another 30 days, which would take me through my birthday month. When I received a call that seemed to come out of nowhere, I knew God was up to something.

Final SCDP gubernatorial campaign convention speech (credit: Associated Press)

U.S. Senator and presidential candidate Kamala Harris and me at the Pink Ice Gala

LESSON FOUR: *Let It Go*

Whatever your "it" is that keeps you stuck and stagnant, let it go. For most of my adult life, "it" was Sickle Cell. After two knee surgeries, a life-threatening DVT and PE, "it" was my blinged-out crutch that gave me something to lean on —and an excuse for walking super slow or hobbling, some days.

"It" was an embarrassing stumble up the steps to the stage to speak at a domestic violence breakfast in Greenville—in front of hundreds of people—shortly after giving up my crutch that later led me to have tremendous anxiety at just the thought of going up steps to stages and podiums to speak without it.

"It" was a brief "Twitter beef" with the house minority leader.

"It" was being vilified and disrespected by establishment Democrats at state and county party levels—*especially* the ones who looked like me.

"It" was learning that DNC Chair Jaime Harrison admitted to nationally syndicated radio host Karen Hunter that he didn't even bother to vote in South Carolina's gubernatorial primary, although he had an unprecedented two weeks to do it.

"It" was always feeling like I had to fight my own people— my Democratic legislative delegation, House and Senate Caucuses, and state party—just to fight *for* my own people.

"It" was constantly having to prove myself to the same people who gave my opponents a pass.

It was a local businesswoman named Diane who called when I first announced my candidacy for the S.C. Senate District 22 seat to let me know that she and a dozen of her closest friends met with Republican Susan Brill, my Senate opponent, and found her much easier to get along with than me.

While I was serving in the S.C. House, Diane told me she thought my references to the Old Guard or the OG were personal. As a new House member, I was constantly fighting the OG. Some of my colleagues had been serving in the S.C. House for almost as long as I had been living, so I led a public awareness campaign to enlighten voters with the popular tagline, "Tell the OG, they've got to GO!" People loved to see it on T-shirts and read about it in my blogposts. Although I had already explained to Diane that my OG references had nothing to do with age and everything to do with regressive, self-centered mindsets and actions, she was determined to be angry about it.

When I ran for Senate District 22, Diane called me and said, "I see you're running for the Senate. If it was up to me, I wouldn't invite you to my office because I don't like the tone of your emails, but since a dozen of my closest friends and I have already met with your opponent, they want to meet with you too. So, I'm calling to see if you're willing to meet with us at my office."

Always eager to stand up to bullies like Diane, I replied, "Absolutely!"

I asked Trav, my campaign manager, to follow up with her regarding the meeting details, not realizing that having him call was going to piss her off even more. When Trav and I arrived at her office for our meeting, she got really nasty and told him that he couldn't stay. That bothered both of us because Diane knew he was coming and agreed when they spoke that he could stay for the meeting. Since he drove me there, he was forced to wait outside the room for over two hours.

She seated me at the head of the conference table so I would clearly be in the line of fire. Most of her closest friends were only familiar with who she told them I was. By the time the conversation really got going, I wasn't nervous or fearful at all, even though the host did her best to ensure that I was both.

I tried to address all of their questions and concerns. And as only God would have it, Diane posed the final question. It was a game changer. First, she told me how disappointed she was that a Black female student at Spring Valley High School was violently thrown out of her desk by a white school resource officer for allegedly refusing to put her cell phone away when her teacher asked her to.

"Why have you said nothing about *that* in your blog," she blurted.

Before I could answer, Ms. Marjorie Hammock, who was seated to my left, looked her right in the eye and told her that her comments were not true and that I was the *only* Richland County legislator who *had* spoken about it publicly.

I thanked Ms. Marjorie and shared more details about my blogpost that specifically addressed the incident at Spring Valley and my Disturbing Schools Bill, which I first introduced in the S.C. House after the young lady was violently ejected from her desk. I told the ladies that because of the Spring Valley incident, I learned that over 30,000 South Carolina students had already been sent into the school-to-prison pipeline for classroom misbehavior that wasn't criminal. And Ms. Marjorie was right. I was the only Richland County legislator to speak about it publicly, demand accountability and transparency, and introduce legislation to ensure that no other students could be arrested and sent to the S.C. Department of Juvenile Justice from their classrooms for noncriminal classroom misbehavior.

Suddenly, the room got quiet. The ladies looked stunned to hear that over 30,000 South Carolina students had been sent into the school-to-prison pipeline from their classrooms under this law.

This time, *I* asked a question: "Since you ladies have already met with my opponent, Susan Brill, a self-described, 'moderate' Republican who currently serves on the Richland Two and Spring Valley Foundation Boards, I'm curious about how she addressed this issue when you asked her about it."

The ladies' faces said it all. A woman who was seated to my right and hadn't said much during the meeting leaned toward me as if she was about to let me in on a secret. She stated that the group never even asked my opponent that question and admitted that they should have.

I wasn't surprised and appreciated her honesty. She went on to say how impressed she was with my responses. As we prepared to adjourn, that same lady stood at her seat and became the first to openly pledge her support to me in my race for Senate District 22. Before I knew it, each woman who was seated at the table pledged her support and asked to be added to my email list. Realizing she was out-numbered, Diane reluctantly offered her support as well.

Had I not shown up at all or left when Diane put Trav out because I was afraid of facing a presumably unfriendly audience alone, I would never have had an opportunity to listen, address their concerns, answer their questions truthfully, or earn their trust and support.

Letting go of the "what-ifs" and what I presumed would be an unpleasant experience, actually helped prepare me for the higher office I was seeking. Being grilled by a dozen women for over two hours—women who had only received negative information about me from the meeting host, didn't feel good. Turns out, it *was* good.

I'm not saying that letting go is easy. It's not. And over the years, there were times when my flesh got the best of me. When others went low, I met them where they were. When they came for me, I gave 'em all the smoke.

It wasn't until I finally settled into knowing who and whose I am that I no longer felt obligated to respond. As I reached a higher level of spiritual maturity, everything began to change. Having the courage to let go of the motives, expectations, opinions, and actions of others is what truly set *me* free.

NO crutches. NO fear. NO animosity. NO excuses. And NO regrets.

CHAPTER FIVE
Chosen

Many are called, but few are chosen …
—Matthew 22:14

"WELCOME HOME!" That's what the sign said, as I stepped out of the Tel Aviv Airport and approached the chartered bus with the big green, black, and white banner that had logos of our hosting organizations, Philos Black and the Consulate General of Israel to the Southeastern United States, prominently placed at the top.

After flying for over 14 hours straight and not sleeping a wink on the flight, I was too tired to ask a lot of questions. And although I only knew one person out of the 25 or 30 people around me, my weary eyes kept gravitating back to that sign. *Why does it say, Welcome Home!* I thought. This was my first trip to Israel, and as far as I was concerned, it definitely wasn't planned. At least, I didn't plan it. In fact, I was still wondering why I was even there. Nothing about it made sense to me.

In late July 2022, Representative Annie McDaniel, a Richland County legislative colleague, called to tell me that the two of us had been invited to Israel as part of a 20-member cohort of Black legislative women. The trip was scheduled for early September and they asked her to reach out to me first. Skeptical about why I had been invited and eager to find out exactly who was extending the invitation, I asked Annie how and why we had been selected to be part of this inaugural cohort. Learning that the hosts pulled from one or two national legislative organizations that I hadn't been very active in only fueled my skepticism.

I had recently met one of the event organizers, Jasper Hendricks, at our National Conference of State Legislatures (NCSL) and later spoke with lead organizer, Wendell Shelby-Wallace, by phone. My conversations with them were helpful. I just wasn't convinced that going to Israel was something God wanted me to do. I reluctantly agreed to participate in the hosts' initial Zoom call where I was surprised to meet other elected legislative women from across the U.S. who seemed comfortable and excited to participate in the trip. After glancing at the three-page packing list and hearing about all of the preparations the trip would require, I was even more overwhelmed.

So, I prayed and asked God to show me clearly whether or not I should go.

Neither the trip organizers nor the participants knew that I was low-key afraid of the extra long flight because I knew that high altitudes, overexertion, dehydration, and high stress could trigger a Sickle Cell crisis.

Not knowing how the rest of the world was dealing with the pandemic also made me leery. I was one of only a few people in the entire S.C. legislature—maybe in the entire state—who was still wearing my mask every day, everywhere.

As fear continued to consume me, I could hear my own voice in my head reciting Psalm 91 as I have been doing practically every morning for years. It was in those moments that God reminded me … it's not enough to just recite His Word. I either believe it or I don't. Believing it required me to simply *act* like it because faith is an action. And just like that, I was able to check myself and move on, determined to do and be better.

I did have one more request of God, though. I asked Him to close the door on the trip to Israel if He wasn't the one who was opening it. I needed to be sure that I wasn't acting on my own will or my own desires, instead of His.

When lead organizer Wendell Shelby-Wallace, who I had just met on the Zoom call, mentioned "roommate assignments" at the end of the call, I thought, "Wow, God! You work fast!"

Dr. Marion, my primary care physician, strongly advised me to opt for an individual room, given my medical history and the fact that I didn't know anyone else's COVID-19 protocol. I called Wendell and asked him if there was any way I could pay the other half of the room cost for a private room, if I decided to participate.

When I learned that the room cost had already been paid in full and that I couldn't pay for the other half, I was pretty sure God had answered my question. By then, I was a little disappointed because the trip was intriguing and the other women legislators seemed so excited. Still, after several life-threatening health challenges, I didn't need to be convinced that my health came first. So, if God was closing that door, I trusted Him and was grateful that He answered me so quickly. Once I let my family know I wouldn't be going, I decided to focus on other things. Besides, it was still my birthday month and I wasn't done celebrating!

Imagine my surprise when Wendell reached out about a week after our Zoom call to let me know that one of the ladies had to bow out. Apparently, her schedule wouldn't permit her to go, which left one room empty.

What? Really, God?

It almost felt as though Wendell was going above and beyond to accommodate me. But why? The more I wrestled with it, the more I knew it was God. Time was of the essence because the trip was just over a week away, so I sat with it for a minute and prayed. The next day, I still had peace about God reopening that door, so I tried to shift my mind and actions in that direction. I told Wendell and my family that I would go and finally went ahead and printed that three-page packing list.

Lord knows, it was a doozy.

By the time September 6 rolled up on me, I was exhausted from all the doctor appointments and shopping errands it took just to begin to pack and prepare for the long flight and be gone for approximately two weeks. Surprisingly, after only a few hours of sleep on the day we were to depart for Israel, I woke up feeling amazing!

Cam and I were supposed to leave for the airport at 1 p.m. He reminded me to exhale because I was obviously stressed *and* late. As only God would have it, my flight from Charlotte to Boston was delayed. Instead of leaving at 5:05 p.m., our flight departed at 6:40 p.m., which gave me time to eat a slice of pizza and drink plenty of water before my three-hour flight to Boston. What I didn't realize was that I was in jeopardy of missing my next flight out of Boston because of the delay.

When my flight arrived in Boston around 8:30 p.m., I was still on the plane and my gate was a million miles away. To make matters worse, our 14-hour flight to Tel Aviv was scheduled to leave Boston at 9:30 p.m., and all of the other members of our cohort had already arrived. It took us forever to deplane. I wasn't sure I could make it to the gate in time because it was so far away. That's when I learned that God delayed the flight *again*, this time until 10:30 p.m.

After much speedwalking and many elevators and escalators later, I finally made it to the shuttle that would take me to the gate to meet my group. Alas, there was just "one more river to cross." To get to the shuttle outside that would ultimately take me to my gate, there were multiple sets of super-steep stairs that I would have to drag two extremely heavy bags down. I took a deep breath and started down the first set. It felt as if I was going in slow motion. When I glanced out at the shuttle, practically all of the other passengers were onboard. Yikes!

Before I knew it, a gentleman appeared out of nowhere. With an accent and a kind smile, he said, "Ma'am … I'll take these for you." A mere "thank you" seemed grossly inadequate. Yet, it was all I had the strength to utter in that moment. As he seemed to effortlessly and carefully lift my heavy bags down the stairs and onto the shuttle, I leaned my head back on the seat once I boarded and thanked God for him. And, as only God would have it, when we were getting off of the shuttle, he took it upon himself to get my luggage down from the rack and carry it off of the bus for me. When I told him I was headed to Israel, he politely nodded, "That's where I'm headed too. I will take your bags to the gate for you."

What a lifesaver! God's angels were encamped all around me. It would be the first of many times on this trip that I'd experience His grace in ways I'll never ever forget.

I finally made it to the gate, hoping to see Annie, since she was the only member of our cohort I would recognize. When I didn't see her, I called Jasper, who kindly came to take me over and introduce me to the other members. Finally I could breathe a sigh of relief, knowing that I made it to the gate in time to board the flight to Israel with my cohort!

As expected, the flight was extremely long. My anxiety about having to get up and walk around every two hours to ward off any blood clots and use that tight, nasty little closet of a restroom to relieve my kidneys of all that water I had to drink, made it impossible for me to sleep.

Watching movies and writing some book notes helped pass the time. Some I wrote longhand in my journal. Others, I typed into the Notes app on my phone. As passengers seated around me slept soundly during the night, I thought about my sons, my siblings, and why God seemed so intentional about sending me on this journey. I wish I could say that thinking and praying about it gave me the clarity I needed.

After landing in Tel Aviv and making our way to baggage claim, I was really glad to see that I wasn't the only one who must have felt as if I had overpacked. Everybody's luggage was big, heavy, and full of all of those packing list necessities. Our first stop was the hotel. It hadn't yet occurred to me that the time difference was significant, putting us promptly at mid-afternoon on September 7. I was just glad to get checked into my room and looked forward to taking a shower and resting, since I hadn't slept on the overnight flight there.

When they told us to meet back on the bus for dinner shortly after checking in and that all we had time to do was wash up, I definitely wasn't feeling *that* or Israel. Nothing against the Ethiopian Israeli Heritage Center or our gracious, dynamic hosts, Ashager and Fanta. I simply didn't want food, fellowship, or engagement at that moment. All I wanted to do was rest.

The next morning was better, although the jet lag was still real. As we found a seat on our chartered bus, it was time for introductions. Turns out the beautiful lady who sat next to me the night before at dinner was our chaplain, Lieutenant Colonel Crystal Miller-Davis, who led our first daily devotion that would become part of our morning routine while our driver transported us to each stop. I had no idea what a profound impact Chaplain Crystal would have on me and this journey. As a night owl who detested early morning engagement, especially coming from "morning people" who seemed overly enthusiastic and excited about it, I was too busy wondering why God was punishing me.

And why had He taken me all the way to Israel to do it?

Our first stop was Capernaum on the shore of the Sea of Galilee.

Although I felt like I was still sleepwalking, I'd be lying if I said I wasn't already in awe of the beauty I was beginning to behold. By the time we took our dinner cruise on the Sea of Galilee that evening, I knew exactly what the sign "Welcome Home!" meant at the airport. As the sun began to set and I gazed out at the glory that surrounded me, my eyes and heart were full. It was as if God was personally welcoming me to the Holy Land—my spiritual homeland, and I was extremely grateful.

By Friday, I was once again forced way outside of my comfort zone. Some may not know that I'm a foodie who also happens to be an extremely picky eater. In my world, those two things are not mutually exclusive. I also don't really enjoy eating at other people's homes, especially people I don't know. Before this journey, I was able to control that by just not accepting many dinner invitations.

Sometimes I do make exceptions when I'm familiar enough with the hosts' customs and habits, their pet and COVID-19 protocols, and other factors that could help me make an informed decision.

Of course, that wasn't the case in Israel and I really didn't want to offend well-meaning cohorts or families, just because of my propensity to be pretty persnickety when it comes to food and the environment within which I eat it. So, imagine my angst when I discovered that our itinerary had us dining in the homes of strangers in a foreign land ... during a global pandemic.

When our bus pulled up for lunch at the home of a wonderful Druze Family in Buq'ata, I was low-key mortified. It would be the first of several in-home dining experiences. Obviously, I was still wondering why God was so mad at me.

And more importantly, how *long* was He gonna be mad?

Eating in people's homes I didn't know, who prepared food I didn't recognize, didn't seem like something I could realistically do. While still on the bus, I tried to come up with a plan. I would look for a salad first and put only that on my plate, if possible. If there wasn't any, I would simply scatter a sampling of different foods around my plate to disguise that I really wasn't eating.

My plan could've worked because I actually did try the salad first ... and almost spit it out instinctively. It looked so colorful and edible, until I tasted the mint. Who puts *mint* leaves in salad? Ugh! I started thinking about the pounds I had been wanting to shed. If this was the cuisine I'd be forced to consume for the next 12 days, I'd definitely be a few sizes smaller when we returned to the United States.

After dinner, the family asked us to remove our shoes and gather around the floor in a different room, so that they could share information about their faith, beliefs, and customs. We sipped hot tea and were fascinated as we listened to stories of reincarnation. By the time we made our way back to the bus, several of my cohorts mentioned that they noticed I didn't eat and asked if I was okay. I told them I was fine and we laughed. Thank God, they waited until we got back on the bus to out me.

When I saw that we were dining with yet another family that evening for dinner, I tried to prepare my mind and stomach for what I thought was inevitable. Turns out, the dinner we had at a couple's home in Yesud HaMa'ala in Upper Galilee was, by most accounts, one of the most delicious meals of the entire trip! The family's neighbor was an executive chef who prepared an absolutely exquisite experience for us.

Every single course was God's perfect reminder to keep my mind and my palette open.

There were several other in-home dining experiences with families who were kind and gracious enough to invite us in. Of course, some foods were much more appealing and enjoyable than others. With each visit, it became less about the food and more about the ability to briefly immerse ourselves in the culture.

I learned so much during those visits. When I realized how different our experiences would've been as everyday tourists, I appreciated these unique, invaluable opportunities all the more.

Each day brought its own new adventures. When I finally got back to my room, I thought about my previous conversations with Texas Representative Rhetta Bowers-Andrews and Atlanta-based CEO Deborah Scott on the bus, after dining at another family's home. I had just met these two women who wouldn't take no for an answer when they asked me if I was excited about being baptized in the Jordan River. I politely responded that I wasn't planning to get "re-baptized" since I had already been baptized as a teen at Shiloh Baptist, my home church in Bennettsville.

They both looked at me like, *"Are you serious?"*

"Yeahhh?" I murmured, sounding almost as unsure as I was, apologetic and wondering why they even cared.

To my surprise, neither of these ladies would let it go. Rhetta asked me why again. I could tell her questions were cloaked in love, not judgment. Deborah's were too. She even went one step further.

"Do you think you'll regret it when you get back to the United States, if you don't get baptized in the Jordan?" she said. "I mean, we don't know if we'll ever have this opportunity again."

Because they seemed genuinely concerned, I admitted to them that the main reason I decided not to get baptized in the Jordan River was because I wasn't prepared and didn't feel like messing with my hair. I had brought very few hair products with me. I left my blow dryer at home. My flat iron wasn't heating up right with the adapters we had to use. When I admitted to them that I didn't plan to get baptized in the Jordan River because I was concerned about what my hair would look like afterward, they chuckled. I did too, probably because I was embarrassed as I heard those words coming out of my mouth.

Really, Mia? I thought. *You gotta come better than that, girl.*

Without flinching, they started polling our cohorts to find out who brought hair care products. Within minutes, I had everything I could possibly need—shampoos, conditioners, gels, mousses, and yes, even scrunchies. Still, they left it up to me, suggested that I pray about it and vowed they wouldn't try to convince me to participate if I really didn't want to. Deborah's question about whether I might regret it kept replaying over and over in my head. I regretted not running against Lindsey Graham when God told me to, so I knew firsthand that "obedience is better than sacrifice."

When we got back to the hotel, I was overwhelmed by the love and support Rhetta, Deborah, and each of the ladies in our cohort had shown me. Exhausted, I went straight to my room. After praying, I realized my hair was just a convenient excuse. I knew it, and my cohorts did too. In the stillness of the night when it was just me and God, He showed me that fear was once again the driving force.

What was I so afraid of? Did I really wanna go back to the U.S. without getting baptized in the Jordan? What if I was opting out of the very reason God sent me to Israel? What if these ladies hadn't fought for me when I didn't have the energy to fight for myself? What was God ultimately trying to show me? As I wrestled with all these questions, it was only getting later, so I tried to close my eyes and get some sleep. We would have to rise early again tomorrow.

The next morning, I woke up with peace and felt refreshed. As I made my way over to Wendell, our lead event organizer, we had a brief conversation before boarding the bus to depart for the day's events. The reason I remember our exchange that morning is because I asked Wendell a question that had been nagging at me. I said, "Wendell, you didn't know me before this trip and I didn't know you. So, why did you go out of your way to make sure I was a part of it?" He looked at me with a calm, reassuring smile.

"Because God wouldn't let me let it go," he said. "I could tell you weren't convinced that this trip was for you, but God made a way. And I just believe your healing is here."

His answer wasn't at all what I expected. To be honest, it totally messed me up.

"My *healing* is here?"

What does *that* mean?" I wondered. And why would someone who doesn't know anything about me say that?

I hate the thought of regret. For me, that word has always been intertwined with fear. Some of the same feelings and emotions I had in 2002 came rushing back. That was the year God told me to "step out on faith" and leave the stability of my "good government job" to start my own public affairs firm. To even consider leaving a salaried position to become an independent, registered lobbyist, something I wasn't even sure I knew how to do well, was beyond scary.

Add to that the pressure I felt to make sure my sons would have what they needed, since their dad and I were going through a divorce. It meant I'd have to trust God in ways I could never have imagined. Moving forward in faith required me to push past my fears, even if I was scared as hell. And I was. That's when I promised myself I would never let fear be the driving force in my life because I knew it would lead me to regret.

For eight solid years, I kept that promise. As my business continued to grow, I was healthy, earning good money, advocating for issues I cared about, and happier and more fulfilled than I had been in years with enough time and flexibility to be actively engaged in my babies' lives.

That began to change after I became an elected official. The fights I was taking on seemed to rob me of my health, my financial stability, and my time. By 2020, I was serving in the S.C. Senate, still working hard to overcome the physical and financial challenges caused by the life-threatening health issues I faced while serving. Although I subconsciously knew that overcoming fear isn't a "one and done" approach, not running against Lindsey Graham when God clearly told me to set my "faith walk" back significantly.

All the hell I encountered from the Democratic Party establishment when God gave me yet another opportunity to be obedient and led me to run for governor of South Carolina in 2022 helped strengthen my faith. Yet, I had become even more cynical about self-serving politicians who consistently put their own interests above those of the people they purport to represent.

As I thought about the magnitude of the challenges I had recently faced, it occurred to me that all of those things may have been why Wendell sensed I needed God's healing. Was it obvious that baggage from the gubernatorial campaign was still weighing me down? At the hotel the night before, I asked Wendell whether it was too late for me to get a robe and be baptized. He assured me that it wasn't.

When we arrived at Qasr al-Yahud (also known as Al-maghtas), the western portion of the Jordan River where John the Baptist was baptized according to the New Testament, it was another scorching hot day. Wendell and Jasper advised us to keep hydration packets and water handy, lather on sunscreen, and sit under covered shelters, if possible.

When I saw the Jordan River, it didn't look anything like I expected. As I prepared to be baptized, a myriad of thoughts ran through my mind. To describe the water as murky was an understatement. For a country girly-girl who is anything but outdoorsy, the fact that snakes and other reptiles or amphibians could've been lurking underwater didn't even occur to me. That was a first. Instead, I was more concerned about the murky water itself getting into my eyes, nose, and mouth. As I caught myself being distracted by the "what-ifs," I took a deep breath and decided to "cast my cares" before taking the first step into the Jordan River.

Much to my surprise and dismay, the water was freezing! How could it be 150 degrees outside and the water in the Jordan River be ice cold? At that moment, I was just past the last step and, without trying, my body was already making a U-turn. For over half a century, every time I immersed myself in cold water or did anything that shocked my body, regardless of how hot it was outside, I had *always* ended up in the ER with an excruciatingly painful Sickle Cell crisis.

Think, Mia. Think about how this story ends. You already know what's about to happen if you don't hurry up and get outta this cold water. And now you're in a foreign land where doctors probably have no clue how to treat someone who is having a Sickle Cell crisis.

My mind kept telling me to turn around and go back to the river's edge where it was safe. Why had I listened to Deborah and Rhetta? No hair products or scrunchies were gonna fix this. I felt as if I had just made the biggest mistake of my life.

And yet, something in me kept whispering, *Keep going. I've got you. Trust Me. Keep going!*

I took a deep breath and looked up toward heaven because I needed God to hear me. As I exhaled and slowly took another uncertain step forward, I could feel my legs shaking. Think I literally froze in that spot for a few seconds.

And these were the words that came to my heart, "I trust You, God. I'm leaving it all right here."

With that declaration, I looked straight ahead at Chaplin Crystal and the event leaders who were baptizing us in the Jordan River and nervously took another step. As I slowly made my way over to them, I paused and prayed silently again, thanking God for allowing me to leave everything with Him that I had dragged into the Jordan—Sickle Cell, every physical, mental, spiritual, emotional, and financial challenge I faced, and all of the hurt and pain that had been weighing me down. I asked Him to "wash away" my tears, my fears, and make me new and whole again. By the time I reached everyone and prepared to be fully immersed, it was obvious to me that God heard my prayer.

After being baptized, I wiped my eyes and made my way over to the stairs to walk out of the Jordan. The heaviness I had previously felt was gone. The water was still cold. Yet, my body seemed to have adjusted and I was no longer overly concerned. Unlike my previous experiences, I had not even the slightest hint of pain in my limbs. Instead, God's peace enveloped me like a warm blanket.

After all of us had gotten changed, we headed to the Dead Sea for lunch and a boat ride. Beholding the crystal blue waters of the Dead Sea was so different from the murky waters of the Jordan River. Warning signs were posted everywhere reminding us not to ingest or expose our eyes, ears, noses, or mouths to the highly concentrated salt water, despite how magnificently beautiful and inviting it was. I wondered whether the stark contrast between the two was a subtle metaphoric reminder of the way life is sometimes.

It's often the most alluring, attractive people, places, and things that are the most dangerous.

After lunch, we lathered up in the Dead Sea's mineral-packed mud and carefully rinsed it off before boarding the boat.

Similar to icebergs, the Dead Sea has "saltbergs." Some of my cohorts exited the boat to get a photo of themselves sitting on a saltberg in the middle of the Sea. Although we were advised that it's impossible to drown because of the highly concentrated salt content, just immersing yourself in the Dead Sea could be deadly.

When we got back to the shore, all of us gathered at the edge of the Dead Sea for a few rounds of the Electric Slide. Still no Sickle Cell pain. No heaviness. And no hint of any of the health issues I had grappled with in the past.

The next day we visited Manger Square in Bethlehem. For no apparent reason, we were accosted by a tour guide who became loud and indignant with one of our event organizers, as we lined up to go into the cave that marked Jesus' birthplace. To keep the noise and distractions out of our ears so that we could stay focused and together, our event organizers had already given us earbud "whisperers." For reasons unknown to us, the tension began to escalate between our group and the tour guide. Chaplain Crystal's voice and the serenity of "whispered" Scriptures in our ears was the calming reassurance we needed to redirect our attention from the tour guide's antics to the beauty of Jesus' birthplace.

When I finally got to kneel and touch the exquisite 14-point star in the floor that marked Jesus' birthplace, I was reminded that all of the stress and frustration we endured to get there was so worth it!

The next destination on our tour was a Palestinian refugee community. The environment on the West Bank was drastically different from Bethlehem. Armed militia. Curtains closing each time villagers caught us looking at them, looking at us. Palestinian children walking and riding their bikes nearby, waving, and smiling as if to say, *You're welcome here and we're glad to see you!*

Somehow, that wasn't exactly the energy we got from the larger community. Our Palestinian tour guide spoke to us before we got off the bus about the challenges these communities faced with the government's rationing of water and other essential resources. That's when I better understood their plight and why the tension that surrounded us in that moment was palpable.

For me, so was the connection. The inhabitants of these communities were people of color. Their living conditions were subpar, especially when compared to the living conditions of the people whose homes we had visited or seen from afar in Israel. I was even more intrigued when our tour guide shared some of their stories. Large banners featuring photographs of Palestinian men lined the streets. As we walked, a friendly, excited boy ran up to our tour guide and wrapped his little arms around our guide's legs. We could tell the boy was obviously familiar with and fond of him.

When our tour guide stopped to introduce the boy to us, he told us that this beautiful little guy was the son of one of the men whose picture was prominently placed on a banner that lined the street. He pointed up to the banner that featured a picture of the boy's father and told us he was killed by government officials who were looking for his uncle. When they didn't find him, they killed the boy's father to send his uncle a message. Our tour guide and his family had been helping raise and support this young boy, and others like him, who had lost parents.

He was careful to point out to us that our tour was neither "pro-Israel" nor "pro-Palestine." It was refreshing to hear that. The phrase that stuck with me then and reassures me now was one our event organizers and tour guides consistently used to describe themselves individually and us, collectively: "We are pro-justice and pro-peace."

I took those words to heart because the phrase—pro-justice and pro-peace—is both inclusive and aspirational. As we left Palestine, I began to reflect on the day. In spite of their challenges, the Palestinian children we encountered seemed optimistic and hopeful. That type of resolve and resilience is why I felt a genuine connection to them. And I was grateful for the experience.

* * *

The next day, we visited SodaStream, one of the top sparkling water brands in the world. When I saw Israelis and Palestinians working side by side with mutual respect and admiration, I understood and appreciated our tour of the West Bank and how this company's mission and core values were strategically aligned with the change it wanted to see. To hear the testimonials of SodaStream employees was sobering and inspiring, considering that they would otherwise not have had an opportunity to meet and get to know one another. By working at SodaStream, they were able to gain the enlightenment and exposure that helps pave the way for genuine connection, collaboration, and camaraderie.

We spoke with some employees who credited SodaStream for the friendships they had forged. By allowing people to connect in a work setting, SodaStream had become a change agent. Barriers were broken. Biases were challenged. And perspectives changed. These types of Israeli-Palestinian interactions are basically forbidden by the government, unless a job requires it.

We went on to enjoy a very interesting and enlightening visit with the African Hebrew Israelites of Jerusalem who live a communal lifestyle in the town of Dimona. I was intrigued by how self-contained and self-sufficient they were. After our vegan luncheon, community members spoke candidly to us about their diet, educating their children on site, providing medical treatment to community members, growing their own foods, developing their own medicines, and designing and sewing their own clothes and jewelry. As I made my way back to our chartered bus, enjoying vegan ice cream, books, jewelry, clothing, and a few nonperishable items from the market, I knew this experience was one I would always cherish.

Later, we were introduced to members of a Bedouin community and enjoyed learning about their culture at dinner with a husband and wife who founded an organization that empowers women—an unusual practice for their culture.

The view from the Mount of Olives in East Jerusalem the next morning was breathtaking. As we began the final days of our journey, tracing Jesus' footsteps up the steepest of hills and following The Fourteen Stations of the Cross to His crucifixion, we were given a glimpse of how brutal His journey really was. Carrying His cross in the sweltering heat was almost inconceivable as we struggled to retrace His steps. By comparison, we only carried a water bottle and a hand towel to wipe the sweat from our faces. When a young boy walked past us and spat on the arms of two of our cohorts, we were reminded of the hatred Jesus faced and the remnants of that hatred that were still present in this sacred space.

A cool breeze gave us a brief reprieve from the heat. I ordered a refreshing freshly squeezed pomegranate juice from a street vendor as we walked away from the site. Sipping slowly, just to savor the taste, gave me a much-needed moment to reflect on God's grace and the remarkable experiences we were having.

When we arrived at the Yad Vashem: The World Holocaust Remembrance Center the next morning, it was already scorching hot. Our tour guide greeted us with a smile and invited us to wait in the shaded area. The children's entrance was closed to the public that day, and because we were "U.S. dignitaries" taking a scheduled tour, the museum had arranged for security. Rather than have us wait in the sweltering heat, our tour guide told us she would find out whether we could enter the building a few moments early.

Shortly afterward, she walked up with the same cheerful demeanor she had when she first greeted us. Because we were a little early for our scheduled tour, she decided to take us through the children's entrance. As we approached that entrance, a gentleman from the security team ran up to her, essentially blocking us from entering. He whispered something in her ear and she looked perplexed. After a brief exchange, she reluctantly shared that we weren't allowed to use the children's entrance. She then asked us to follow her, and we did.

As we headed toward another entrance, two members of the security team ran past us to stop us from using that access point as well. By this time, our tour guide was noticeably frustrated. The three of them had what appeared to be a brief, slightly heated exchange. She asked us to huddle up afterward so that she could explain. She told us that the security team was confused because the two entrances we attempted to use were reserved for U.S. dignitaries who would be accompanied by security and tour precisely at our scheduled time.

When she realized that their security team didn't recognize us as the U.S. dignitaries they were waiting to accompany, their conversation became more intense. With tears rolling down her face, she turned toward us and apologized profusely for the confusion. We appreciated her heartfelt apology. By then, all of us were sweating from standing in the heat.

Somehow, 20 Black women with braids, natural locks, ponytails, T-shirts, shorts, jeans, sneakers and flip-flops obviously weren't what the museum's security team envisioned or expected. Because of the hot temperatures and amount of walking we were doing, the event organizers had advised us to dress casually and comfortably. And since every tour guest on site that day was wearing very similar comfortable attire, I couldn't help but wonder whether it was our attire or our race that threw them off.

A visibly frustrated, embarrassed tour guide admitted that she was disheartened by the way we were treated. She said she had never seen staff behave that way before. We assured her that it wasn't her fault as security proceeded to escort us to the same access point they had just denied us entry to moments before.

No one on the security team apologized. It was another sobering moment for us and certainly not an unfamiliar one.

As we prepared for our visit to the Western Wall for Kabbalat Shabbat, I wasn't sure what my prayer would be. Quite frankly, this journey had already begun to awaken something in me that I had neither the words or the ability to articulate.

When we arrived at the Wall later that evening, I expected to see hundreds of people. Instead, there were thousands. Annie was kind enough to hand me a sheet of paper from her notepad and this is how my prayer began:

Dear God,

Help me see myself the way you see me. Help me harness the power (your power) within me to do everything you've created and called me to do …

When I was done, I walked over to the Wall, gently folded the paper that contained my prayer, and carefully nestled it into a small crevice. Then, I bowed my head and rested my face against the Wall to talk with God for just a little while longer before rejoining the festivities behind me.

Celebrating Shabbat, a Jewish holiday that is also known as the Sabbath, were literally thousands of people of all ages dancing and singing together! I learned that Shabbat is a holiday celebrated every week from sunset on Friday until sunset on Saturday. Stores close. Restaurants and entertainment venues close. And the people of Israel spend their time with family. Some rest, study, or attend synagogue. For them, it's more than just a day off from work. It's a time of reflection, rest, and spiritual illumination of the key concepts of their faith.

As a believer in Christ, it was fascinating to see the Jewish people shut down everything in observance of Shabbat. In the U.S., we barely close grocery stores, restaurants, shopping centers and entertainment venues on Christmas Day.

It reminded me that Thanksgiving, my favorite holiday, had become less about fellowshipping and feasting with family and more about Black Friday sales.

If I could pick one of the Jewish community's customs to emulate and practice at home, it would definitely be Shabbat. I absolutely love the concept and the emphasis the holiday places on quality time, regardless of whether you spend it alone or with family and friends. Because the collective has made it a priority, other options and distractions are removed from the equation.

The soul food Shabbat we enjoyed at a couple's home that evening only solidified my love and longing for this type of holiday in the U.S. The decor and the food were exquisite. We enjoyed steak, salmon, shrimp, and the best yams. It was truly a feast.

Saturday, September 17, our last full day in Israel, rolled around before we knew it. I had no idea that we'd have a check-in that morning after breakfast. After checking out of the hotel, I walked into the meeting room and discovered a circle of chairs. I sat in an empty one and waited on the rest of our cohorts. When organizers Wendell and Krystal asked us to come up with one word to describe our experience on this journey, I was relieved that they started to my left because I needed a little more time to think of one word that would describe all of the amazing experiences I'd had over the last 12 days. By the time I heard from everybody else in the circle, I hoped I would be able to come up with one word. It seemed like such a tall order at that moment.

One of my cohorts said *love*. Another said *gratitude*. Someone else said *connection*. Before long, I heard *grace*. And although all of these words described my experience as well, none of them fully captured the essence of what this journey had been for me. I still didn't have a clue what my one word would be. As we made our way around the circle, I was up next. A feeling of dread came over me because I had no idea what my one word was.

When I opened my mouth, the word *chosen* came out and the circle erupted with, "That's it!" to let me know that chosen wasn't just *my* word. It was **the** word! Wendell and Krystal stopped to ask me why chosen was my word and I briefly shared that I didn't know why I was there at first. I didn't know anybody. I didn't have any reason that I could think of to have been invited to be part of the journey. And because of that, I spent the first day or two thinking that I was there by accident or mistake.

God must've been mad at me because I was someplace I wasn't supposed to be. As the days progressed, God made it clear to me that my being there was no accident. No mistake. I was chosen by Him "for such a time as this..."

For the first time, I felt as if He handpicked me precisely for this journey. Looking around the circle, there wasn't a dry eye. As we hugged each other, the tears flowed. My word wasn't just for me. It resonated with each of my cohorts and event organizers. Yeah ... chosen was **the** word. And that word would become an ever-present echo in my spirit for days, weeks, months, and years to come.

When we arrived at the Garden Tomb, I couldn't wait to see where Jesus' body was laid to rest. Located just outside the city walls of Jerusalem, seeing the garden and cave that housed the tomb where Jesus' body was placed made me feel so connected to His journey. Climbing into the extremely tight space that was supposed to be His final resting place and seeing the stone that was rolled away, reminded me of all of the "stones" in my own life that God had rolled away and the "mountains" in my own life that He continues to move.

If God took me all the way to Jerusalem just so I could know and never doubt that He lives and that His power and His plan are so much bigger than I can even begin to fathom, it was more than worth it! This experience was precisely the confirmation I needed, because even when our challenges seem insurmountable, as they often do in my life, Jeremiah 32:17 reminds me that "Nothing is too hard for You (God)." As we enjoyed our closing dinner in Jaffa and headed to the Tel Aviv airport for the first leg of our flight home, there were at least three things that I knew in my heart with unmistakable clarity: I was chosen by God for such a time as this; no part of my journey was an accident; I will never, ever be the same.

My baptism in the Jordan River

Philos Black chartered tour bus, Israel

LESSON FIVE: *Trust the Process*

Let's be real. It's hard to trust the process when it seems like we're losing. We're not always sure what the rules of engagement are, so trusting a process we're not in control of can be tough and, at times, terrifying. Sometimes you win, sometimes you learn. What the world defines as winning and what God defines as winning are very different.

The Bible says, "You shall know the truth and the truth shall set you free." That's why so many of us struggle and cower in the face of truth. It's not that we're comfortable losing or enjoy being in bondage. It's that we've subscribed to the world's definition of winning, even when the world's scorecard usually measures us against someone whose gifts, talents, and divine destiny couldn't be further from our own.

In politics today, truth is the new hate speech. The minute someone disagrees, it becomes a tug of war between winning ideas and losing ones. No one likes to lose. It can be embarrassing, humiliating, demoralizing, and even stigmatizing. We feel like we're being judged, branded, and rejected, usually by people who don't even know us. The fact that there's a lesson in every loss often escapes us. We're so blinded by an insatiable need to win.

Not possessing the courage to take hard stances or do the right thing, even if we must do it alone, says more about us and our lack of conviction, character, and commitment to truth, than it says about those who may call us losers.

Having the courage to trust the process and to speak and live truthfully should be the universal standard for whether we're winning or losing.

Most of us assume that feelings of fear are negative. And whether you dread speaking publicly like I did or confronting an issue or person you would rather run away from, feeling fear is natural. All of us deal with fear during our lifetimes, some of us more than others. Being a public servant who leads with courage means I get to **choose** to acknowledge, confront, and overcome my fears, even when I have to do it alone.

Feeling fear and being afraid aren't the problem. It's our response to fear and our reluctance to trust a process when we don't know and can't control the outcome that determines whether we view a situation or opportunity as a negative (loss) or a positive (win).

Not winning the gubernatorial primary taught me more about myself and others, about life and faith, than any other lessons I've learned as an adult. I wouldn't trade the life lessons of my journey for anything. So what if I didn't get the party's nomination. I had already discovered that my vision and values were no longer aligned with the State Democratic Party.

The question I should've asked myself wasn't, "Why does the Party establishment keep embracing a losing strategy?" But rather, "What did I gain from the experience? What did the process teach me? Have I learned the lessons?"

Answering those questions truthfully tells me everything I need to know about whether I'm winning or not. I'm proud of myself for running hard, staying the course, and ignoring the naysayers. Even if I didn't "win," by the world's standard, I did what God told me to do this time. Was it easy? No. Still, the pain pales in comparison to the wisdom I've gained.

Running for governor in a state like South Carolina takes a level of faith, courage, obedience, and sacrifice that I hadn't yet reached in my House and Senate runs. Sure, taking an "L" can be tough. Likewise, giving in or giving up in those moments when we feel fear also ignites feelings of insecurity, embarrassment, shame, and inadequacy, especially when it's obvious to us, even if it's not to those around us, that we've defeated or sabotaged ourselves. That's what I learned from not running against Senator Lindsey Graham.

My free will allowed me to avert God's plan because I was overcome by the "what-ifs." Some people knew. Some didn't. What matters to me is God knew. I knew. And I let my fears about my mobility on crutches paralyze me. When I realized that I was solely to blame, that I couldn't possibly win a race I didn't run, I promised God that I would never, ever sabotage myself again.

Fear is like a school bully we would rather run from and avoid at all costs. Yet, losing is not an option when we dare to face our fears. Surrendering to a process we don't control can be painful and euphoric. Yet, each time we choose to trust it, we strengthen our determination, resolve, and ability to transform our lives and the lives of those around us.

Think about how you felt when you decided to run for office, start that business, or quit smoking. What about when you finally mustered the courage to speak publicly for the first time and got a standing ovation? Overcoming fear ultimately makes us stronger and more confident so that subsequent battles or tests become progressively easier.

Once you punch bullies in the nose, you already know they're less likely to come for you again. And if they do, they'll find a very different person than the one they originally encountered.

Wiser. Stronger. Fearless. Unstoppable.

No one said the process would be easy. We only need to trust that "still, small voice" that pushes us to move forward *anyway* and believe beyond a shadow of a doubt that it'll be worth it. Wisdom is my new definition of winning. That's all I need to remember to push past my fears and truly trust the process.

CHAPTER SIX
Free

Whom the Son sets free, is free indeed.
—John 8:36

Even I couldn't believe I was dialing his cell phone. Yet, there I was less than two weeks after returning from Israel calling House Minority Leader Todd Rutherford. During my trip, I had an opportunity to reflect on our Twitter exchange and I simply wanted to apologize—not for *what* I said but for *where* I said it. At the time, I didn't think of it as a partial apology, but as I continue to grow and mature spiritually, I imagine he would have. And he would've been right.

Thankfully, Todd didn't answer my call. He sent me a text message asking me to text him and I was reminded of an incident that happened in 2020 after George Floyd's murder. Out-of-state agitators posing as protesters vandalized several Columbia businesses, assaulted protestors, and set Columbia police vehicles on fire. A local media outlet interviewed a few elected officials who represented the Columbia area to discuss it.

Days after Todd and I were interviewed, several people sent me a lengthy Facebook video he posted. Apparently, he was incensed by my interview responses. Instead of coming to me directly, he chose to vent his frustrations publicly on Facebook. I watched in disbelief and was prepared to respond in kind until I watched the last few minutes of his video.

And just like that, I went from feeling blindsided by the attack to having compassion for him. Although I had more healing to do, my reason for calling Todd was to simply acknowledge and accept responsibility for responding on Twitter and ask him to forgive me. Instead of texting him, I thought it best to not reopen old wounds. So, I whispered a prayer, asked God to forgive me, and decided to let it go.

I may never really know why I was the target of his ire in 2020 or 2022. And that's okay. I don't have to know.

Before I knew it, 2023 was here. And so was the first day of the legislative session.

"Please pick up, Margie. I really need to talk to you before we hit 'send' on this email," I mumbled under my breath, as her phone rang for the third time. Margie Bright Matthews is my Sister-Senator and bestie in the S.C. Senate. After three rings, I braced myself for the inevitable because, like mine, her voice-mail is almost always full.

Think I audibly gasped when she answered.

"Heyyyy Margie! You in the car?"

"Yep, I'll probably be late for the caucus meeting because traffic is barely moving. You going?"

"Not sure I'm gonna make it either. I need to tell you something, though, so I'm glad you picked up. I'm about to announce that I'm leaving the State Democratic Party."

"What?! Please don't do that. It'll make you a target."

"Ha! Too late! Girl, you know I've been a target for 13 years."

"Yeah, but why do you have to announce it? I just don't want you to do that."

"I know and I get why. I just don't feel like I have a choice. I can't quit quietly. Some won't like it, but I've prayed about it and I really can't go back into the Senate chamber today wearing an SCDP jersey. I just can't do it."

There was a loud sigh and then a long pause. Margie had seen a lot of what I went through with the state party. Although everything she said was true, this was something I *had* to do.

I let Trav talk me out of it in 2016, but God wasn't easing up on me this time. There was no way I was gonna allow fear to keep me in bondage another day. I knew exactly what Margie meant. A public departure from the state party could cost me, politically. And if God told me to run for reelection to the Senate, I was prepared to deal with that. What Margie didn't realize was starting the 2023 legislative session as a member of the S.C. Democratic Party was no longer an option, at least not for me.

Finally, Margie broke her silence and said, "Okay, if that's what you feel like you need to do, I got your back."

I don't think she had any idea how much I needed to hear that.

I had already written the email draft, not knowing when or if it would ever see the light of day. When I woke up on that Tuesday morning and re-read it again and again, I knew in my spirit that *that* day was the day. As soon as we hit send, I gotta admit, just the thought of it was a little scary.

New Year, New Direction!

After two long years of campaigning ... I took some much-needed time to pray, rest, reflect, and recharge. And although I wasn't the S.C. Democratic Party's (SCDP's) gubernatorial nominee, I'm grateful to all of you who supported me ... and those of you who didn't. I mean that sincerely because I trust God's Plan for my life.

In September, I was one of 20 Black women legislators from across the country who was invited to travel to Israel! It was a life-changing journey and one you'll hear more about because I'm super excited to be writing my first book!

After seven months of prayer and reflection, I've decided to leave the S.C. Democratic Party because it no longer espouses the values my constituents and I hold dear. I want you to be the first to know that my decision isn't meant to disparage anyone who identifies as a S.C. Democrat, but the SCDP's "party focused" approach doesn't work for the people.

And if it doesn't work for you, it doesn't work for me.

My parents taught us to **always vote for the person** whose vision and values were most aligned with ours. I've stayed true to that by working with and supporting honest, compassionate, empathetic servant-leaders of both parties. But after fighting Republicans and Democrats for the past 12 years … it hurts to admit how often I've had to fight my own party, just to help my own people.

And I'm not just talking about people who look like me. My House and Senate districts have consistently been among our state's most diverse. So, my people are hard-working South Carolinians of all races, genders, ethnicities, generations, faiths, political ideologies and socioeconomic backgrounds who believe as I do that their lives and livelihoods matter … too.

Yes, I've run as a Democrat, while serving my constituents with integrity and independence … the latter often putting me at odds with the SCDP establishment. But working alongside some amazing colleagues, candidates, and community members who genuinely give your all to improve our state

reminds me that, like my parents, many of you have sacrificed and worked hard to help build and strengthen the S.C.
Democratic Party.

And sadly, you're the very people the party seems to have
forgotten.

Childhood memories of welcoming Democratic Party
and NAACP members into our family's funeral home
for meetings and community events and my Dad serving as Bennettsville's first Black city councilman after
Reconstruction are always with me. Whatever his challenges, the SCDP worked with him ... not against him. They
were unified by their individual and collective mission to
improve the lives of every person they served.

As the first woman to represent House District 79, first
woman and African American to represent Senate District
22, and first Black woman to run for governor of S.C., my
mission is to advance a "people-focused" platform that genuinely improves lives, since I'm now even more enlightened
about the true state of our state and why so many of us lack
the representation and resources we need to thrive here.

And the more my sons talk about their desire to live anywhere but South Carolina, the more it hurts that our best
and brightest continue to leave our state in droves and have
for decades.

Meanwhile, the SCDP establishment hasn't made any significant changes or won a gubernatorial race in 20 years. By not
engaging, enlightening, or expanding the electorate ... refusing to publicize the June primary and getting a historical top

of the ticket "shellacking" on November 8, the party ensured a Republican supermajority and the losses of eight Black legislators in the S.C. House, five of whom were Black women.

Yet, a recent SCDP fundraising email acknowledges, "Black voters are the backbone of our party..." which makes me cringe because I've experienced first-hand how the party treats Black voters and Black women who run statewide.

If the definition of insanity is doing the same thing year after year, election after election, and expecting a different result, then the S.C. Democratic Party is the poster child for what a losing strategy on repeat looks like. Even a "first in the nation" presidential primary designation won't change that.

You deserve a strong voice in your government ... one that's authentic, bold, and courageous. That's what you'll always have in me. And with so many unprecedented and systemic challenges, none of us can afford to be blinded by party loyalty, silent on critical issues, or content with the status quo. Ever.

This is a new year. It's time for a new direction. So, with unprecedented clarity and perspective, I'll continue to move forward in faith ... **boldly, fearlessly** and yes ... **independently**—always eager to work with any person or party that prioritizes our people ... ever mindful of who and whose I am and why God has placed me in this space, "for such a time as this ..."

As soon as the email hit people's inboxes, my phone started ringing. Ironically, the same media outlets that didn't cover any of my efforts on the Senate floor while I was running in the gubernatorial primary, were now lined up outside of the Senate chamber waiting to interview me about why I left the SCDP. And since I was invisible to them just a few months before, they were invisible to me on that Tuesday afternoon when Margie, Senator Mike Fanning, and I took the back exit to avoid them.

My statement was crystal clear about why I left the S.C. Democratic Party. The media wanted a fight. Apparently, so did the SCDP. I'm not one to *start* a fight, but I definitely ain't running from one either. Right outta the gate, Joe Bustos with *The State* interviewed a few of my Senate colleagues and created his own narrative about why I left the SCDP.

On January 29, this was *The State* newspaper's headline: "SC Sen. Mia McLeod says she left the Democratic Party because it didn't support her governor bid. Party officials say she ran a bad campaign."

When I texted Joe about it, asking him to show me where and when I said that, he never replied, apologized, or retracted.

Since they obviously had nothing else to talk about, Joe and the SCDP kept the chatter going. The Richland County Democratic Party (RCDP) chair at that time, who was also a Black woman, had practically begged me to join Joe Cunningham's team as his number two because she believed all of her Republican tennis buddies thought Joe Cunningham was sooo cute and would cross over to vote for him.

I just didn't realize until then that she obviously had an axe to grind after I refused to lend credibility to a candidate who I believed only wanted to exploit Black Democratic voters for his own political gain. When I publicly left the SCDP she issued an RCDP Statement, without the county party's knowledge or approval I'm told, insisting that I resign from the Senate because the people of Senate District 22 elected a *Democrat*, not an Independent.

So there I was, still having to fight the Democratic Party. If I was such a horrible candidate, you'd think they would *want* to let me go. Yet, they fought harder to keep me than they ever did to expand, engage, or empower the Democratic electorate.

Everybody knows I fight hard for my constituents, even the establishment Dems who were trashing me because I left the SCDP publicly and told the truth about why. When local media personality Cynthia Hardy asked me to be on her show to talk about my decision I didn't think I needed to, since my published statement was clear. When she told me that my segment would give me an opportunity to reiterate my statement for those who may not have had a chance to read it, I agreed. After watching part one, which featured some of the SCDP Establishment Dems and was by most accounts, a "bash Mia fest," I was kinda glad I did.

Cynthia and her husband, Jim, gave me an opportunity to appear solo on part two of her show. I was grateful to them because it allowed me to address some of the lies and intentionally misleading comments that some of her guests offered the previous week. I hoped that once both segments aired we could finally stop talking about the issue. Unfortunately, some folks weren't quite ready to let it go yet.

Here's my email response to *The State's* long list of lies about why I left the S.C. Democratic Party.

In Sunday's edition of *The State* (January 29, 2023) ... the same newspaper that has for years consistently gone out of its way to make me seem insignificant, there's a front-page, top-fold story ... full of speculative and anonymous contributions. Not sure why *The State* is still writing about me weeks after my announcement that I've left the S.C. Democratic Party (SCDP) or why any reputable newspaper would rely on "anonymous" sources, but as always ... I'm happy to set the record straight. ICYMI ... here are some of the highlights:

1. You failed me and I quit.

The State presented this lie right out of the gate as if it were a direct quote, knowing that I've never said or implied it. What I have said ad nauseum is that the SCDP failed the people ... not me. The only thing "I quit" is a state party that repeatedly places party loyalty above the needs and interests of the people it purports to serve.

2. Is McLeod's announcement part of a plan to replace the current party chairman—who reportedly turned down an offer to run her campaign—with someone she views as more friendly?

No, I've publicly left the SCDP, remember? If nothing changes, doesn't matter who's captain of the Titanic—it's still the Titanic.

3. Meanwhile, sources within the S.C. Democratic Party said McLeod's campaign was seriously flawed with no infrastructure, inexperienced people, and no plan to overcome a lack of money and poor name recognition.

By "sources" within the SCDP, *The State* is obviously referring to the SCDP chair because only he had firsthand knowledge about my gubernatorial campaign "infrastructure," which was originally organized and staffed with his people. For months, I begged him to help me find key campaign staffers who genuinely understood S.C., reflected the uniqueness of my perspective, and could help convey the authenticity of my voice. I believed a person of color from this region could best understand the unique challenges I faced as the first Black woman to run for governor of our state. But he insisted there were no qualified, capable people of color who could do the job. So, over his objections, I found my own … a phenomenal core team of Black, white, and Latina S.C. women who were small in number but brilliant, compassionate, qualified, and more than capable. They could've been much more effective if the SCDP had at least done its job and let them do theirs.

4. (McLeod) lost. She's not a good candidate, she's M.I.A. in the Senate, and she was M.I.A. in her gubernatorial race, the state representative said. Now she wants to blame everyone but herself. It's time for some self-reflection.

Let's be clear … M.I.A. was stolen from the SCGOP's anti-Mia TV ads and mailers in 2016 and 2020 to try to keep me out of the S.C. Senate. Using my first name as an acronym didn't work for the SCGOP either, since I won big in 2016 and bigger (by 24 points) in 2020 against moderate Republicans with significant name recognition and money. In fact, my senate race outperformed every other Democratic House and Senate race in 2020 … the same year a former SCDP chair lost his U.S. Senate bid with an unprecedented $130-plus million … while we lost three Democrats in the S.C. Senate and two Democrats in the S.C. House. The SCGOP has spent hundreds of thousands of dollars trying to keep me out of the Senate seat and not a dime to keep these "anonymous" haters out of theirs. But why would the SCGOP spend money against SCDP lawmakers it already controls?

5. One S.C. Democratic Party source with knowledge of the campaign contended McLeod did not like asking for money and "she didn't like campaigning."

Ironically, *The State* printed this lie along with a photo and caption of me enjoying my time on the campaign trail. And since money is everything to the SCDP, perhaps it can explain why it's already crying "broke" in 2022 after a former SCDP chair's 2020 U.S. Senate bid brought in a record-setting $130-plus million of game-changing, anti-Lindsay Graham money from all over the country. How do you lose a race with that kind of money and still not expand the SCDP's footprint, infrastructure, or the electorate in your home state ... let alone move the needle for struggling South Carolinians?

6. Robertson ran McLeod's campaign for state senate in 2016, and, according to Robertson, McLeod wanted him to leave his chairmanship to run her gubernatorial bid. Robertson declined. Robertson declined to say whether McLeod's statement was about revenge for not taking the job.

Yes, I did ask SCDP Chair Trav Robertson to consider running my gubernatorial campaign since he was my campaign manager in 2016, and at the time, I considered him a close friend and trusted advisor. Until 2022 when I stepped out on faith and ran for governor, his guidance and motives were never in question, but that changed dramatically last year. Had he simply declined, I would've respected his decision and quickly moved on to find someone who could fill that critical role. Instead, he acted as my de facto campaign manager to control and ultimately sabotage any hires we could've made in a timely manner. According to him, there were no women or persons of color who were "qualified," so we spent a tremendous amount of time debating why his referrals and recommendations were always white men who weren't from or connected to South Carolina. Later, my team (the one I hired over his objections) and I discovered why, but by then, the damage was already done.

My faith reminds me that vengeance is God's, not mine, so my announcement wasn't about revenge. It was about providing my constituents with the same transparency they've always gotten from me. I just chose to leave publicly while other Democratic candidates and incumbents continue to leave quietly.

7. Tyler Jones, who worked as Cunningham's general campaign consultant, said McLeod's announcement may unintentionally sabotage the state's chances. It makes it look like there are deep divisions in the party, when in reality, the divisions don't exist within the Democratic electorate, they exist within the party establishment ...

Most S.C. Dems already know this guy overtly uses the SCDP as his political "GoFundMe" account, despite the fact that his losses far outnumber his wins. What better way to have unfettered access and opportunities to exploit the Democratic base for his own financial gain? God forbid, he misses out on those exorbitant "consulting" fees now that the SCDP has secured its "first in the nation" presidential primary designation. And those deep divisions exist in both the party and the Democratic electorate, but don't take my word for it. I'm just a sitting S.C. Senator who has never lost a House or Senate race, even in swing districts. My record speaks for itself. So does his.

8. **State Rep. Gilda Cobb-Hunter, D-Orangeburg, lamented the losses of Black Democratic women Krystle Matthews, Kimberly Johnson, Wendy Brawley, and Chardale Murray from the legislature, saying they were future leaders of the party … The thing that is so distressing about it for me, Cobb-Hunter said, is that they were pretty much all very strong women who didn't just go along to get along and who didn't just do what they were told, and therein is part of a problem of why they are no longer here.**

I share Representative Cobb-Hunter's frustrations, which provides further proof of the plight of strong, independent-minded Black women within this S.C. Democratic Party. I can think of several others who were vying for seats at different levels of government and have suffered the same fate for the same reasons. Regardless of the outcome of the gubernatorial race in November, I'm confident that had I been at the top of the ticket, we wouldn't have lost five more Black legislators in the S.C. House … some of whom the SCGOP didn't even actively target.

9. **I just don't think those challenges we had last year and the difficulties we faced last year gives anyone an out or an opportunity to simply abandon the Democratic Party, our value system, our beliefs, our goals, one county party chair said.**

Sounds like this "anonymous" county party chair is the same one who emailed me about her future aspirations to run for the Senate seat I currently hold and practically begged me to abandon my own race for governor to run as Cunningham's running mate before the primary because her SCGOP tennis buddies thought he was "so cute" that they'd cross over and vote for him in the Democratic primary. When I declined, she used her "county party chair" position to ensure that Black voters in Richland County didn't know who the candidates were or when the primary was. Sad, but her motives and actions accurately represent the current State Democratic Party. And if 12 years of fighting to change the SCDP from within isn't long enough, then how many years is?

10. At the end of the day, the party needs to help motivate and inform voters on the issues, and the candidates are on their own to stake their claim on those issues. I did not see that at the statewide level, Brawley said.

Thank you, Representative Brawley. While I'm grateful to have initiated these long overdue conversations, it's exhausting to have to keep the spotlight on the SCDP and its responsibilities. In every primary and general election before 2022, the SCDP at least attempted to meet its basic obligations to the people of S.C. Why was 2022 different? Obviously, it was the first time in S.C. history that a Black woman ran in a S.C. gubernatorial primary and also the first time four Black women simultaneously ran for statewide seats. Yet, the 2022 Democratic Primary was the first and only time the State Democratic Party failed to let S.C. voters know: who the candidates were, what the candidates' platforms and voting records were, and when the primary election was.

If the state party continues to be disingenuous and deflect, I'll keep putting the truth out there for the people because the SCDP can't keep calling itself the "big-tent" party if party establishment leaders are the only ones under the tent.

Margie was right. Leaving the SCDP publicly and telling people why made me an even bigger target. Fortunately, the SCDP establishment's antics couldn't override or overshadow the freedom and peace I had after leaving the SCDP publicly. Although I didn't realize it then, doing so was ultimately one of the boldest, most courageous, authentic actions of my political career—a reminder that God put me in the arena to do just that—**disrupt** the status quo. And with each challenge He has allowed me to overcome in my life. I've emerged stronger, wiser, and yes, even more courageous.

No fear. No regrets. And no turning back.

Funny how all of my rebranding efforts in 2020 kept redirecting me to the word "courage." Discovering that courage is my brand has truly been affirming for me personally, professionally, and politically. And just in case I needed confirmation, God sent me a sign that was undeniable.

On September 7, 2023, Shari, my Senate executive assistant, called me more than once as I traveled to Atlanta for my first Philos Project Conference, one year after Philos Black sponsored our trip to Israel. I was excited to reconnect with some of the women and event organizers who I had gotten to know on that life-changing journey.

As soon as I finished the conference call, I planned to call Shari back. And before I could wrap up the call, Shari was calling ... again.

"Hey Shari," I answered. "Stuck in traffic in Augusta and still on another call. Just saw that you've been trying to reach me. What's up? Is everything okay?"

"Yes, Senator ... everything's okay, I think. I just want to let you know that Senator Shealy is trying to reach you, and it must be important. So, please call her back as soon as you can."

"Okay ... I think I did see a missed call from Katrina. Will wrap up this conference call and call her right back."

When I dialed my Sister-Senator's cell number, she answered on the first ring like she had been waiting for me to call. I said, "Hey Katrina! Sorry I missed you."

She abruptly answered, "Where are you?" I told her I was on my way to a conference in Atlanta.

"Sandy's in Alaska. You're headed to Atlanta. Everybody's traveling right now, but I need y'all to have your asses on a Zoom call on Friday, September 8, at 11 a.m. Can you do it?"

I chuckled and said, "I'll be in conference sessions on Friday. I'm sure I can take a break and hop on, though." I could tell by Katrina's tone that it was important.

"What's the call about," I asked.

"I don't know what it's about, she said, but it's with Caroline Kennedy and all of us have to be there!"

"Caroline Kennedy? **The** Caroline Kennedy ... as in John F. Kennedy's Caroline Kennedy?"

"Yes ma'am ... **that** Caroline Kennedy!"

Before I could ask if it was legit, Katrina blurted ... "I thought it was some kinda joke or prank or something at first, but her office really called and asked me to get all five of us together for a Zoom meeting with her! And Friday is the day."

Thinking she probably wanted to personally commend us for our bipartisan efforts to defeat the SCGOP's total abortion ban, I said, "Well, alrighty then ... I'll be there!"

What I didn't realize was that Ambassador Caroline Kennedy and her son, Jack Schlossberg, wanted to do that and more.

When we met on that Friday morning, I had made arrangements to use the facility's conference room and was one of the first Sister-Senators to log in to the Zoom call. Just seeing and talking to Ambassador Kennedy and Jack seemed a bit surreal. They wanted to know a little about each of us and how we decided to band together as Dems, Independents and Republicans in a hyper-partisan, red state like South Carolina. They were intrigued that we remained unified on the abortion bill, an issue that is extremely and intentionally divisive, in a male-dominated Senate where we were grossly outnumbered 41-5 at the time.

We talked on Zoom for 20 or 30 minutes. They praised us for taking stands of conscience and putting the people's interest above our own political careers. Ambassador Kennedy commended us for being an example of how elected leaders *can* work together across the aisle to stand up for freedom and individual rights, especially when the country is so polarized.

Jack added that he's really inspired by our willingness to stand together and do something so courageous, in spite of the personal attacks and pushback each of us faced, since courage is the quality his grandfather most admired.

I listened intently because I didn't want to miss anything. It was almost as if time stood still. I mistakenly assumed that *that* was our moment. And if Ambassador Kennedy and Jack had simply stopped there, it would've been everything I had envisioned and imagined.

But they weren't done. Ambassador Kennedy added that she, Jack, and her daughter Tatiana serve on the John F. Kennedy Library Foundation's board and that the board had decided to honor us as their 2023 John F. Kennedy Profile In Courage Award recipients!

The look on all five of our faces said it all.

I could barely process what I was hearing! The reason that's such a big deal is because the Profile in Courage Award is a global accolade that fewer than 100 people in the entire world have received. Past recipients include former President and Nobel Peace Prize winner Barack Obama; former President George H.W. Bush; U.S. Senator John McCain; civil rights icon and Congressman John Lewis; former U.S. House Speaker Nancy Pelosi; former Congresswomen Liz Cheney and Gabby Giffords; Ukraine President Volodymyr Zelenskyy; former Vice President Mike Pence; as well as my friend and mentor, Nobel Peace Prize winner and former S.C. Governor David Beasley.

My Sister-Senators and I were speechless. That alone, is a rarity. In retrospect, it was probably a good thing, since we couldn't tell anybody outside of our immediate families for at least two more weeks.

So when *The Today Show* teased that a big announcement was coming at the top of its 8 o'clock hour, our families, friends, and community members were able to watch along with us as host Savannah Guthrie shared our photos and brief bios, while Ambassador Kennedy and her son Jack explained why we were being honored. Let's just say, the news spread like wildfire in political circles across South Carolina and around the country.

Before long, the five of us were featured on the cover of *The New York Times*, interviewed by *The Washington Post, Good Morning America, CBS News* and numerous other major media outlets.

Just the thought of receiving the same award for political courage that some of my political heroes and sheroes had received was like God's way of saying to us, *Well done, my good and faithful servants ...*

Yeah ... *this* award was indeed the honor of my political life.

When we arrived in Boston for the Awards Ceremony, the JFK Library Foundation's staff and every member of the Boston Harbor Hotel's team treated us like royalty. The cool, crisp October air ushered us into the warmest, most heartfelt welcome imaginable. It was a far cry from the cold, harsh way we were treated by many of our colleagues in our home state. Guess that's what Scripture means when it says, "A prophet is not without honor, except in his own home, among his own people."

The JFK Library Foundation asked the five of us to give brief remarks. Our acceptance speeches were just as different as we were. I don't think any of us expected David Letterman; David Axelrod; retired General and former Chairman of the Joint Chiefs of Staff, Mark Milley; retired U.S. Supreme Court Justice Stephen Breyer; David Gergen; and a host of other VIPs to stand in line, just to shake our hands and personally thank us for putting partisan politics aside and bringing civility back into politics. Banding together in a hyper-partisan, divided state and country, is what brought us to the big stage that night! And we were so grateful.

The best part was that BJ and Cam were there with me in Boston! My Sister-Senators and I learned that our names will forever be enshrined at the JFK Library and Museum—a beautiful reminder to every person who visits the site in Boston!

For me, the Profile in Courage Award symbolized the courage I've always shown, personally and politically, and proved that South Carolina *can* be highlighted on a national stage for something positive and amazing—for a change. The five of us have secured a very special place in history—statewide, nationally, and globally—one that can never be diminished or deleted. Even now, I'm still digesting the magnitude of that moment.

And to think our gorgeous lantern, that prominently features all five of our names—**Senator Katrina Shealy, Senator Margie Bright-Matthews, Senator Mia McLeod, Senator Sandy Senn** and **Senator Penry Gustafson**—won't be displayed or commemorated anywhere inside of the S.C. State House because our Republican colleagues find it "too controversial." Yet, even blatant disrespect couldn't ruin the high we had on that historic night.

Surrounded by our families, a few friends, and yes, some new fans, it felt amazing to finally be seen, supported, and celebrated for what we do and who we are.

Putting partisan politics aside and doing right by the people simply because it *is* right, is what all of us are elected to do. The fact that actually doing it is such a rarity in politics today, speaks volumes about how self-centered and self-serving politics has become. The five of us were not naive about what we were up against or the consequences we would likely face. We understood what was at stake and what the political fallout might be. What I love about us is that we "counted the cost" and had the courage to do it anyway.

Just two months before, SCGOP leaders intentionally stacked the S.C. Supreme Court with five men, making South Carolina the only state in the entire nation with an all-male supreme court at that time. And once the deck was stacked, the court had no trouble reversing its ruling from a few months prior when it held the same six-week abortion ban unconstitutional. Suddenly, our all-male supreme court reversed itself. And nothing had changed, except the makeup of the court.

Back in August, one of the newspapers published a story about how regressive South Carolina had become. "South Carolina is one of the worst states to live and work in for 2023, a new CNBC report says ..."

Ironically, it was published on the same day as the S.C. Supreme Court's decision to abandon its prior ruling and hold that the state's six-week abortion ban is now constitutional. I remember being asked to speak about the changes on several national media outlets. My message was basically the same each time I spoke about the ruling of the newly configured, all-male supreme court.

Yes, South Carolina's six-week abortion ban is a devastating
blow to our state's women and girls. No, the abortion issue
is **not** a priority for most South Carolinians. The SCGOP has
made it a priority to pander to its base in hopes of getting its
members re-elected. And yes, I was the first female legislator to vote against the South Carolina Supreme Court's newest male justice, since the legislature elects judges in South
Carolina. My "no" vote had nothing to do with the candidate
or his qualifications. It was obvious that the SCGOP's goal
was to politicize and weaponize the court on the abortion
issue. And I wasn't about to "rubber stamp" or assist in that
effort. After rigging the court, the SCGOP's efforts were
successful.

Whether we're in the Senate or not, my Sister-Senators and
I won't stop fighting until every S.C. woman and girl has
the freedom and autonomy to make her own healthcare
decisions.

Clearly, that message was enough to incite the craziest of the
crazy religious zealots across our state. Here's an example of a
MAGA election denier who described the 2020 election as "stolen"
and said he heard one of my media interviews and decided that
he needed to weigh in. This is a brief clip of the long, rambling
voicemail message he left at my Senate office:

Yeah … this is for Mia. Mia, I just saw you on the news
talking about the abortion thing. Y'all need to try not to get
pregnant and … ahhh … not be so … ahhh … you know …
willing to spread your legs for lack of a better term. Ahhh

... and you know, I got a daughter. She's been sexually active since she was a teenager. She never got pregnant. You know, women know ... they know when it's their time to do that. They need to wise up and not get drunk and get knocked up. But when you have a human being in you, he has ... they have ... she and he have rights too. And I'm tired of hearing about a woman's rights ... a grown woman ...

Messages like this never surprised me and Lord knows, I've received more than my share of them. The God I serve, in His infinite wisdom, gives all of us free will. Unfortunately, the S.C. Republican Party doesn't. So, the level of hypocrisy is staggering, especially when it comes to divisive issues like abortion and the death penalty. My Republican colleagues literally identify as "pro-life" on Tuesdays and "pro-death" on Wednesdays. And despite my best efforts, I have yet to find one Republican in either chamber who can explain, justify, or Biblically reconcile these juxtaposed stances.

Not one in 14 years.

Ironically, our Profile in Courage Award wasn't about abortion. It was about five women of different races, ethnicities, political ideologies, and party affiliations who put our personal and political differences aside to stand up for women's rights and freedoms ... irrespective of the political consequences.

When I accepted the prestigious John F. Kennedy Profile in Courage Award in 2023, I reminded everyone who was watching that:

Courage isn't summoned in the absence of fear. Courage is what summons us to act in spite of fear.

I've always been honest and transparent about where I stand on the issue. I've said it many times before and I'll say it again. I'm not pro-abortion. But I am anti-hypocrisy. And when I see the flagrantly hypocritical actions of my colleagues who use God's name to camouflage their ungodly actions, I have to speak up. If not, my constituents won't have a voice.

Back in 2014, I penned a blogpost titled "My God" because I was tired of the deceptive, disingenuous rhetoric that was being spewed by so-called Christian conservatives to curry favor with voting members of the faith community who had no idea that they were being duped. Here's an excerpt:

Must we be hypocrites about everything in this state? I mean … since we wanna wear the Bible Belt like a badge of honor, shouldn't some of our actions reflect it?

Think about it. Your lawmakers love to protect fetuses in the womb. Why? Because the gift of life is one of God's most precious, of course. But there's nothing Godly about our refusal to assist or help protect that same precious life, once it is manifested outside of the womb. In South Carolina, when the umbilical cord is cut, so is the concern and compassion. Funny how one goes from being "God's Chosen" to society's forgotten by simply passing through the birth canal.

And when I receive legislative emails from "Christian" coalitions that spew hatred for others in His name for their own political purposes, I can't help but wonder what "God" these people serve.

Surely not mine …

Saying we're Christians is one thing. Behaving like Christians is another. Deliberately disenfranchising voters, denying healthcare, equal educational and economic opportunities to certain South Carolinians, refusing to pass tougher gun laws, and failing to protect our state's most vulnerable are just a few examples of ways in which God's will has been preempted by power-hungry, good ol' politicians who carelessly and callously hide behind His will to invoke their own.

And for the record, I don't believe abortion is right … for *me*. That's why I didn't have one.

If you don't care about life from the womb to the world, you shouldn't describe yourself as pro-life. In spite of the very real possibility of life-threatening complications because of a Sickle Cell diagnosis that made each of my pregnancies high risk, I chose to carry both to term because I was blessed to have access to quality, affordable healthcare, and physicians who wouldn't have been criminalized, barred from the practice of medicine, or imprisoned for treating me if I required life-saving emergency medical treatment during my pregnancies. Fortunately, I also had a loving, extremely supportive village of family members and friends to help me.

Every woman or girl should have those resources available to her and the freedom to make that deeply personal, life-altering decision for herself, just like I did.

Unlike many of my Republican colleagues, I recognize that I'm not God. "His thoughts are not my thoughts. Neither are His ways, my ways."

The difference is, I understand that adding a senator or representative prefix to my name doesn't give me the right to "play God" on legislative Tuesdays, Wednesdays, and Thursdays.

When I introduced the nation's first Erectile Dysfunction Bill —dubbed the "Viagra Bill"—in 2016 I wasn't prepared for the national media frenzy the bill ignited. Speaker Lucas appointed me to serve on a committee that was supposedly tasked with creating a safer, more equitable state for women. Somehow, it quickly morphed into a covert mission to defund Planned Parenthood.

Spending the entire summer in those committee meetings showed me that our state's Republican majority wasn't interested in addressing the real needs of the majority of South Carolinians. For many of them, this seemed to be a game of political expedience where women and girls were being used as political pawns. After discovering that women in our state who sought legal and sometimes life-saving abortion services were subjected to a 24-hour waiting period, mandatory celibacy counseling, and forced to submit a sworn affidavit from her sexual partner detailing why she was seeking an abortion—I was done.

My Viagra Bill imposed the same ridiculously intrusive and humiliating requirements of men seeking erectile dysfunction drugs. *Time Magazine, The Washington Post,* NBC News, CBS News, and practically every major media outlet in South Carolina and across the country, covered it.

As the S.C. General Assembly got closer to passing the six-week abortion ban, I introduced the Pro-Birth Accountability Act, another groundbreaking bill that gives Republicans every opportunity to put their money where their mouths are and prove that they are, in fact, pro-life, by helping cover the escalating costs of childbirth and child rearing from conception to college. And just as expected, these so-called pro-lifers have consistently denied any meaningful support to the very women and girls they're forcing to give birth.

When my Sister-Senators and I received the John F. Kennedy Profile in Courage Award seven years after my Viagra Bill initiated a much broader, more inclusive conversation about whether government should make critical healthcare decisions for women *and* men, I knew that what the five of us had done was much bigger than us and the abortion issue.

Individually and collectively, we chose to do the right thing for the right reasons even if it cost us. At the end of the day, it's courageous leadership, not the labels some have tried to affix to our names, that will ultimately define us and our legacies.

Receiving the John F. Kennedy Profile in Courage Award

The Sister-Senators and the Kennedy family at the 2023 JFK PIC Awards ceremony, Boston

LESSON SIX: *Lose the Labels*

I didn't realize until I publicly left the S.C. Democratic Party that for some people, party affiliation trumps their own identity and sense of self. It made me think about the professional, political, and personal labels others have attempted to affix to my name over the years.

Which ones had I accepted? Embraced? Rejected?

In addition to "Democrat" and "DINO" (Democrat In Name Only), I've been called other names over the last 14 years. Pro–birth, right-wing extremists have called me a "baby killer." Status-quo defenders prefer: "Bitch." "Trouble-maker." "Angry Black woman." "Confrontational." "Aggres-sive." "Controversial." And my new fave: "Mean girl."

When all else fails, they love using my first name, Mia, as an acronym to lie about my attendance at the State House. Suggesting that I'm "Missing In Action" or "M.I.A." is clever and probably would've worked if my voting record didn't prove I was always present *and* voting. Even after the Re-publican caucus spent hundreds of thousands of dollars on mailers, digital, and TV ads using the acronym to try to keep me out of the Senate ... I won. BIG!

A few disgruntled Democrats tried to recycle the M.I.A. slogan in 2023, when I publicly left the S.C. Democratic Party. Didn't work for them either.

Despite all of these tactics, the one thing they can't call me is scared.

I've served with women and men on both sides of the political aisle who act as if life wouldn't be worth living without their legislative tags and titles. They carry themselves as if they have no other identity, nothing of value to offer without senator or representative prefixes attached to their names.

While most Senate and House members proudly and prominently don legislative license tags on their vehicles to showcase their political prowess and stature, I've never affixed a legislative tag to my vehicle or my sons'. I don't need to. I'm a state senator with or without the license tag. Drawing extra attention to myself or to them would've made us easy targets, especially for a Black woman who unapologetically disrupts the status quo.

When I ran statewide, my team and I had conversations about safety and why we needed to be careful about publicly disclosing where we would be and when. What happened to my friend, Clem, and eight of his parishioners at Mother Emanuel, proves that race-based hate is still alive and well in South Carolina. As a vocal Black woman and former Democrat, in a state that proudly identifies as MAGA country, I don't have that luxury. Thankfully, I don't need a legislative tag or title to know who and whose I am.

In the late '80s when I was a page in the S.C. House of Representatives, public servants were held in high esteem. Their names meant something to them and to the people they represented. Elected officials were held to a higher standard. Public service was a privilege ... not a power grab.

Those days are coming to an end.

Back in 2016, when anti-Mia ads flooded the airwaves and saturated every media market in the greater Columbia area, it was the negative attack ads saying I was M.I.A. that were most concerning. They ran ad nauseum. My Republican opponent had the support of status quo defenders on both sides of the political aisle, so I was concerned about whether my messaging was getting through to everyday people. Two separate encounters told me everything I needed to know.

The USC Homecoming game was the Saturday before the general election. Although I hadn't planned to go, my team and I had done all we could reasonably do to earn the support of District 22 voters. So, after knocking on a few more doors that morning, I decided to head to the tailgate that afternoon. Some of my sorority sisters had "Mia for Senate" signs with my face and campaign logo prominently placed on their cars, SUVs, and tents. I was still sporting my campaign T-shirt.

A young Black man came over to me and introduced himself. He said, "So you're Mia? Yeah ... I saw all those TV ads saying you go M.I.A. and don't like showing up for work."

My heart dropped as I anxiously waited for him to finish so I could tell him the truth. Before I could, he said, "Mannnn ... I looked at those ads and thought, now that's the woman for me right there cause I don't like taking my ass to work neither! Just want you to know that I voted for you already and I hope you win."

By the time he finished, I was mortified *and* relieved. Both of us laughed so hard. The SCGOP's messaging had backfired. The irony of it all was a beautiful reminder that, "If God is for me ... who can be against me?"

That conversation rejuvenated my faith and gave me permission to exhale, relax, and truly enjoy the rest of my time at the tailgate. And God wasn't done.

A few days later, I walked into my polling place at Lake Carolina Elementary School and cast my vote in my very first race for the S.C. Senate.

As I exited the building to head to my car, a gentleman with a news camera approached me. He held his camera down by his side. I didn't know or recognize him. He greeted me with a warm smile and what he said to me in that moment was God's way of reminding me that none of the negative labels the opposition attempted to affix to my name, stuck. That's because His Word says, "No weapon formed against you will prosper."

On that election day morning, I discovered that my name can't be hijacked.

The gentleman said, "I've been reading about you and what you stand for. And I've seen the negative attack ads that use your name as an acronym. But I have a better acronym for your name: Mission. Impossible. Accomplished."

I thought, "Wow ... MIA ... Mission Impossible Accomplished!"

More proof that this is truly spiritual warfare, because "What the enemy means for evil, God will turn around for good." I won the State Senate seat by 10 points that year against a moderate Republican woman in a swing district.

And by the grace of God my name, Mia, was the only "label" I needed.

CHAPTER SEVEN
Stop the Insanity

The many broken promises I have made to myself have created
wounds I am still discovering.
—Sarah Jakes Roberts

While campaigning statewide in 2021 and 2022, I often personalized the definition of insanity to remind S.C. voters that if we keep doing the same things year after year—election after election—we'll keep getting the same results. Not winning a statewide gubernatorial race in about 20 years is all the proof any of us need to know that what Democrats are doing here in South Carolina and across the nation isn't working.

What I hadn't yet done consistently was apply that definition to the losing strategies and practices in my own life.

As someone who has always identified as a night owl, I was constantly complaining that there just weren't enough hours in the day to get everything done. For years, I convinced myself that if I didn't have an early morning meeting, there was no need to wake up at the crack of dawn. Besides, I've always been above average when it comes to productivity. Truth is, morning people get on my nerves, especially the ones who are super energized and overly excited about it.

After a series of brutally honest conversations with myself at the beginning of 2023, I finally decided to do something different because I wanted something different. To jump-start that painful process, I read books like *The High 5 Habit: Take Control of Your Life with One Simple Habit* by Mel Robbins, *The 5 AM Club: Own Your Morning, Elevate Your Life* by Robin Sharma, *Don't Settle for Safe* by Sarah Jakes Roberts, *Battlefield of the Mind: Winning the Battle in Your Mind* by Joyce Meyer, and *The Power of Consistency: Prosperity Mindset Training for Sales and Business Professionals* by Weldon Long. To simply refer to any of these resources as enlightening or impactful would be an understatement.

Slowly, but surely, I started setting my alarm for 5 a.m. It didn't take me long to realize I also had to go to bed earlier than 1 a.m. As I've learned to adjust my schedule and manage my time better, I've discovered that I really can get a lot more done by simply getting up earlier and being intentional about what I plan to accomplish each day. Before I knew it, I was working out again and walking three to four miles a day again. Sleeping better. Feeling better. Suddenly, I had time to read and listen to an inspirational message every day. Messages by Pastor Radhika, Pastor Michael McClure, Jr., and Sarah Jakes Roberts are a few of my favorites.

One of those early mornings with God stands out to me more than others. It was about a year after I returned from Israel. Cam and I were preparing to discuss some Scriptures when God revealed something so poignant and powerful—I couldn't believe it had never occurred to me until that moment! I was thinking about the word, *chosen*. That one word is such a pivotal and personal depiction of how I'm beginning to see myself in God's eyes and how resonant it was with every woman in our cohort the minute I said it out loud.

Cam and I had just re-read Isaiah 43. He was back in Colorado, so we planned to talk about it afterward. I remember sitting quietly for a minute when my mind inadvertently went back to those first few steps into the Jordan River. I could see myself vividly, as if I were reliving that moment. The water was so cold that it stopped me in my tracks. It was like I couldn't take another step because everything in me was saying, *Go back! Get out of this cold water, girl! This is gonna end very badly. You know you can't afford to have a Sickle Cell crisis over here.*

That's what 50-plus years of precedent taught me. It was as if time stood still for a moment, leaving me virtually paralyzed. My body was partially turned toward the steps I had just taken to enter the Jordan River. My mind kept telling me to retreat, to run in the opposite direction back to the safety of the river's edge. Yet, my heart kept telling me, *Trust God and keep going.*

As I re-read Isaiah 43:2, that's when it hit me—a whole year later! In those first few seconds after stepping into the Jordan River, I had a choice to make. A choice that I didn't realize would ultimately change the quality and trajectory of the rest of my life.

I could've chosen the safety of familiarity and the comfort of knowing my own limitations. Or, I could trust God fully and completely, like I had never trusted Him before.

Even if I had chosen to turn around and not go further into the cold Jordan River to be baptized, I believe I would've survived and been okay. For 54 years, I had always been, "okay." Honestly, I was tired of just being okay. I wanted to experience God's best because His Word says:

The thief comes only to steal, kill, and destroy. I came that you might have and enjoy your life … and have it more abundantly.

As I meditated on those Scriptures that morning sitting at my kitchen table, I realized that Sickle Cell has been the biggest "thief" in my life. And just being *okay*—at times barely surviving—is definitely *not* living the life of abundance Jesus promised. In my heart, I wanted to thrive. And for the first time ever, thriving seemed to be within my reach.

Taking that next step forward, talking to God with each subsequent step, I finally decided to truly let go of what I thought I could control like Isaiah 43:18–19 describes:

Do not remember the former things; neither consider the things of old. Behold, I am doing a new thing! Now, it springs forth. Do you not perceive it? I will make ways in the wilderness and rivers in the desert.

Submitting myself fully to God meant the shackles of Sickle Cell had to go.

The blinged out crutches I clinged to for support for well over two years had to go.

More than half a century of limiting beliefs about myself had to go.

Those recurring doubts and fears about who God is, what His Word says, and how it applies to me, had to go.

Was I going to believe *Him* this time, or was I still too comfortable believing the lies I told myself about me?

With each step forward, the shackles began to fall as I made my way toward the chaplain and others who were baptizing us a few feet away. And I knew I was in too deep to turn back.

As they took my hands and prepared to immerse me in the Jordan River, I finished my prayer by leaving all of it right there. Every pain. Every worry. Every fear. Every doubt. Every health concern—strokes, blood clots, Sickle Cell, a family history of cancer—every financial challenge, every rejection, every betrayal, everything that had robbed me of my peace, my faith, and His promises over the years.

That must've been what Wendell was talking about when he said, "I just believe your healing is here." Choosing to trust God instead of leaning on my own understanding, my own beliefs, my own thoughts, my own experiences, and yes, my own history. *That* was the divinely ordered pivot that would ultimately heal, empower, guide, and transform me.

Wendell was right. My healing *was* there, right there, in the Jordan River. And I was only able to receive it because I continued to step forward in faith and *chose* to trust God!

Didn't realize it then that simply making the right choice was the defining moment that changed everything.

Choosing Him on that hot September day in Israel opened my eyes to see that He had already *chosen* me.

I've always said that my steps are ordered by God, so He put me to the ultimate test to see if I would stand on what I said I believed. The easiest path, and seemingly the best option for me at that moment, was to turn back to what was familiar and comfortable, guided by my own thoughts, my own understanding, my own insecurities, my own experiences, and my own limiting beliefs.

Obviously, trusting and believing God is a lot harder than it sounds. I was so close to doing what was comfortable and familiar, *again*. Somehow, in the stillness of that moment, I mustered the courage to do something different, something rare, something unfamiliar, and much harder and scarier than I ever imagined.

I decided to take another bold step forward and then another and then another, not knowing the outcome and just, "Trusting in the Lord with all my heart, leaning not on my own understanding, acknowledging Him in all my ways and (believing that) He would direct my path." That was the beginning of a whole new way of life for me, a life powered and guided by Him alone.

There I was a year later, realizing that my decision that day, at that time, was precisely *why* God sent me to Israel.

It was to break the cycle of "insanity" in my own life.

And I have not had one hint of Sickle Cell pain since. Not one Sickle Cell crisis. Not one doubt in my mind that I *am* God's chosen, that my steps are indeed ordered by Him, that He really has "called me out from among them" and prepared me "for such a time as this!"

What a life-changing revelation.

When the 2024 legislative session convened on Tuesday, January 9, I planned to reach out to Governor McMaster to ask when he would reappoint my magistrate since the bogus complaint filed against her was dismissed right after we adjourned last year. The Senate had to be in session to reappoint magistrate judges, so I knew we had to wait until we reconvened in 2024. Still, knowing it and liking it were two totally different things. And after everything some of my Richland delegation colleagues had put her through, I was eager to get her reappointment done.

Around 8:30 a.m. that morning, I called the governor on his cell phone. Wasn't sure he would answer and was glad when he did. He sounded super energized and excited about our first day back. "Well good morning, Senator!" he exclaimed.

I was excited and energized too, probably for very different reasons. Time was of the essence, so I asked him how he was doing and reminded him about the bogus, retaliatory complaint that a Richland County legislative delegation member had orchestrated against my magistrate.

"Now that the complaint has been dismissed, when will you reappoint her?" I asked.

He paused and said that her situation sounded familiar, and that he needed to reacquaint himself with the issue. He told me he would work on it that day. Not exactly the response I was hoping for, but I thanked him anyway and told him how much I appreciated that. He could tell that I was eager to finally put this matter to rest. Governor McMaster knows me well enough to know that when an issue is important to me, I won't stop until it's resolved. And I'm sure he didn't wanna hear from me every day until then.

Fortunately, I got a call from Sym Singh, Governor McMaster's legislative liaison at the time. He told me that the governor had inquired about my magistrate's issue, and he had briefed him. Sym asked if I had time to meet with the person in the governor's office who handles appointments to state boards, commissions, and magistrate courts. I assured him that I would make time. That afternoon, and over the next two weeks, we worked together to get the requisite documents signed. And by the third week, my magistrate's reappointment paperwork still hadn't made it to my Senate desk.

A few days later, a different Richland County legislative colleague, who voluntarily insisted that he didn't want to run for Senate District 22, sent me a text message asking me to call him. I had no problem with Representative Ivory Thigpen running if that's what he chose to do. The Senate seat didn't belong to me. It belonged to the people of District 22.

For months, Black Caucus colleagues warned me that he was planning to run for the Senate seat, since I announced my independence from the State Democratic Party. Some Caucus members were upset that he would run against one of his own caucus members. They said they were warning me because they didn't want me to be blindsided. After 14 years in this arena, I was confident that I couldn't be blindsided by anything or anybody, anymore.

When I returned his phone call, our conversation was really no different from our previous conversations, except this time he said, "God told me to go ahead and announce my run for the Senate on January 22."

Still preoccupied with my magistrate's reappointment, I replied, "Great! Thanks for letting me know. Hope everything goes well."

"So I'm guessing you still haven't made your decision," he lamented.

I thought, *Why does my decision matter if God already told you to announce your run on January 22?*

I wasn't bothered by his decision, so I decided to leave it alone and simply reminded him that members of our legislative delegation were trying to destroy one of my best magistrate appointees, and I couldn't even think about finalizing and announcing my decision until I was able to get her reappointed. Not surprisingly, he said nothing in response, so I wished him well again and politely ended the call.

When I walked into the Senate Chamber on January 23, I noticed a folder on my desk and was elated to see that it was my magistrate's reappointment paperwork! Finally!! Once I was able to find four Senate delegation colleagues and get their signatures, she would officially be reappointed to another four-year term. With all that going on, I completely lost track of time. Had my magistrate been reappointed sooner, I probably would've remembered to reach out and congratulate Ivory on his January 22 announcement. Although we might have been vying for the same Senate seat, I never considered him my enemy or my adversary.

When he announced his intention to run for the House District 79 seat that I vacated in 2016 to run for Senate District 22, I supported him because I thought he would fight for the people. When I hosted town halls and community forums across my House and Senate districts, I always invited him to participate, so that our constituents would have an opportunity to get to know him.

It was only after hearing from those who *did* attend his campaign announcement, that I felt blindsided. Yep—*blindsided*—the one thing I didn't think I could be anymore. It wasn't because he announced he was running. I knew he planned to do that. What I didn't realize was that the majority of his announcement speech was about me.

One newspaper reported, "But he suggested McLeod was not as pragmatic a lawmaker as she could have been in the State House, and that he was potentially more capable of working with Republicans in the Senate to dilute more aggressive conservative policies."

Well ... damn.

Didn't I just receive a global award for working across party lines in the Senate? And if a total abortion ban doesn't qualify as "more aggressive conservative policies," I'm not sure what does. My colleague had served in the House for eight years. I guess I mistakenly assumed he would be honest about *his* record. Instead, he chose to lie about mine.

Sadly, shade and disrespect from establishment Democrats in "leadership," had become the norm, not the exception. The version of Mia that I left in the Jordan River would've been quick to clap back. Lord knows, I wanted to. And although I had made significant strides, I was definitely a "work in progress."

This time, God told me to *Be still.* Staying quiet when I'm being attacked is not easy for me. Thankfully, by that time, obeying God was. And although it took everything I had to be obedient, He gave me the strength. So, I said nothing.

Phone calls and text messages were already coming in from constituents and colleagues, asking if I planned to seek re-election. By the time he announced, I knew where I was leaning. I just wasn't going to say or do anything until I received confirmation from God. Besides, in the 14 years I served, I had never announced that early. The filing deadline was April 1 and we were just approaching the end of January. That four-year commitment is no joke for those of us who work as hard as I do for my constituents, so I was gonna take my time and be sure I was making the right decision.

As only God would have it, the governor "officially" reappointed my magistrate on January 24 two days after my colleague announced his run for the Senate. At that point, I was grateful to be able to exhale and think clearly as I patiently awaited God's confirmation about whether to seek re-election.

When the April 1 filing deadline finally came, I was ready. God was crystal clear about what I was to do. I was thrilled about His confirmation and stressed about how my beloved Senate district and Sister-Senators would fare if I didn't run. My day started super early. I knew that Emily Harold, who had been filming my Sister-Senators and me for a documentary since the beginning of 2023, was meeting me at the Richland County Election Commission on Hampton Street to record me walking into the commission. She wanted video footage of me proudly paying the filing fee and signing my name to seek another four-year term in the S.C. Senate.

As much as I hate cameras, I had almost grown accustomed to Emily and her camera guys. Doing a documentary on the five Sister-Senators couldn't have been easy. She had been filming us since the beginning of 2023, never imagining that we'd become Profile in Courage Award recipients and get as much national media attention as we did.

It was around 11 a.m. and Emily was wearing me out with phone calls and text messages, sounding a bit panicked about the time because, by then, it was obvious that I was cutting it super close to the noon filing deadline.

As I approached the State House, I called Emily to let her know. She and her camera guy were waiting for me in the State House parking garage at my parking space. I asked her to go with me to my office on the sixth floor. When we arrived, I invited Shari in and shut my office door so that I could share my decision with all of them at once.

And when I said those seven words—*I've decided not to run for re-election*—all I could see through my own watery eyes were tears rolling down Shari's.

Although I tried to reassure her that everything would be okay, I was nowhere near done. I still had to call my Sister-Senators. So, one by one, I called them. First, Katrina; then my bestie, Margie, who already knew where I was leaning; then Sandy; then Penry.

That was one of my toughest days in the South Carolina Senate.

The difference was … for the first time in 14 years, God allowed me to do what was best for *me*. And it felt amazing!!

When the filing deadline closed at noon, calls from the media and others poured in. There were three candidates who filed for the Senate District 22 seat and for the first time in eight years, I wasn't one of them.

I promised my Sister-Senators I would do everything I could to help them. Margie didn't have an opponent, so that meant we could focus our time and attention on helping our SCGOP Sister-Senators Katrina, Sandy, and Penry. Yet, I still had to think about my own district because it was critical that we elect the best possible person to lead Senate District 22.

State Representative Ivory Thigpen, Richland Two School Board Member Monica Elkins, and former Richland County Chair Overture Walker were vying for the District 22 Democratic nomination. Of the three, I immediately knew who I would support. And once again, God told me to *Be still,* as they made their cases to voters. Although it was extremely difficult, I had come way too far to start doing my own thing now.

Meanwhile, at the State House, we were extremely busy, trying to wrap up the legislative session. As the end of my final legislative session approached, I began to think about what I wanted to say to my colleagues. Some, I would be glad to leave and hope that our paths never crossed again. Others, I would genuinely miss.

Still, when May 9 rolled around, it was time to give my farewell remarks. So much to say. So many people to thank. So many reflections. My family and a few close friends were there. I knew it would go well. What I didn't expect was the outpouring of love and support from some colleagues on both sides of the aisle. As the Senate presented me with a resolution to acknowledge the prestigious Profile in Courage Award that my Sister-Senators and I received, some Democrat and Republican leaders stood with me. A few House members did too. It was sobering to see Republicans and Democrats standing together in support of who I am and the legislative work I've done.

As the reading clerk read the Senate Resolution, I felt such a sense of peace and gratitude for the time God had allowed me to serve and for the way He allowed me to serve.

A few moments later, it was time for me to speak:

It was at this well that I shared publicly for the first time that I know the pain and trauma of being sexually assaulted—at a time when there were 41 men in this chamber and only five of us. Some male colleagues ... they wondered why I felt the need to share my pain publicly, knowing that not one heart, not one vote would change. In that moment, I wasn't even sure myself why God led me to share it. But before I could even leave this chamber, God showed me why. It was to liberate others as well as myself. Not just others who are outside of this state house. That day, I became acutely aware that there are many among us, female and male, who know my story all too well because it's their story, too.

When I think about the legacy I want to leave, several words immediately come to mind. Among them: courage, principled leadership, service. Why courage first? Because it takes courage to lead. It takes courage to stand on our principles and speak truth to power. It takes courage to put the interests of others above our own. Truth is, courage always costs us something. My prayer … my prayer for all of us in this room and under the sound of my voice, is that we will always be willing to pay the price. Always choose courage … always. Always … choose courage …

As Primary Election Day approached, I found myself getting agitated when some organization leaders told me that Ivory had led them to believe I was supporting him in his election bid for Senate District 22. Apparently, he was getting endorsements because of it. For the first time since my journey to Israel, I began to question God since nobody would have had to guess where I stood on the candidates, if He had just let me put the truth out there.

I soon learned that just because circumstances change, doesn't mean God does. Again, I had to trust Him and not address it publicly.

Although I thought that my SCGOP Sister-Senators and my preferred candidate for Senate District 22 would probably win their primaries without a runoff, I was wrong.

Penry, who beat two-time Democratic gubernatorial candidate Vincent Sheheen in 2020, lost her primary by an unbelievable margin. Sandy's opponent surprisingly managed to beat her by a measly 34 votes. Katrina also found herself in a runoff. It was becoming crystal clear that the SCGOP delighted in "eating its own," so I was getting a little nervous.

WIS-TV news anchor Judi Gatson asked me to serve as a panelist on the station's election night live-stream coverage.

Thankfully, Representative Russell Ott won his primary race for the S.C. Senate. He would have to face a Republican challenger in November. Councilman Overture Walker, the candidate I was quietly supporting for the Senate District 22 seat, also had a runoff. I couldn't believe what was happening. Results from Senate Districts 22 (mine) and 23 (Katrina's) dominated the primary runoff headlines. Everybody seemed to be watching those two races closely. After low-voter turnout during the primary, I wondered whether the runoff numbers would be even more abysmal. Instead of focusing on that, I made phone calls for Katrina and thanked God for allowing me to weigh in publicly about my support for Overture in the runoff election for our beloved Senate District 22.

When June 25 arrived, my day started super early again and went nonstop until almost midnight. Judi asked me to join her as a guest panelist at WIS again to discuss the runoff election returns as they came in. I agreed, thinking we'd have lots to talk about and celebrate at the end of the night. As I parked my car on Bull Street, in front of the WIS studio, Margie and I were on the phone. She was headed to Katrina's watch party in Lexington. Both of us had heard that Katrina might be in trouble. Neither of us wanted to believe it.

By the time I made my way into the WIS studio and got mic'd up to weigh in on the runoff election results, Judi and her co-anchor Greg Adeline shared with me that Katrina had just conceded to her opponent. We hadn't even started livestreaming yet.

What a gut punch.

After taking a minute, I whispered a prayer about Overture's Senate District 22 race, and before I knew it, the livestream was up and running. Watching Katrina's interview from my seat at the studio seemed weird and surreal. I wanted to be there with her and my Sister-Senators because I knew she needed all of us. Meanwhile, the results from the Senate District 22 runoff were still trickling in, so I got it together and prayed my way through the numbers. One minute, Ivory was in the lead. The next minute, Overture was.

As soon as I came to terms with the reality of what had happened in Katrina's race, an unmistakable peace came over me. God's peace. And it felt good to just rest in it. The other guest panelists, SCGOP Chair Drew McKissick and SCDP Executive Director Jay Parmley, and I engaged in a very thoughtful, civil discourse about the primary and runoff elections, the abortion issue, and the candidates. It was one of the most engaging exchanges I'd had at WIS. And I've had many over 14 years.

We left the studio that night without the Senate District 22 runoff results. I knew because of the peace I had, that everything would be fine in the race for my beloved Senate District 22. After doing another brief interview with Seth, Emily's camera guy, I got back into my car to call Margie and ask if they were still in Lexington with Katrina.

A few seconds after I turned the ignition on, my phone rang. It was Overture. All I could hear was the excitement in his voice, "We did it, Senator! We won!!"

Whew … I needed some good news! And God never fails to give us exactly what we need … exactly when we need it.

Overture told me where they were and asked me to meet him at his victory celebration on Richland Street just a few blocks away. Many of his supporters were gathered there to celebrate with him and his family and I was grateful to God for allowing me to play a small role in electing someone who, I believe, will truly fight for the people of Senate District 22. It was a bittersweet end to a grueling month. After making sure Katrina was okay and realizing that, with Overture Walker's election, the people of Senate District 22 should be too, I continued to rest in God's peace.

As the new year quickly approached, I began to focus more on my health and wellness by working out three days each week, walking four to five times a week, changing my diet and re-enrolling in physical therapy to improve mobility in my knee. No complaints, though. I was just thankful. If some of my colleagues and critics knew how close I've been to death, literally and figuratively over the last 14 years, they would've tried a little harder to finish the job.

The Sister-Senators (left to right): Penry Gustafson, Margie Bright Matthews, me, Katrina Shealy, and Sandy Senn after my farewell speech at the State House.

Delivering my farewell speech, May 2024

LESSON SEVEN: *Take Risks*

Speaking truth to power can be scary, especially when you're one of the only ones who is doing it. Years ago when I served in the S.C. House, I received a call from a constituent who wanted to thank me for going against the majority of my predominantly Democratic legislative delegation after Richland County voters on both sides of the aisle were disenfranchised by the County Election Commission during the 2012 Presidential Election. I appreciated her for reaching out and reminded her that I simply did what I was elected to do. As our brief conversation came to an end, she said, "You're exactly the kind of elected leader we need and I'm so glad you're our representative. I just hate that you don't have higher political aspirations."

I thought, *You just hate that I don't have higher political aspirations?*

What in the world does *that* mean? I was confused because this was our first and only conversation. I really *didn't* have higher political aspirations. So, how did *she* know that? I shared her comments with Millie and we laughed when we discovered that what she meant was, *You can't possibly want to go any higher than the S.C. House because you went against those in power.*

I had never thought about it like that. Yes, politics can be dirty and some of my legislative colleagues were already threatening me because I sided with the people. Sadly, working *for* the people meant that I was, in fact, working *against* those in power.

And those in power in Richland County, happened to be members of my own party.

After that conversation with my constituent, if I ever saw a need to have a bigger voice and platform, I wondered whether I would be brave enough to pursue it. And yet, that's exactly what I did four years later when I voluntarily vacated the House seat to run for Senate District 22. Winning the Senate seat that year taught me several things. The most valuable lesson was:

Don't play it safe. Always take risks.

Any time we choose to step up, speak out, or stand up for the right reasons, it's risky. Some won't like it. Others may try to hurt us because of it. Being the only member of my legislative delegation to boldly speak out about what our constituents experienced and call for transparency and accountability, was a risky move—especially for a new legislator, like I was at the time. It was the right move, though. Quite frankly, it was the *only* move. And because voters were the beneficiaries of my bravery, they didn't forget who fought for them.

That's why I've never lost a House or Senate reelection bid —even when both parties ensured that I had opposition.

Was it risky to run in a swing district for the S.C. House in 2010 with no prior elected service, no name recognition in the district, and no S.C. Democratic Party support?

Was it risky to stay in the race when some rural Kershaw County constituents literally slammed doors in my face after they realized I was Black, a woman, *and* a Democrat?

Was it risky to choose authenticity and ignore my campaign manager's advice in 2010, when she told me to rent a less expensive car to drive in Kershaw County, insisted that I camp out in Kershaw County from 7 a.m. until 7 p.m. daily and warned me to never describe myself as a lobbyist to Kershaw County residents?

Was it risky to go against members of my own party in 2012 to advocate for disenfranchised constituents on both sides of the political aisle?

Was it risky to fight for a Spring Valley High School student who was violently ejected out of her desk by a school resource officer, knowing that I would be fighting solo, since most of my legislative delegation considered the incident a "school board issue?"

Was it risky to vacate the House seat in 2016, since I didn't have to, and run for the S.C. Senate against a moderate Republican, knowing that the incumbent Democratic senator and his family were supporting my Republican opponent?

Was it risky to announce my intention to run statewide in 2021 and officially file to run in 2022, understanding that the S.C. Democratic Party wasn't likely to stand down and let the primary process play out fairly?

Was it risky to travel approximately 17 hours to Israel with the life-threatening health challenges I knew I could face?

Was it risky to immerse myself in the cold Jordan River, when exposure to extreme conditions had caused acute Sickle Cell crises for me every time, since I was seven years old?

Was it risky to leave the S.C. Democratic Party publicly in 2023 and tell people why?

The answer to all of these questions is—absolutely.

Yet, each time I've pushed past fear and dared to do it anyway, my confidence *and* my courage soared.

CHAPTER EIGHT
A Different World

Harpo ... who dis woman?
—Mary Agnes "Squeak," *The Color Purple*

One of my favorite lines from the movie *The Color Purple* reminds me that although I barely resemble the fearful person I once was, some of the personal struggles I've encountered are still very real in my life. The difference is, I now know how to push past them. And after everything I had been through and overcome, seeing myself in a new light was like doing a double take.

Pastor Radhika always reminds us that we are spiritual beings going through a natural experience. In fact, God's Word says that "We are *in* this world, not *of* it." When I reflect on my spiritual journey in South Carolina politics, my pastor's references to the Book of John have helped guide me through some tough, lonely days at the State House.

After I was first elected, I thought that because I had lobbied for eight years before and had already worked in the executive and legislative branches of government, navigating my new role inside the legislature wasn't going to be as difficult for me as it was for some of my colleagues who were entering the State House for the first time. I was familiar with the players and processes.

While some of my legislative colleagues struggled to navigate their way around the State House complex and get back to their cars in the parking garage, I had worked in or around every building on the grounds by the time I was first elected in 2010. Serving in the South Carolina Legislature wasn't gonna be nearly as challenging for me as it may have been for others.

At least, that's what I thought.

I knew how dysfunctional our government was, how racist and misogynistic many of our systems were, how antiquated, regressive, and oppressive many of our public policies were. What I didn't realize was how complicit, complacent, and comfy too many of our legislators were on *both* sides of the political aisle.

Perhaps I should've known that speaking out on behalf of my constituents and calling out the wrongs that were being committed against them by Republicans *and* Democrats would essentially make me public enemy number one.

I knew pretty early into my first term in the S.C. House that I was different from many of my colleagues. When we started the redistricting process in 2011 and the SCGOP packed my swing district with Black voters, it never occurred to me that I would be the only Democratic legislator at the time to publicly fight the redistricting plan.

And although I initially thought it was the Republican's plan, I soon learned the truth when neither the House Democratic Caucus nor the S.C. Democratic Party lifted a finger to help me protect my swing district from being gerrymandered. Having to fight for my swing district as a civilian, didn't stop *The State* from penning a story with the salaciously misleading headline:

"Representative ... Doesn't Want Any More Black People in Her District."

Again, crickets from the State Democratic Party.

Over a decade later, when *ProPublica*, an independent Pulitzer Prize-winning investigative media outlet published the story, "How Rep. James Clyburn Protected His District at a Cost to Black Democrats," it shed much more light on some of the alleged actions of our 6th District congressman that had contributed to the marginalization of Black voters. What *ProPublica* revealed is definitely consistent with what I'd experienced and, if true, helped ensure that South Carolina would have only one congressional seat held by a Black person ... his.

The redistricting plan the congressman allegedly proposed to the SCGOP was race-based and deprived Black voters of fair and balanced congressional representation. It also strengthened the Republican majority's stronghold in our state. For everyday voters, terms like "redistricting" may be a bit confusing. That is intentional. Both parties want to keep it that way. The less the public knows about the strategies behind redistricting or the way voting districts are drawn, the better for incumbents.

Simply put, redistricting is the process whereby voters should get to choose their elected officials. Instead, it's now the process whereby elected officials get to choose their voters.

After reading *ProPublica's* article, albeit years later, I understood so much more than I did back in 2011. In fact, that article helped fill in the blanks for me. And by 2023, there weren't many blanks left.

I already knew firsthand that no other elected South Carolina Democrats dared publicly acknowledge, let alone address, the biggest elephant in the room. The question I've always had is, why not? Why wouldn't the South Carolina Democratic Party engage and enlighten its base about how the state's redistricting plan directly impacts them? Why was I one of the only legislators who did? Why didn't Democratic Party loyalists question the SCDP's unwillingness to challenge the state's redistricting plan?

Sure, SCDP operatives love to play the victim and put all of the responsibility on the Republican Party, since it is the majority party and has been for 20-plus years. But if S.C. Dems have absolutely no say and no sway on critical issues like fair elections, why are they so afraid to expose the truth about the impact of unfair and imbalanced representation on South Carolina voters?

I've heard some S.C. Democratic leaders talk about how horrible the Republicans' redistricting plan was in 2011. By 2021, many of the same Democratic leaders couldn't seem to find anything wrong with the Republicans' redistricting plan. Those of us who weren't directly involved in the redrawing of the district maps deferred to our colleagues who were. Even if the SCDP didn't suspect that the gerrymandering was a collaborative effort between the congressman and the SCGOP, why not fight to share the truth about how the proposed plan would impact the people of South Carolina?

Year after year I struggled with being the voice on issues that the majority of my party, caucus and legislative delegation chose to ignore. And while I was fighting for the people, the majority of my party at the time, was fighting *me*.

That's when I began to blog about the difference between politicians and public servants and why I'm offended when anyone inadvertently refers to me as a "politician."

It's also when I began to appreciate the fact that I'm different.

After I announced my decision to not seek reelection to the S.C. Senate in April of 2024, and the candidate I supported won the Senate District 22 seat in the June runoff, I was elated and ready to exhale.

Then, June 27 happened.

That was the night President Biden debated Donald Trump for the first time during the 2024 Presidential Election. By most accounts, it didn't go well, at least not for President Biden. What stood out to me most about that night was the President's voice. It was more like a faint whisper. He looked and sounded physically ill. It was obvious that he wasn't feeling well.

I wondered why his team had him participate in a nationally

televised debate at 9 p.m. with a known pathological liar who has to be fact-checked in real time, when it was obvious that President Biden wasn't at his best. Was it a setup by his own party to force him out of the presidential race? I didn't wanna be cynical. Those who know me know that's not my nature. After watching that first presidential debate, though, I admit that I just couldn't seem to shake the thought.

Ironically, it was five years to the day that then Vice President Joe Biden engaged in what many thought was a game-changing presidential primary debate. Then U.S. Senator Kamala Harris hit Biden with, "That little girl was me," to highlight his previous stance on busing as a means to desegregate public schools across the U.S. That same year, I witnessed firsthand the way Biden was undermined by key members of his campaign team when his presidential campaign made stops in South Carolina. I was serving my first term in the S.C. Senate at the time.

At S.C. Senator Dick Harpootlian's home in Columbia, Vice President Biden and his wife, Dr. Jill, talked with me privately about doing some communications consulting for his presidential campaign. I was intrigued by the opportunity, yet reluctant. Although I had deep respect and admiration for the vice president—a Black woman who was aptly qualified, capable and happened to be my sorority sister, was also vying for the presidency. I was honest and transparent with them about what Senator Harris' candidacy meant to me. And although this was a bona fide business opportunity, I wasn't naive about the fact that many would see and distort it as an endorsement.

Vice President Biden told me he understood and asked that we continue to communicate.

Our subsequent conversations were brief. Each time we met, he spoke to specific members of his campaign staff in my presence and asked them to follow up with me. I rarely heard from his staffers, although they always promised to get back in touch.

When I arrived for what would be our third and final meeting, I could hear the crowd cheering as the vice president spoke. A member of his team walked me in and took me to a small meeting room. On our way there, I caught a glimpse of a Biden campaign staffer I knew and recognized from South Carolina. We briefly acknowledged each other from a distance as I was escorted to the meeting room.

When the vice president walked in, he greeted me with a hug and thanked me for coming. After taking his suit jacket off, he sat down beside me. When the staffer who escorted me left and it was just the two of us, we talked about what had and hadn't happened since our last meeting. Vice President Biden seemed relieved to reconnect with me and was honest about how much Senator Harris' busing comment hurt him. He told me he still admired and respected her immensely and that if she wasn't successful in the presidential primary and he was, he would definitely have a place for her if he became our next president.

As he reflected on how close Kamala and his late son, Beau, were, it was obvious that he was extremely fond of and felt a real connection to her. I knew from our conversation that if he won the Democratic nomination, she would likely be his running mate. His genuine compassion and concern resonated with me because both are rarities in today's political arena. That's ultimately when I realized that, like me, Biden was different.

When he reiterated that he wanted me to be an integral part of his campaign team going forward, I believe he was sincere. Although I hadn't been officially asked to join his campaign as a consultant, Vice President Biden summoned one of his executive staffers to the classroom and directed her to promptly follow up with the campaign's legal team to ensure that there were no legal or ethical issues that would preclude his campaign from contracting with my firm. She assured him that she would and asked that we exchange cell numbers.

A few days later, I did receive a call from Biden's campaign. It wasn't the staffer he asked to call me, though. It was the South Carolina staffer I recognized and acknowledged on my way to meet with the vice president. The staffer was obviously surprised to see me at the event and asked why I was there. Although cordial and respectful, I sensed that somehow I had inadvertently infiltrated this staffer's turf, and they weren't exactly thrilled about it.

Even after Senator Harris ended her presidential campaign in December of 2019, Vice President Biden's campaign and I never got to the point where I had to make a decision, which wasn't surprising after I received that phone call. Realizing that the former vice president of the United States seemed to be undermined by some members of his own campaign staff was an interesting insight for me, but not a surprising one.

Five years later, after President Biden's devastating debate performance, I was reminded that many of the Democratic Party operatives I've encountered during my 14 years in elected office seemed to be more about self-preservation and protecting their own little democratic kingdoms within the larger party apparatus.

When questions about President Biden's age, mental acuity, and fitness to run began to emerge, it wasn't surprising that this type of chatter would precede a slow, steady leak of information from those in his inner circle, ultimately fueling more speculation and cynicism about his ability to endure a second four-year term. When I tweeted that President Biden's debate performance would be hard for him to overcome, it wasn't because I questioned his mental acuity. Based on my interactions with him, I had no reason to. It was because I understood better than most what he was up against within his own party.

By July 24 of 2024, President Biden relented and gave defiant, disillusioned establishment party operatives what they wanted by stepping aside and almost immediately endorsing Vice President Kamala Harris as the Democratic Party's nominee.

Suddenly, there was renewed interest in the Democratic Party that excited establishment Democrats. Initially, polling data appeared to align with what Democratic Party operatives wanted us to believe.

The Bidens were slowly fading from the spotlight and a new generation of leadership was emerging—almost seamlessly. Although I believed the Democratic Party's treatment of the President was cold, harsh, and overtly disrespectful, I had already voiced my opinions about the party's politics when I left the State Party publicly in January of 2023. For over a decade, I had seen and experienced firsthand what the Democratic Party had become and how it operated.

Even as an Independent, I could never support Donald Trump, so President Joe Biden would've continued to have my support if he had stayed in the race. I believe him to be a true public servant and genuinely good human being. When he bowed out, of course I supported my sorority sister Vice President Harris and hoped that the party would use this shakeup as an opportunity to focus on reconnecting with working people across America.

I left the Democratic Party because the Democratic Party left the people of South Carolina. Period. If I had run and served as a Republican, I would've left for the exact same reasons—only sooner.

Ultimately, when the novelty of Vice President Harris' presidential campaign and record-breaking fundraising numbers began to wane—the shift was almost palpable.

Still, Democratic Party operatives did nothing different.

As tensions continued to intensify between Israelis and Palestinians, the Democratic Party remained hopelessly divided about whether to continue to send military aid to Israel, impose sanctions, or demand a ceasefire to help put an end to the devastation in Gaza.

I warned SCDP leaders at our Senate caucus retreat in Charleston that the administration's failure to take a firm, balanced approach to stop the carnage in the Middle East would surely impact the general election, especially in larger swing states. Even in South Carolina, I found myself conversing with more voters who were planning to "sit this one out" because of it.

While Republicans continued to hammer Democrats on inflation and the economy, as well as mounting challenges at the U.S. border, the GOP's attacks basically went unchecked and unchallenged. Only a few strong democratic surrogates emerged to help Vice President Harris tout the historic policies and funding that the Biden-Harris Administration had successfully championed to lead our nation through the devastation and havoc that was exacerbated by the Trump Administration's mishandling of the pandemic.

On the evening of the presidential election, I was back on WIS-TV as a guest panelist. As reports began to trickle in from S.C. Democratic operatives who insisted that Vice President Harris would win by a landslide, incoming numbers suggested otherwise. By the end of the night, it was obvious that Donald Trump would soon be back in the Oval Office. Many down ballot races for congressional and statewide seats in South Carolina and in other states around the country, would also go to Republican candidates.

The Democratic Party would be forced to reckon with its own demons and yet another self-inflicted demise. As a postmortem assessment became imminent, I quietly braced myself for the inevitable. Based upon my experience, a very fractured, disconnected Democratic Party would soon begin to point fingers, play the blame game, and predictably return to its very comfy and familiar version of insanity.

Accurately forecasting the actions of Democratic and Republican Party operatives reminds me of just how enlightening my political journey has been. Politics today is a different world, so daring to be different in this arena can be exhilarating and excruciating. And I wouldn't have it any other way.

Introducing Vice President Joe Biden at the SCDP's annual dinner, 2013

LESSON EIGHT: D.A.R.E.

Acknowledging and leaning into the qualities that distinguish us, can be tough. All of us long to be loved and appreciated for who we are. Often, we stand out because we're different, which can make us extremely uncomfortable.

When the spotlight is on us, we usually wish it wasn't. Without even trying to be different, we just are. And people tend to gravitate toward authenticity, especially in politics. The flip side is that being different sets us apart and may be threatening to some. When we're getting what colleagues and critics may consider to be too much attention or recognition, they often feel threatened and act or react accordingly.

Being different can be lonely. To avoid the pain or discomfort of feeling isolated or ostracized, we often master the art of shrinking and blending in just to make others feel comfortable, only to realize that diluting who we really are, makes us uncomfortable and consequently, is grounded in fear.

Take political party affiliation for instance. Identifying as a Democrat or Republican shouldn't define us. Neither should it prevent us from seeing, acknowledging or speaking the truth. When it does, fear is usually to blame. I know people who have long-since distanced themselves from the Democratic and Republican parties, albeit privately. Some are actively serving in public office and some aren't. Regardless, party affiliation is a personal choice. No one should feel like they must be affiliated with one party or the other to have relevance, value, and a voice in our political process.

In this country, we are free to vote for the person whose principles and platform are aligned with our values. The freedom to make our own decisions and exercise our own choices is inherent in a true democracy—or should be. Yet, too often, that freedom is censored by party affiliation, hijacked by self-serving politicians or clouded by our own fears.

Even now, when I feel myself becoming fearful, I practice my personalized version of truth or dare, a fun game I played with friends as a child. This is usually how my conversation with myself goes:

Truth is ... I'm afraid of ______. So, I'm daring myself to ______.

Like our fears, the adult version is not a game. It's a method I've developed to remind myself of the divine power I have within to face and overcome any obstacle or adversity.

DECIDE beforehand how I'm going to deal with fear each time it shows up.

ACT in a way that is consistent with my decision.

REMEMBER how I defeated fear last time.

EMPOWER myself with the knowledge that I've already kicked fear's butt at least once.

And D.A.R.E. (DECIDE, ACT, REMEMBER, EMPOWER) myself to do it again and again ...

Overcoming fear is not a "one and done" approach. We must practice these fear-fighting techniques until fear is no longer a dominant factor in our lives.

CHAPTER NINE
Be Still and Know

If you wait until you feel ready, you'll never do it.
—Frances Morris Flournoy, my "Auntie"

I'd be lying if I said there weren't times during my years of public service that I truly felt like an outcast, as if I didn't belong in either chamber. And although our state government is predominantly white and male, it wasn't just because of my race or gender. I had long since grown accustomed to being the only Black person in some rooms and the only woman in others. In some settings, I was the only one in the room who checked both boxes.

Maybe that's why I instinctively began to count the number of Black and brown faces in each room I was blessed to enter. And right after that ... the number of women. I'll admit the practice was born primarily out of a genuine longing to see someone ... anyone ... who looked like me. Even now, it's sometimes unusual to see another Black woman in the spaces I get to occupy. I can't wait for the day when I no longer feel the need to count—a day when the occupants at these tables, in these rooms, truly reflect the diversity *and* demographics of my state.

Because representation really does matter.

Early in my career, seeing someone who looked like me in certain spaces gave me something I didn't even realize I needed ... **proof** that it was possible. And **permission** to pursue paths I had been misled to believe were not within reach ... *my* reach, anyway. Even after being nominated and invited to participate in national leadership initiatives and global public leadership fellowships, I've still struggled with feelings of inadequacy and wondered if I was supposed to be in *this* room or at *that* table with leaders who wielded significant influence and impact, nationally and globally.

Although I realize I'm not where I am by chance, to see myself fully, faithfully, and finally, I continue to do the work to dismantle decades of limiting beliefs I've held about myself because of others' inability or refusal to "see" me.

Over the years, I've spoken to tens of thousands of people about my experiences. During many of those talks, two words that sound alike, but have very different meanings, were my focus: "no" and "know." I penned "The Know Factor" over a decade ago and it has become one of my favorite go-to messages when I speak to young people who, like me, have probably heard more than their share of that dreaded two-letter word in their lifetimes:

No! You have Sickle Cell, so you might not wanna take on that challenge because it's probably way too strenuous and stressful for you.

No! You're a single mom, so if I were you ... I wouldn't try to start my own business. You'd do better to stick with the job you've got so you won't have to worry about a steady paycheck, health insurance benefits, or retirement.

No! You're not ready to run for office just yet. You should wait. I mean, this is a swing district and it'll be hard to get white voters to vote for a Black woman. Get some more experience. Get your name out there a little more first.

I've heard the word, "no!" too many times to count.

Yet, the more I heard it, the more determined I was to prove that the naysayers had no control over my path, my purpose, and my destiny. Lord knows my path hasn't been an easy one. When you have an independent mind, a bold voice, compassion for people, and a true heart for public service, the political world can be a very lonely place.

Somehow, I knew my faith was stronger than my fear. And if I wanted to do the amazing things God has called me to do, I'd just have to do it afraid.

Every day, we get to show ourselves and the world who and whose we are. We are who God says we are, so our options and opportunities are unlimited. We are free to be selfless servants and fearless warriors …

Admittedly, undoing half a century of limiting beliefs didn't happen overnight. I've had a few "stops" to make on my journey of discovery and healing.

First, I had to stop being loyal to the past.

Second, I had to stop saying, "yes," to people who have never truly seen, valued, or cared about me … only how my "yes" benefits them and their agendas.

And last, but not least, I had to set and stick to my own boundaries.

People want a fighter. And because I've always been a fierce and fearless advocate, I seem to have been on everybody's short list to call, whether they lived in my district or not, anytime there was "good trouble," the kind civil rights icon Congressman John

Lewis referred to as necessary to challenge injustice and create positive, meaningful change.

Yes, public service is a noble calling for those of us who use our political superpowers for good. But it can lead to burnout if we're not careful, especially since standing up, speaking out, and fighting for what's right has become the exception, not the rule.

When we serve for the right reasons, there are so many "wrongs" that demand our attention. We often don't feel the impact of the imbalance, until it's too late.

Here I am 14 years later, just coming to grips with the fact that I could no longer continue to neglect my health, financial stability, or physical, mental, and emotional well-being. Even after all the fights I've led and sacrifices I've made to serve the people of South Carolina—an unlikely encounter in 2020 with a woman I didn't know, followed by an unplanned journey to Israel in 2022— were the catalysts God used to challenge some of my thoughts, perceptions, and beliefs about *me*.

Absent those two experiences, I probably would've continued to accept the opinions of others about whether I'm living up to *their* expectations. I could've easily defaulted to the path of least resistance and allowed myself to be governed by and submissive to oppressive systems and people whose mission is to ensure that I never truly see myself the way God sees me, never discover the divine purpose for which He created me, or tap into the Divine power that lives within me.

When Margaret Seidler reached out to our family's funeral home, neither of us had any idea my response to her email would cause our journeys of self-discovery to collide in such a profound and impactful way. As the two of us began to talk regularly, it was obvious that our connection went beyond our ancestries and ignited a sisterly bond that we couldn't have foreseen or imagined.

The more Margaret learned and shared about her ancestors, the more I was able to discover about my great-great-grandfather Joseph W. Morris. Her research picked up where Daddy's left off and revealed the missing pieces I needed to better understand and appreciate the recipe for that "good stock" Daddy always talked about. Who I am. What's in my DNA. And why God **chose** to place me on this path, retracing my great-great grandfather's footsteps on some of the very trails he blazed.

Because he persisted, persevered, and prevailed in the 1800s, I know I can too.

I am reminded of when Sophia in *The Color Purple* says, "All my life I had to fight." Having to fight my own people just to help my own people makes me think about all the boxing matches I used to watch on TV with Daddy. He would order pizzas and we'd sit and watch boxing matches for hours. "Fight Nights" quickly became one of my favorite things for us to do together. I remember how Sugar Ray Leonard, Evander Holyfield, Larry Holmes and Mike Tyson had different weight classes, stances and styles, but all of them fought equally hard in my eyes. And unlike basketball, my other favorite sport, boxers never get to call a time out during a televised match. Only the referee is able to pause or stop a fight, usually when it's obviously not safe for the boxer to continue without medical attention because of an injury.

Likewise, I couldn't call a time out while I was serving. In politics, we don't have referees, although the public will often cry foul if someone's actions are flagrantly out of bounds. These days, even that isn't enough to delay or stop the fight. People are so desperate for someone who will truly fight for them that they often miss, minimize, or look past the fact that their champion is battered, bruised, and bloody. They're just grateful to have somebody who's not afraid to jump into the ring.

I knew it was time for a change when constituents and community members heard that I might not run for re-election in 2024 and began to reach out to "affectionately" say, "You can't leave us now." Or, "You've gotta run. We need you in there!" Comments like that weren't meant to be mean or hurtful. In fact, they were intended to be just the opposite. Yet, each time my phone rang and someone ran down all *their* reasons I couldn't leave the legislature, it pissed me off. Not because the people who were saying it knew how "wounded" I was after decades of imbalance, but because I knew. And I could no longer continue to "pour from an empty cup."

Until then, it hadn't occurred to me that it also takes courage to leave or exit any arena on your own terms when you know it's time. I could have taken the easy path and not announced publicly that I was leaving the S.C. Democratic Party to become an Independent in 2023. And guess what, I would've easily won a third term to the S.C. Senate. In fact, I probably would've breezed through without serious primary or general election opposition.

Because we have a two-party system in the U.S., many elected officials just smile and wave publicly, knowing they've quietly quit fighting for the people they purport to represent, and coast through the next decade like they've coasted through the last one.

In a state like South Carolina, where there are no term limits, elected officials at state and federal levels can stay in office until they die. Some do.

I've introduced term-limit bills that had bipartisan support. Yet, most incumbents won't vote against their own interests, so there was never enough traction for passage. I've also encouraged voters to always hold their elected officials accountable, starting with me. If not, too many incumbents will do nothing to challenge the status quo or draw attention to themselves. They would much rather play it safe. And an electorate that is not engaged or informed will be at their mercy, wondering why their communities are faring worse now than they did 20 or 30 years ago. It's too easy for politicians at state and federal levels to get elected and then do nothing but keep the seat warm until they're ready to give it up.

When Daddy told me, *You come from good stock,* I thought I understood what he meant. Yet, it was Margaret's research about my great-great-grandfather that gave me the clarity I needed to hold my head high and refuse to believe or entertain the notion that I'm inadequate or insufficient. To deny or diminish God's power and presence in my life is no longer an option, now that I "know" better.

Daddy's City Council re-election campaign ad

LESSON NINE: *You Belong Here*

While serving in the S.C. House and Senate, I've been in some rooms where nobody seemed to notice. And others where everybody seemed to notice.

And yet, my presence wasn't acknowledged in either.

I've walked into other rooms where women understand innately who I am and what I'm up against in this male-dominated, hyper-partisan political arena.

I remember when I first "saw" me. The day I first looked myself in the eye to affirm what I inherently knew but never dared to verbalize. As I stared at my image in the mirror, thinking about at least seven generations of greatness that runs through my veins, I smiled and said calmly and confidently, "You come from good stock. And you are enough."

As much as I needed to give voice to those words and desperately wanted to believe them, even that audible acknowledgement couldn't silence the relentless whispers that screamed, *You know you're not enough and probably never will be.* Still, I somehow managed to keep moving forward with just enough courage and confidence to convince myself and others that I was.

Then, God sent me to Israel.

The loneliness and isolation I've often felt here in the U.S., paled in comparison to the loneliness and isolation

I expected to experience on that trip. Honestly, it was one of several reasons I didn't wanna go.

Little did I know that after years of focusing on everybody else, God was actually isolating me to give me the time and space to focus only on me. It was on that healing journey that I finally began to understand what the words *you are enough* really meant.

You are enough didn't mean that I wouldn't make mistakes or that I wouldn't fail. It meant that my mistakes and failures wouldn't define or defeat me.

You are enough didn't mean that I wouldn't feel fear anymore. It meant that I would develop real courage and confidence, the kind that allows us to move forward, in spite of fear.

You are enough didn't mean others would see, acknowledge, or appreciate my value. It meant I needed to see, acknowledge, and appreciate my own value instead of depending on or expecting others to do it for me.

Growing up in Bennettsville, I was pretty sheltered from what was going on in other parts of the state and nation. Mama and Daddy didn't have much in terms of money and material things. The funeral business was very demanding of Daddy's time and I can remember him having what I now know to be slow months financially, where the business and household expenses exceeded his income. Even then, they always made sure the bills were paid on time. I remember hearing them talk about how important that was. Mama's salary as a public school teacher and librarian wasn't even close to what it should've been. Yet, somehow, they made it work.

I always looked forward to family dinners at my Great-Aunt Frances' house on Sundays. Frances Morris Flournoy was the matriarch of our family. Affectionately known as "Auntie," she was the glue—the constant in our lives that kept everybody and everything together.

I was so excited when I got to sleep over at Auntie's some weekends. We'd sleep in on Saturdays and she'd make me milk coffee to drink with breakfast. Sometimes, she'd even fry me some oysters to go with my grits! I'd stick close to her in the kitchen, just to see how she made everything taste so good. It has been over 30 years since Auntie passed away and I still haven't had mac and cheese that comes anywhere close to hers.

And everybody knows how much I love mac and cheese.

When she wasn't cooking, we'd sometimes drive about 15 minutes away to Laurinburg, North Carolina, to check on her Aunt Ola and Aunt Dot, or go shopping to buy clothes and food for children in our community who didn't have either. It was normal for Auntie, who was also a public school teacher, to invite some of her students and their siblings into her home to eat, take a bath, do laundry, get tutored in subjects they were failing, or just take a break from their daily struggles.

Auntie was always on the go and I was her sidekick, so much so, that my nickname in the community was Lil' Frances. On weekends, she took me with her to check on community members who were sick or had recently lost a loved one. We visited others who had mobility challenges or didn't have family members close by and just needed a helping hand.

Like my parents and hers, Auntie was the epitome of a true servant-leader before I ever even knew what a servant-leader was.

Back then, I didn't feel a difference between my immediate and extended family. Everybody worked together as a team. Our village was strong, loving, and fiercely protective. Neighbors, church, and community members genuinely cared about one another. Anyone in the community was more than comfortable chastising, redirecting, and disciplining me, especially if they saw me doing something I shouldn't have or hanging out somewhere I shouldn't be. Early in my life, that village concept created and cultivated in me a sense of belonging and accountability to my community and my elders.

In spite of all the love and support I had, I still sometimes struggled with feelings that I wasn't good enough, smart enough, pretty enough, worthy enough, especially when compared to others. I don't ever remember sharing those feelings of doubt, insecurity, or inadequacy with my parents, my teachers, or Auntie. I must have thought they would dissipate when I reached certain milestones, blazed certain trails, or broke through certain barriers.

I've always been self-motivated and fiercely competitive. And yet, it's almost embarrassing to admit that with each new achievement, each new accolade, I've still struggled with the same old recycled feelings that somehow, my being there must be by accident.

Mama and Daddy loved us and did the best they could to provide a strong foundation. Of course, they were human and made mistakes too. I just don't remember them talking about them. In retrospect, talking about their mistakes and failures was probably taboo, since both of them strived for excellence and instilled a can-do attitude in all of us. To Tracey, Erica, Jimmy, and me, they were superheroes. I just wish they were still here so I could ask them how they overcame their own fears and struggles.

Daddy served a brief stint on Bennettsville's City Council and was the first Black man to occupy that space after Reconstruction. I was too young to remember what he said or how he felt about his experience. Mama loved the news and current events. I watched the news on TV sometimes with one or both of them, not really understanding how the political arena worked and never imagining I would ever be a part of it.

I chuckle now when I think about how I stayed in trouble with Daddy during my middle and high school years, for not keeping up with current events. He was politically active and "woke," before I knew what activism was.

I remember pleading with him to let me shop at downtown stores with my friends, the stores he had forbidden us to patronize because of the way they treated Black people in our community during the Civil Rights Movement. He understood the power of protests and economic boycotts, especially when it came to how he spent his hard-earned money. None of that stuff made sense to me then.

But man, do I get it now.

Back then, children were seen and not heard, especially when grownups were talking. I was privy to many conversations I didn't fully understand. What I'd better not do was interject my thoughts, opinions, or ask questions about any of the issues grown folks were discussing. They may have had conversations *around* me, but I understood that those conversations didn't *include* me.

I sometimes wonder if being physically in the room, yet outside of the conversations, may have contributed to my feelings of invisibility when I became an adult, although I'm confident that's not what the grownups in my life intended.

And even though I still occasionally wrestle with feelings of inadequacy, it's not nearly as often as before. Each time doubt and fear try to creep in, I hear Daddy's big voice saying, "You come from good stock and don't you forget it." I see Mama's warm smile, and hear her sweet voice saying, "I love the way you speak up for yourself when you need to. I admire that about you."

Meditating on what I know to be true, reminds me that regardless of what I think, what others say, or how I feel ...

God created me in His Image. I am fearfully and wonderfully made. I am who God says I am. That means, I'm more than a conqueror!

My identity and my destiny are anchored in His promises. I have no reason to fear—He has called me by name. I am His.

And what I now know for sure is … I belong here.

CHAPTER TEN
The Mia Rule

The question isn't who is going to let me; it's, who is going to stop me?
—Ayn Rand

As I prepare to step into the next chapter of my journey, I'm realizing just how much people wanna know about what's next for me. I can't seem to go to the grocery store or out to eat without somebody stopping me to say, "Hey Senator … we're really gonna miss you at the State House," or "Thank you, Mia, for everything you've done for us. Hope this is only, 'so long,' and not 'goodbye' forever." Or, "You're gonna run for office again, right?"

Before I respond, I have to remind myself to never say never because, when God speaks, I listen. That means, I can't rule out another run simply because I don't *wanna* run. Lord knows, I don't. But whatever God leads me to do, is what I'm gonna do.

Often, I hear people talk about their calling, or what they feel they were created to do. Over the years, I've even heard some say they're in the positions they're in because they've "answered the call" of God for their lives. I haven't always known what my calling was. I'm just grateful that I do now.

Truth is … advocating, disrupting, and speaking truth to power is extremely uncomfortable for an introvert like me. Yet, these are precisely what God created me to do. Instead of embracing the call, I spent the first few years of my political life running away from it. What kept me locked in, was that I couldn't look the other way or keep my mouth shut when there were injustices and hypocrisies that hurt my constituents and community members.

There were many times I wish I could've stayed in my lane, like so many of my colleagues, and let somebody else do the advocating … the disrupting … and the truth-telling. Obviously, that wasn't God's plan.

Although I'm not nearly as concerned as I used to be about what people think or how they feel about me, being different in the ways that I am, isn't easy. The struggle is real. And stress is stress, even if it has a positive stimulus or yields positive outcomes. The difference now is, I'm no longer running away from the unique, distinctive qualities that make me, me.

Even though I'm crystal clear about who and whose I am and what God has called me to do, occasionally I still pick the scabs of old wounds that haven't fully healed and lament the "what-ifs" of hopes and dreams deferred.

As I prepare to leave public service in the traditional sense, some refer to it simply as retiring. Others prefer to call my departure from the S.C. Democratic Party in 2023 and subsequent decision not to seek reelection in 2024, as a "principled resignation." Regardless, leaving the State House means that the venue within which I've operated for over a decade, will drastically change, but my calling won't.

I was created to lead and advocate with courage and authenticity. My pathway to purpose has been excruciating, enlightening, and engaging—equipping me with everything I'll need to share my wisdom, knowledge, experience, and insights with others. Many women and men who are among our world's most impactful servant-leaders and status quo disrupters have never served a day in elected office. So, it feels good to know that I don't have to hold a seat to take a stand.

For the first six years of my elected public service, it felt like all I was doing, without even trying, was pissing people off. Not the people I served. They loved me. The people I served *with*.

When I first met Trav in 2015, I had already announced my plans to run for the S.C. Senate. Anton knew I didn't have a campaign manager yet and suggested that I meet with Trav. At our first meeting, Trav sat in the empty seat across from me, leaned in with a serious, concerned look on his face and said, "Representative McLeod, Is there anybody in this county you *haven't* pissed off?"

He was referring to my predominantly Democratic Richland County legislative delegation. We laughed about that for years. I hired Trav on the spot to manage my Senate campaign. We worked well together and were excited to win the election pretty handily. As a freshman in the S.C. Senate, I was eager to revamp South Carolina's Disturbing Schools Law. While I'm super proud of the Disturbing Schools Bill that I revamped and helped pass in 2018, there's one fight we still haven't made significant progress on yet.

Hate crimes.

Right now, South Carolina and Wyoming are the only two states in the nation that still don't have enhanced penalties for hate crimes. Even after the Mother Emanuel Massacre claimed the lives of nine beautiful souls in Charleston, the Hate Crimes Bill that bears the name of our beloved colleague, Senator Clementa Pinckney, has yet to even be debated on the floor of the very chamber he served in. Ironically, the bill has passed the S.C. House multiple times already and arguably has enough SCGOP support to pass the S.C. Senate too, if a few Republican colleagues hadn't blocked us from debating and voting on it.

In 2022, Reverend Nelson Rivers told me that Mother Emanuel Survivor Polly Sheppard had made a video that he wanted to share with me. Mrs. Sheppard is the person the Mother Emanuel murderer allowed to live "to tell the story."

And tell the story she does. Courageously. Poignantly. Passionately.

Reverend Rivers asked me if I would be willing to show Mrs. Sheppard's video to my Senate colleagues. At the time, there were at least five senators whose names were listed in opposition to the bill, which prevented us from bringing it up for debate on the Senate floor.

In the S.C. Senate, each senator can exercise a moment of "personal interest" when we're in session. So, on Wednesday, April 27, 2022, I went to the well and respectfully asked our Senate staff to play the video on the big screens that hang prominently to the left and right sides of the chamber. No advance notice. No prior discussion about the video's subject matter. No permission was required or requested.

As Mrs. Polly Sheppard calmly and graciously reflected on the tragic evening of June 17, 2015, every single one of us who was in the chamber that day, couldn't help but be captivated by her courage and candor. Yet, as she began to call out the names of the senators who were blocking us from debating the Hate Crimes Bill, the vibe in the Senate chamber changed drastically.

Some of my Republican colleagues' faces turned bright red. The majority leader stood up multiple times while the video was playing. His movements seemed a bit frantic, as if he were trying to see if there was any way to stop it. Fortunately, the video continued to play until the end.

Her words were so powerful. So painful. Some of our Republican colleagues stormed out of the chamber. Others were visibly upset with me, as if I had violated some unwritten, unspoken Senate rule or protocol.

Every senator's name that was listed on the Senate calendar was public information. Anyone could've gone onto the State House website and seen the names of senators who opposed the Hate Crimes Bill. Unfortunately, too many South Carolinians don't realize that and too many incumbents on both sides of the political aisle would rather keep it that way, knowing that it insulates them from accountability. In my neck of the woods, when people feel outed because their actions are exposed or highlighted, we call that "throwing a rock and hiding your hand." And for those who were pissed off enough to storm out of the chamber, we have another saying, "A hit dog will holler."

If I did somehow, inadvertently violate a Senate rule, maybe it's because I was a member of the Senate Rules Committee for four consecutive years. And the Committee *never* met. Not even once. Yet, the Senate rules kept changing on the floor.

How does *that* happen?

One "rule," I'm told, was put into place after I showed the video of Mrs. Sheppard on the Senate floor. As a member of the Senate Rules Committee, I had no idea, until I had a casual conversation with my Sister-Senator Sandy Senn. Somehow, the topic of showing videos on the Senate floor came up and Sandy joked that I had basically ruined it for everybody. After I showed Mrs. Polly Sheppard's video, the rules changed *again*. Now, anytime a senator has a video he or she wants to show on the Senate floor, it has to be pre-screened and pre-approved by Senate leadership.

I was like, "What? Are you kidding me?"

Sandy laughed and assured me she was serious. Even told me she had a name for it.

She called it, "The Mia Rule."

As crazy as it was to hear that there was yet another backroom Senate rule change, thank God I was bold enough to share Mrs. Polly Sheppard's video on the floor of the S.C. Senate chamber and Senate leadership was forced to take notice. I knew Mama and Daddy would've been proud of me because whether I'm ready to embrace "my calling" or not ...

I am a status quo disrupter.

Daddy used to tell us, "If you see me in a fight with a bear, help the bear!" In other words, "Don't worry about me. God's got me." That kind of confidence made me think he was invincible. And with all that I've already overcome in my life, I'm starting to feel pretty invincible too.

The Mia Rule provides the perfect segue into my next chapter—one where I trust God enough to embrace my uniqueness, fearlessly confront any obstacle in my way, and take bold, decisive action. No permission required or requested.

Still from video featuring Mother Emanuel Massacre survivor Polly Sheppard

LESSON TEN: *Make Room*

It's almost time for the general election and I'm elated that for the first time in 14 years, my name isn't on the ballot. Was hoping to relax and exhale for a bit, but two words have been lingering on my mind and in my spirit: make room. Perhaps God is telling me to prepare for something bigger, something better, or both.

In Dr. Henry Cloud's book, *Necessary Endings,* he reminds us that:

> Getting to the next level always requires ending something ... leaving it behind, and moving on. Growth itself demands that we move on. Without the ability to end things, people stay stuck, never becoming who they are meant to be, never accomplishing all that their talents and abilities should afford them.

I'm a firm believer in the Biblical principle that we can't expect to receive the new things God has for us if we continue to hold onto the old things. In other words, we can't walk into something new if we're afraid to walk out of something old. In about a month, I'll enter into a new season, one in which I continue to be fully and faithfully submitted to God's plan. Boldly stepping into a new chapter and not knowing exactly where God is taking me requires a different level of faith and courage.

Although I look forward to rebuilding my business and regaining my footing financially, I still struggle with the time I've sacrificed and the toll it seems to have taken. Leaving the legislature is one thing. Figuring out how to make room for what's next, is another. Change, even if it's positive or welcomed, can be difficult to navigate.

Taking the first step to embark upon a new path or journey into a new season, can ignite a myriad of emotions. In these moments, I've found myself entertaining all kinds of "woulda, coulda, shouldas," as fear creeps back in and whispers, *What if you didn't really hear God? What if you've missed it and continue to struggle once you're officially out of the Senate? What if your best days are behind you?*

Sometimes, we would rather stay in the comfort of the familiar, even when we know we can do better, be better, or deserve better. Rather than risk venturing into unknown territory, we often convince ourselves that we have autonomy or are at least in control where we are. I've told myself that lie too many times to count.

Early in my political career, I used to think that being courageous was simply not backing down from a fight. Not backing down doesn't mean we won't get knocked down. At some point, everyone goes through adversity. It's a necessary part of life. Going through adversity is not optional. *Growing* through adversity, is.

True courage is about getting back up, understanding why we got knocked down and choosing to grow through it anyway. Holding on to a comfortable, familiar version of ourselves is cowardly and counterproductive. It stifles our personal growth and transformation. And like any other baggage, weighs us down.

Those of us who believe in God understand that although we have free will, learning to trust God's will for our lives and take action that is in alignment with His Word, paves the way for us to bask in the fullness of who He has called and created us to be.

For me, making room means letting go of good enough to free up space for God's best.

It presses me to release the lies I've told myself about myself, to push past the limiting beliefs and behaviors that have kept me in bondage for far too long, so that I can make room for the truth.

Making room nudges me to let go of broken promises and broken people. It gives me permission to unapologetically remove myself from the places, politics, practices, and preferences that no longer serve me.

Making room allows God to "redeem the time," by giving Him the space and freedom to do His Will in my life without interruption, interrogation, or interference.

Simply put, making room gives me the opportunity to get out of my own head and out of my own way, to create space for God to be God in my life.

His plans for me are so much bigger, wiser, and better than my own. Being intentional about making room for everything He has for me is by far one of the most liberating and exciting aspects of my journey. Having the courage to lead, serve, live *and* leave different seasons of my life on my own terms, has strengthened my faith in numerous ways. Even when doubt and fear try to convince me otherwise, Dr. Maya Angelou's wisdom reminds me that, "I may encounter many defeats, but I will not be defeated."

By the time November rolled around and I was officially free from the South Carolina legislature, I found myself re-reading my notes from Pastor Radhika's sermon earlier that fall. Weeks later, the message she shared that day, helped me shift my focus, push past my doubts and fears, and get back on track.

> Today is the youngest you'll ever be. Why wait? Years from now, you'll wish you had done it today. Stop being distracted by things and people who aren't serving you. Stop swimming in regret. Sometimes we have to lose some things to find ourselves. Redemption doesn't mean recalling or recounting what you've lost. It means "making room" for God to maximize what you have. Stop holding on to people and places God is trying to free you from. Some things will break our hearts, but fix our vision. We must acknowledge the part we've played in our own suffering and forgive ourselves, so we can "make room" for God's Plan to manifest in our lives.

And there it was again—make room—that timely, two-word phrase that had been on repeat in my head for weeks.

Although I'm not sure where God is leading me next ... I trust Him. Besides, my focus in the next chapter will be very different from my focus in the last. Now that I'm able to better understand the impact of my own limiting beliefs and behaviors, nothing is beyond my reach. And I can't wait to make room for all of it!

"How did I get here?"

The ICU nurse checked again to make sure there was no bleeding from the incision site that was flagged with a bright red label affixed to the thick plastic doughnut-shaped protective covering that encased my right wrist. She looked at me with such compassion before attempting to answer the question I didn't realize I had verbalized. Glancing at both arms, I couldn't help but notice the IV lines that served as evidence of what happened.

September 15, 2025, was busy like any other Monday. As usual, my day began with a brisk morning walk to pray, reflect, and think through what I needed to get done that week. Four and a half miles later, I was back at home to shower, cook a quick spinach and cheese omelet and catch up on some work. Two days before, I had driven to Bennettsville, South Carolina, to do a presentation for Cousin Martha's pastoral gala. Her senator couldn't attend, so I told her I would be honored to do it since my sister Tracey and I were planning to go and celebrate with her anyway. Once I got there, I suddenly started to feel lightheaded and weak. When we arrived at the event venue, I noticed a dull ache in my left arm and my heart started to race. I've heard others describe similar symptoms when they were having a panic attack, but I had never experienced anything like it.

Since Tracey and I arrived at the gala early, I sat quietly in the back of the room and prayed that the symptoms would pass so that I could do the presentation. After about 30 minutes, just before the program was about to begin, the symptoms disappeared as quickly as they had come. I thanked God that I was starting to feel like myself again. The presentation and program went really well. I drove back to Columbia that night and was excited to head to church for Baptism Sunday the next morning. The issues I experienced the day before were becoming a distant memory. On Monday, as I was preparing dinner, my left arm started to ache again. I sat at my kitchen table for a minute hoping it would subside like it did on Saturday and wondered what could've caused it. A minute or two later the ache escalated into more intense spasms. I went into my bedroom and leaned back on my bed pillows praying that the pain would ease up.

Instead it got worse.

Thankfully, Cam walked in just in time to call Dr. Marion for me. When we described my symptoms, he advised us to go to the nearest emergency room.

As BJ and Cam drove me to the hospital, I closed my eyes and continued to pray silently. I was in too much pain to talk. They were concerned, and yet, I wasn't.

When we arrived, I was able to walk in and let the desk personnel know the symptoms I was experiencing. They wasted no time taking me back for tests.

After the tests, I was taken into a different area where multiple people moved and talked with a sense of urgency. They told me that my tests indicated I was having a heart attack. The first nurse calmly advised that she was on one side of me and another nurse was on the other. She said that they would need to act quickly. They each started an IV line in my arms, removed my clothing and personal belongings, and put me in a hospital gown to prepare me to be transported to the main hospital.

Surprisingly, I wasn't afraid. My prayers in those moments were different from the prayers I prayed in 2018 when I had another life-threatening medical emergency. This time, they were bolder. I wasn't pleading with God to heal me like I had before. I'm a living, breathing testament to God's Healing Power. In that moment, I decided to meditate on His Word and believe in faith that "... by His stripes (or wounds), we are healed."

That's why I couldn't allow myself to accept what the doctors and test results were saying. Although I heard them clearly, I reminded myself to stay focused on what God said.

As they quickly prepared me for the ambulance ride, I continued to silently regurgitate God's Word back to Him and could feel His Psalm 91 protection covering me. The ER team kept talking and working. I kept praying. And I knew in my spirit that I would be okay. I could see the ER doctors talking to BJ and Cam, so I fought back the tears because I didn't want my babies to worry any more than they already were.

After the ambulance personnel introduced themselves, they gently transferred me onto the gurney and rolled me out of the ER and into the ambulance. I closed my eyes again and asked God to give BJ and Cam the same peace He had given me.

When we arrived at the hospital, the cardiologist and his team were waiting for me. I had never been treated by a cardiologist before and the experience in the "cath lab" was a bit overwhelming. The cardiologist explained that they would insert a heart catheter through an artery in my wrist to assess what was happening with my heart. If that didn't work, they would go through my groin. I'll admit that the latter point of entry did sound painful and much more invasive, so I prayed that the artery in my wrist would suffice.

The cardiologist reiterated that all of the tests indicated I was having a heart attack and that it likely meant my coronary arteries were blocked or clogged. I just couldn't bring myself to take any ownership of that diagnosis, so I waited patiently to hear what God said. Meanwhile, the cardiologist assured me that if clogged arteries or blockages were the issue, he could fix it. The next thing I remember was him telling me that the procedure went well.

They discovered during the heart catheterization that the usual plaque buildup that clogs or blocks arteries and leads to most heart attacks wasn't there. He said he believed he would've done more harm than good to try to fix a problem I didn't have.

That's when I knew in my heart that God was the only one who could fix the medical issue I was experiencing.

When I asked the cardiologist what caused it, he explained that he didn't really know, although he ruled Sickle Cell out. Tests revealed a tear in my coronary artery. According to him, the only thing that would fix it was time and rest. That sounded bizarre. A *tear*? Time and rest? This was definitely sounding more and more like a "God thing."

As expected, there was no sleep for me in the ICU. By the next day, the pain in my left arm had subsided. Although I felt a little drained, I was so grateful that God had gently tapped me *again* to get my attention. And although I wasn't willing to totally dismiss what the medical experts were saying, there was just no way I could accept a heart attack diagnosis. During the night, I looked at all of the equipment that was connected to my body and chuckled when I thought about the boxes I'll now have to check each time I fill out a medical profile. Stroke ... check. Deep Vein Thrombosis ... check. Pulmonary Embolism ... check. And according to the cardiology experts, heart attack ... check.

Over the last 10 years, I've received a myriad of life-threatening medical diagnoses, and yet, God has allowed me to live to tell the story of His grace, mercy, favor, and healing.

When the cardiologist made his rounds the next morning, he attempted to explain the diagnosis in more detail, using an acronym I had never heard of before. He said that SCAD (Spontaneous

Coronary Artery Dissection) is considered a rare type of heart attack. Research suggests it is likely triggered in some individuals who experience extremely high stress, are pregnant, or run marathons. Because I could easily eliminate the last two triggers, I thought about all of the stress I had been under recently.

A little over a year before, I retired from the State Senate. Then, I took the lead to close our 111-year-old family business while rebuilding my consulting business and living paycheck to paycheck.

Add to that, student loans with exorbitant monthly payments that have been the bane of my existence for decades.

Yep, God was definitely up to something. I just wasn't sure what yet.

You would think that spending a few days in the ICU might be enough to make me want to slow down and not test the limits, mine or His, any time soon. Funny how stubbornness works, though. Before being discharged, I was already feeling well enough to gently challenge the cardiologist about what I could and couldn't do.

And his list of "couldn'ts" was long.

No exercise. No strength training or lifting anything.

Those restrictions would be hard enough. When he hit me with no driving and no travel, I just couldn't help myself.

"For how long?" I asked, almost in disbelief.

I already had a flight and hotel booked for a big documentary fundraising event in New York City with my Sister-Senators, and I *had* to be there. Besides, the event was roughly three weeks away. Surely, that would give me enough time to rest and heal.

So, I asked the cardiologist a more direct question. "Will I be able to fly to NYC in three weeks?"

He paused for a few seconds, smiled, and said, "As much as I would love to say, yes, I'm gonna have to say, no."

"No?!"

Panic was starting to set in. "What about a late-September strategy session in Charleston with a new client? Yes, it's a two and a half hour drive, but I could have someone drive me."

"I'm afraid not," he answered in an apologetic tone.

"Well, I should still be able to go to Wofford College in Spartanburg overnight on September 29 for a speaking engagement with my Sister-Senators, right? It's closer than Charleston and I wouldn't have to drive."

Again, his answer was no.

He must've sensed that I was struggling and sat down in the chair next to my hospital bed. We talked at length about the important and necessary role rest would play in my healing and recovery. Obviously, I needed that reminder because I could literally feel my left arm tingling and my stress level rising. Whatever this latest medical challenge was, I agreed it must've been stress induced. And there I was, stressing again before I was even discharged.

Those three events had been on my calendar for months. And I caught myself tensing up at just the thought of having to bow out of them.

God had His reasons. I may never know what they were, but I trusted Him. In spite of my best efforts, there were still aspects of my life I acted as if I controlled, and, despite my best efforts, had clearly taken for granted.

Among them were my health, my livelihood, and my schedule.

Obviously, that needed to change.

Sometime between the moment the cardiologist left the room and the discharge nurse entered it, I realized that my temporary new normal was orchestrated by God. It was not an option to not accept or follow His instructions. I've lived long enough and through enough to know that God has many ways to get my undivided attention if He chooses, and I definitely didn't want that.

"Casting my cares upon Him" would require a level of faith and trust I had leaned into many times before.

This was the divinely orchestrated wake-up call I needed.

After all the heart monitors and IV meds were unplugged, the nurse removed the IV lines from both arms and wrapped the sites securely to prevent bleeding. He also explained the importance of the new prescription medications the cardiologist ordered for me. And because I hate taking medicines, I reminded myself that the medications and the barrage of doctors office visits that awaited me over the next several months were necessary *and* temporary.

When I walked into my house after all I had been through and overcome, yet *again,* my heart was filled with gratitude. God hadn't just spared my life. He had used this rare medical emergency to save my life. Before all of this happened, rest was something I knew I needed and hoped to get one day. The only problem is that "one day" never comes when we're more committed to our preferences than we are to God's plan.

Until September 15, it felt normal to keep pressing, keep pushing, and keep going, no matter how tired, overworked, or overwhelmed I was.

But God's Word says, "Come to me, all you who are weary and burdened, and I will give you rest."

After everything He had brought me through, I decided to take Him at His Word.

* * *

In November, I was back at the hospital for a scheduled appointment. The cardiologist ordered a scan of the arteries in my heart. He told me that this scan would reveal just how much damage the heart attack caused to my heart, which he believed was inevitable.

About a week later, I had my follow-up appointment with him to discuss the results of the scan. When the cardiologist and nurse practitioner entered the room, they had noticeably different looks on their faces.

With a look of sheer amazement in his eyes, the cardiologist gave me the results. "The tear is completely healed," he said. "*And you have zero percent calcification in your arteries.*"

I thanked God audibly for always keeping His promises. Full restoration and healing are what I prayed for and that's exactly what He gave me. Then, I said, "Sooo, let me make sure I'm clear. Was it SCAD?"

"Yes, it definitely was SCAD," the cardiologist replied.

"And now, it's like it never happened?"

They glanced at each other before acknowledging the miracle of God's healing power that defies logic and medical science.

"Yes, like it never happened."

PATH OF SERVICE

Executive Branch

1996–1997 — Director, Violence Against Women Act (VAWA) Program, Office of South Carolina Attorney General Charlie Condon

- First person to lead this premier statewide initiative at a time when South Carolina led the nation in women murdered by their male partners
- Developed South Carolina's first statewide, evidence-based protocols and curricula for law enforcement, prosecutors, judges, and victim advocates to use when investigating, prosecuting, and adjudicating domestic violence, sexual assault, and stalking cases

1998–2001 — Director, State Office of Victim Assistance (SOVA), Office of South Carolina Governor Jim Hodges

- First woman to lead the State Office of Victim Assistance
- Opened rural satellite offices to expand access to the state's multimillion-dollar Crime Victim Compensation Fund, garnering national recognition; program components were showcased as a model for other states

2002 — Director of Governmental Affairs, South Carolina Department of Probation, Parole & Pardon Services

- Led the government affairs department for a cabinet-level state agency
- Advocated successfully for passage of the agency's landmark Interstate Compact legislation, which had state and national implications

Private Sector

2003 — Founded McLeod Butler & Company, LLC, a boutique public affairs consulting firm

2003–2010 — Government Relations and Lobbying

- Co-authored and lobbied for landmark legislation that facilitated more than $100 million in recurring South Carolina Education Lottery funding for four-year Historically Black Colleges and Universities (HBCUs) across South Carolina

2011–present — Public Affairs and Political Navigation

- Represents diverse disciplines and sectors, including a global Fortune 500 corporation, nonprofit associations, and municipalities in multiple states

Legislative Branch

2010–2016 — South Carolina House of Representatives, District 79

- First woman to represent House District 79, one of South Carolina's fastest-growing swing districts at the time
- Advocated for a diverse constituency in education, healthcare, infrastructure, economic and workforce development, public safety, fair district maps and systemic reforms

2016–2024 — South Carolina Senate, District 22

- First woman to represent Senate District 22 and the first Black woman to represent the capital city (Columbia) and Richland County in the South Carolina Senate; sponsored and passed bipartisan legislation to reform the state's antiquated Disturbing Schools Law, impacting the trajectory of over 750,000 South Carolina students
- First Black woman in South Carolina to earn global distinction as a Rodel Fellow in Public Leadership after completing the Rodel Fellowship in 2017
- 2023 John F. Kennedy Profile in Courage Award recipient

2021–2022 — Statewide Campaign

- First Black woman to run for governor of South Carolina

ACKNOWLEDGMENTS

Growing up in Shiloh Baptist Church in Bennettsville, South Carolina, I remember watching the older church mothers cry out to God during the service and say, "When I think of the goodness of Jesus and all He's done for me, my soul cries out, Hallelujah, thank you God for saving me." As a child, I hadn't quite lived long enough or been through enough to understand their words or their reasons. Now, I do.

Thank you, God … *For every mountain you've brought me over. For every trial you've seen me through … for every blessing, Hallelujah … for this, I give you praise.*

I'm thankful for my parents, Jimmy and Shirley, who raised me with unconditional love, corrected me with healthy doses of discipline and accountability, instilled in me empathy and compassion for others, and reminded me that "I am my brother's keeper."

It's hard to imagine life without my big sister Tracey, little sister Erica, and baby brother Jimmy. You guys taught me how to speak, hear, and receive the truth in love—exactly what God knew I would need to become the fearless warrior I am today.

I'm so grateful for my grandparents: Otis and Signora Jeffries, Leah and Jim Worrell, and James Phillip McLeod; my aunts and uncles: Frances Morris Flournoy, Faye Jeffries Hester and Ralph

Hester, Barbara Jeffries Griffie, Otis "Sonny" and Janis Jeffries, Larry and Sudie Jeffries, Terry Worrell Glover and Darryl Glover, Gary and Cheryl Worrell, and Jimmy and Dolores Washington; and my godparents Mary and Woodrow Jackson. I've always been close to my first cousins on both sides of my family too. In fact, I can't remember a time in my personal and political journeys that they weren't earnestly part of. I'm truly blessed to have a family whose love and support inspire and empower me—today, tomorrow, and forever.

After losing my Mom, I still needed a few more angels on this earth, so God gave me Aunt Barbara, Aunt Faye, Godmother Mary Jackson, Rose Butler, Geraldine McIlwain, Mama Wilson, Geraldine Butler, and Shirley Mendenhall. The unconditional love and prayers of my "bonus moms" continue to guide me through some of life's most tumultuous terrain.

And these days, when life is truly "life-ing," it's my inner circle that helps keep me grounded, grateful, and laughing, even when I feel like crying. Don't know what I would do without y'all, and I hope I never have to.

More than three decades after our undergraduate years at the University of South Carolina, my sorority line sisters (a.k.a. "Silhouettes of a Dream") have been there, for and with me, every step of the way. Thank you, SOADs, for always having my back. Love y'all with ALL my heart!

Senator Maggie Glover, I was a first-year law student when you made history as the first Black woman to serve in the S.C. Senate. I'm a Pee Dee girl too and was elated to see someone who looked like me representing my hometown area. Your distinguished service provided proof of possibilities I hadn't yet considered and I'm forever grateful. Love and appreciate you, Senator!

Margie, Sandy, Katrina, and Penry, when I branded us "Sister-Senators," only God knew what was in store. We're more than a brand. We're sisters for life, building a legacy of leadership that cultivates courage and civility to inspire future generations of women leaders around the world!

I'm especially grateful for my primary care physician, Dr. Marion; my dentist, Dr. Loretta Felder McKelvey; my hematologist, Dr. El Geneidy; and all the other brilliant, compassionate doctors, nurses, healthcare professionals, and healthcare systems who ensured I received excellent care throughout the medical challenges I've faced during the 14 years I've served in elected office.

To help regain strength, mobility, and flexion in my knee, my healing journey would've been incomplete without the expert care of my orthopedic surgeons at PRISMA Health; my friend and occupational therapist, Hima Dalal; and later, Dr. Sherman Roberts, Jr. I'm equally thankful for my trainer, Ron Emmons, who pushes me to reach my fitness goals in spite of the challenges. ·

While serving, I often had to be camera-ready for media interviews or press conferences. Thanks to Radhika Patel and later, Tanta Brown, I never had to worry about my hair. Maggie Lin made sure my nails were pretty too—a reminder that I don't just have sisters in the Senate.

I adore my hometown folks in Bennettsville, S.C., and Marlboro County. You guys represent the best of humanity and all the reasons I wouldn't have wanted to be born or raised anywhere else.

Thank you to my teachers, administrators, and community leaders in Bennettsville who poured love into me over the years, always raised the standard, and challenged me to never settle for less than my best. I can't possibly acknowledge all of them by name, but I have to mention Beatrice Dupree, Annie Newton Hilliard, Suzanne Linder Hurley, Debra Settles, and G. Lynn Moore.

No matter where life takes me on this journey, there will always be a special place in my heart for my beloved Bennettsville High School Class of 1986. Go Gremlins!

Speaking of beloved, I have to thank Dr. Carolyn Matalene, my Advanced Writing professor at USC, who taught me that "good writing moves from the abstract to the concrete." Earning an A in her class and knowing that she later recommended me to teach a professional communications course at the University are still among my proudest moments as a USC Gamecock!

When my team encouraged me to do a photo shoot for the book cover, I didn't want to because I hate taking pictures. Now, I'm glad I did. Thanks to Tonya Brown at Total Bliss Hair Studio and Shelia Farrar at Pretty Mugz. My hair and makeup were just the touch of glam I needed!

And finally, thank you, to every member of Team Mia for SC! Some of you have been a pivotal part of my 14-year journey of elected public service from day one. Others, not quite as long. Perhaps you were a resource, event host, fundraiser or much-needed support system for me while I campaigned or served. Whatever part you played, as a volunteer or paid team member, just know that all of the amazing things we've accomplished together, were possible because of you.

ABOUT THE AUTHOR

Mia S. McLeod is a barrier-breaker, truth-teller, political trailblazer and 2023 John F. Kennedy Profile in Courage Award recipient whose courage to lead on her own terms has consistently defied expectations. She was the first woman to represent South Carolina House District 79 and South Carolina Senate District 22 and the first Black woman in her state's history to run for governor. Mia spent 14 years on the front lines of South Carolina's political arena—confronting inequities, exposing hypocrisies, and challenging systemic injustices.

A seventh generation South Carolinian, Mia earned both her Bachelor of Arts and law degrees from the University of South Carolina. She was born and raised in rural Marlboro County, S.C., the second of four children, in the heart of what America has come to know as the "Corridor of Shame." Mia's father, Jimmy, was a small business owner whose childhood memories of the deeply segregated south never left him. He taught her the importance of being a change agent. Her mother, Shirley, a public school teacher and librarian, taught Mia that her voice has power.

From calling out the Old Guard within both political parties to taking principled stands of conscience that often came at significant personal and political costs, Mia has never shied away from speaking truth to power. She completed the Rodel Fellowship in Public Leadership in 2017 and is the first Black woman in South

Carolina to earn this premier public leadership distinction. The fellowship is housed within the Rodel Institute, a nonpartisan center for public leadership.

Her first book, *The Unlikely Disruptor: South Carolina's First Black Woman to Run for Governor,* is a deeply personal account of what it means to lead with courage and conviction in the face of adversity, combined with the lessons she learned along the way. Mia shares the unvarnished truth behind her public battles and private reckonings—revealing how faith, authenticity, and fearlessness fueled her fight to disrupt the status quo.